TEENAGE MUTANT NINJA TURTLES

VENGEANCE, PART 1

VOLUME 12

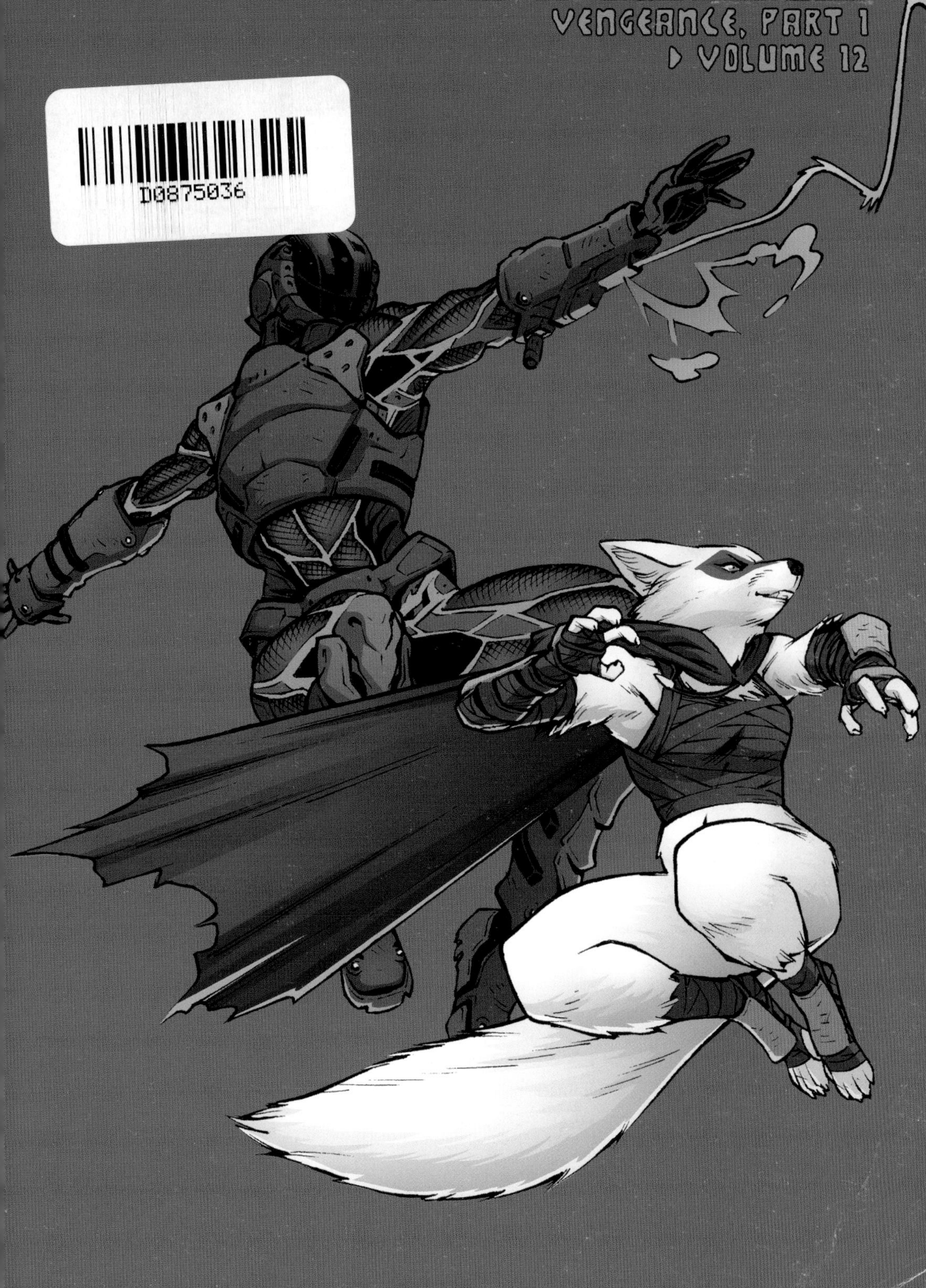

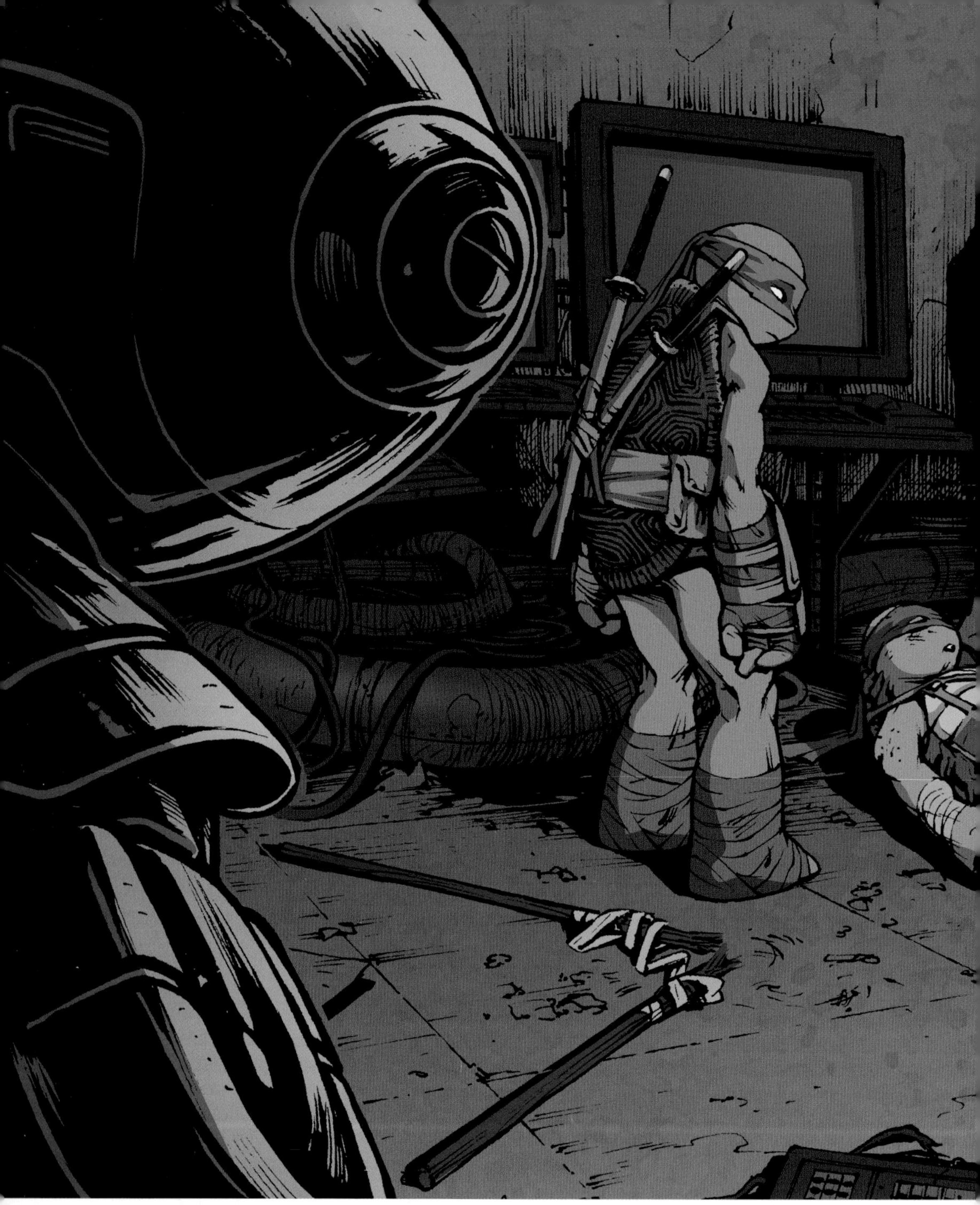

Special thanks to Joan Hilty, Linda Lee, and Kat van Dam for their invaluable assistance.

ISBN: 978-1-63140-450-4

18 17 16 15   1 2 3 4

IDW®
www.IDWPUBLISHING.com
IDW founded by Ted Adams, Alex Garner, Kris Oprisko, and Robbie Robbins

Ted Adams, CEO & Publisher
Greg Goldstein, President & COO
Robbie Robbins, EVP/Sr. Graphic Artist
Chris Ryall, Chief Creative Officer/Editor-in-Chief
Matthew Ruzicka, CPA, Chief Financial Officer
Alan Payne, VP of Sales
Dirk Wood, VP of Marketing
Lorelei Bunjes, VP of Digital Services
Jeff Webber, VP of Digital Publishing & Business Development

Facebook: **facebook.com/idwpublishing**
Twitter: **@idwpublishing**
YouTube: **youtube.com/idwpublishing**
Tumblr: **tumblr.idwpublishing.com**
Instagram: **instagram.com/idwpublishing**

Originally published as TEENAGE MUTANT NINJA TURTLES issues #45–47 and TEENAGE MUTANT NINJA TURTLES FCBD 2015.

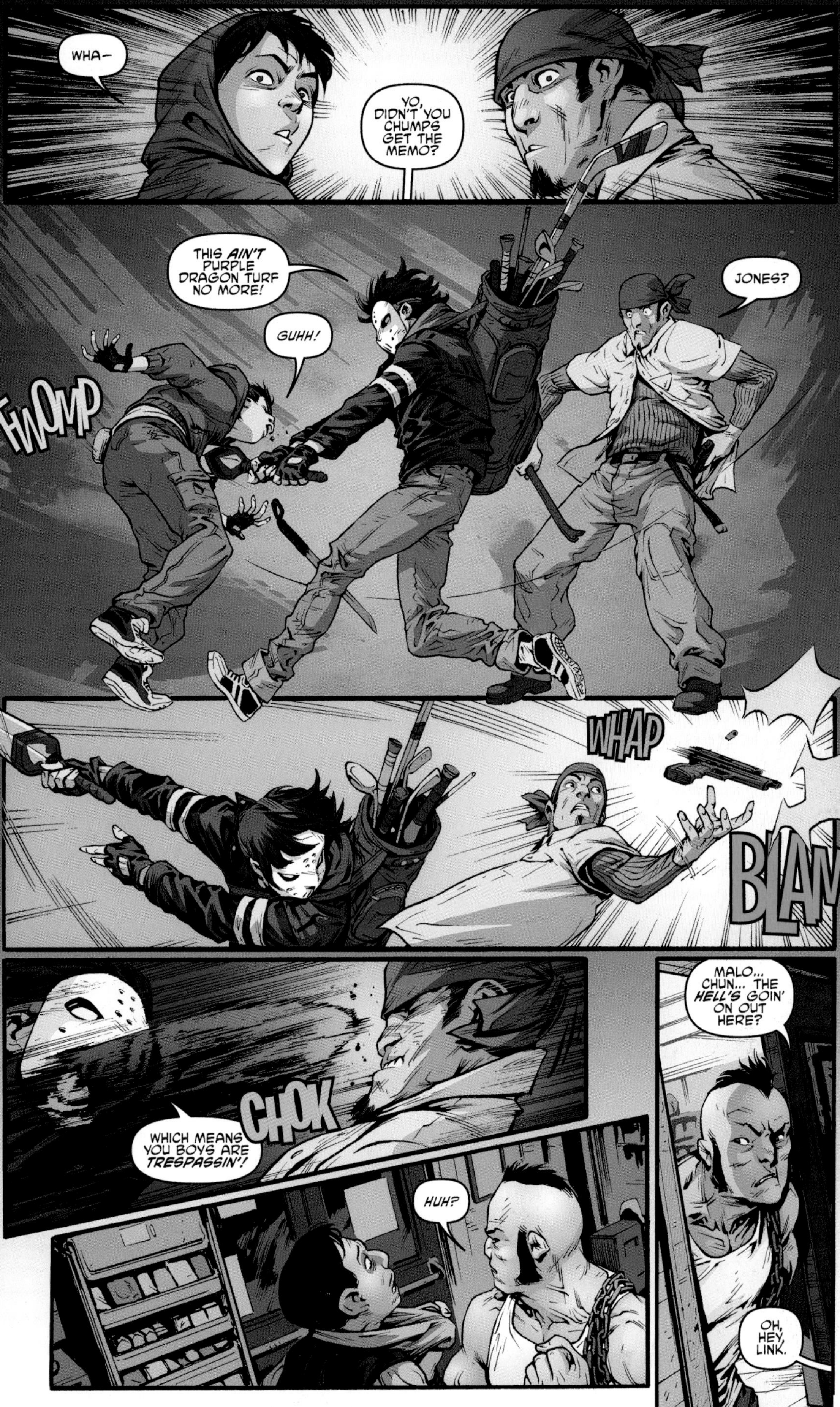
WHA-
YO, DIDN'T YOU CHUMPS GET THE MEMO?
THIS AIN'T PURPLE DRAGON TURF NO MORE!
GUHH!
FWOMP
JONES?
WHAP
BLAM
CHOK
WHICH MEANS YOU BOYS ARE TRESPASSIN'!
MALO... CHUN... THE HELL'S GOIN' ON OUT HERE?
HUH?
OH, HEY, LINK.

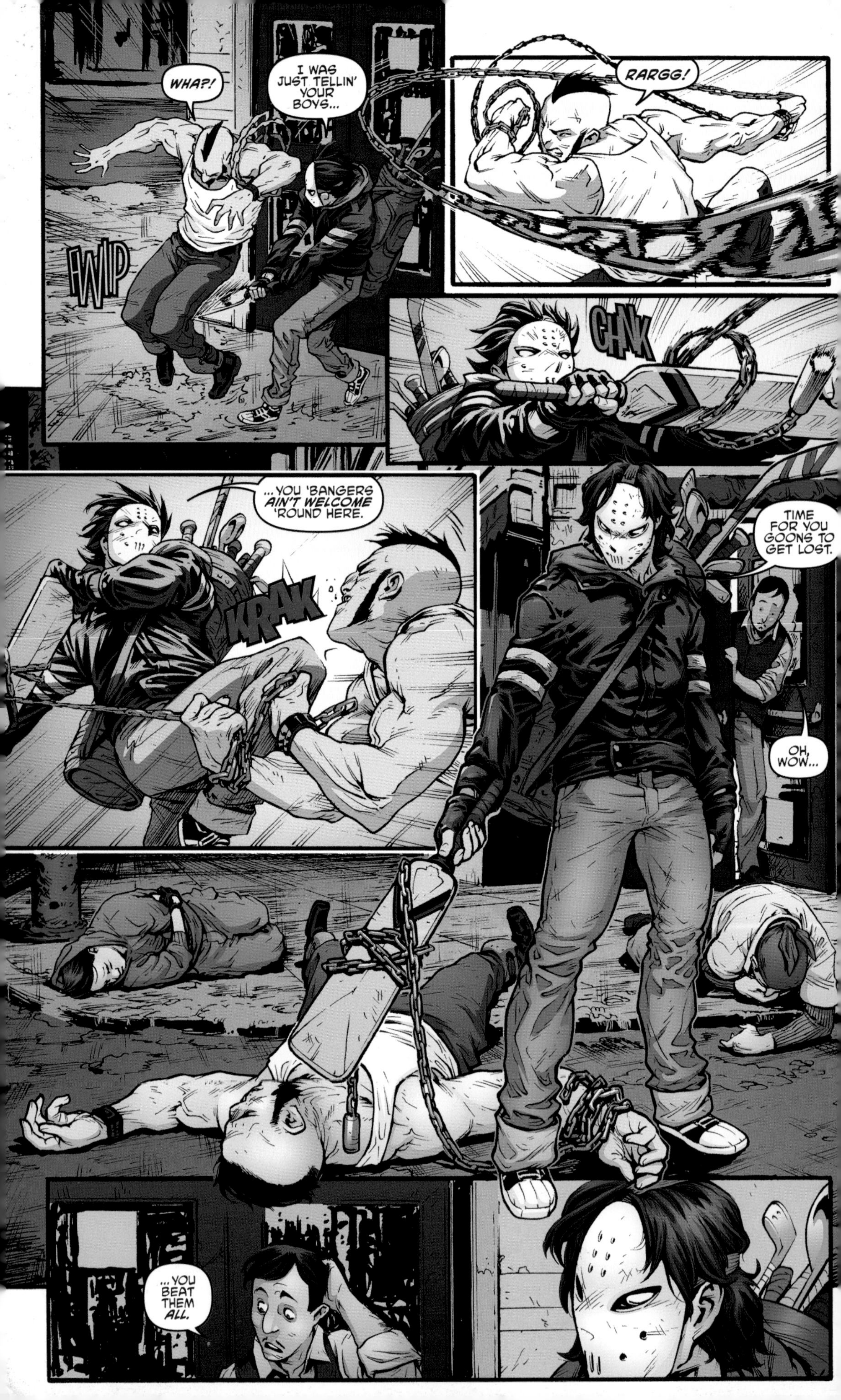
WHA?!
I WAS JUST TELLIN' YOUR BOYS...
FWIP
RARGG!
CHNK
...YOU 'BANGERS AIN'T WELCOME 'ROUND HERE.
KRAK
TIME FOR YOU GOONS TO GET LOST.
OH, WOW...
...YOU BEAT THEM ALL.

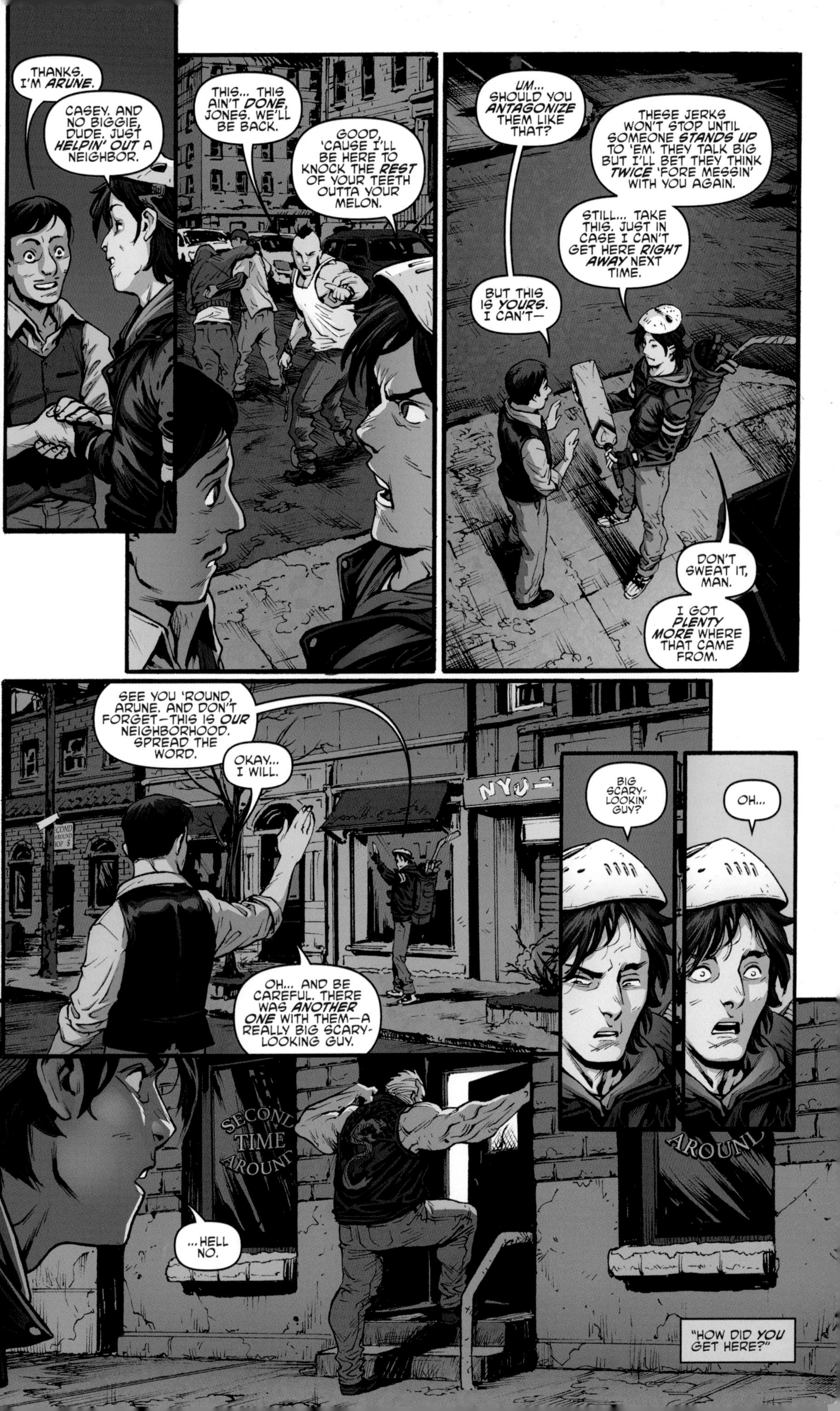
THANKS. I'M *ARUNE*.
CASEY. AND NO BIGGIE, DUDE. JUST *HELPIN' OUT* A NEIGHBOR.
THIS... THIS AIN'T *DONE*, JONES. WE'LL BE BACK.
GOOD, 'CAUSE I'LL BE HERE TO KNOCK THE *REST* OF YOUR TEETH OUTTA YOUR MELON.
UM... SHOULD YOU *ANTAGONIZE* THEM LIKE THAT?
THESE JERKS WON'T STOP UNTIL SOMEONE *STANDS UP* TO 'EM. THEY TALK BIG BUT I'LL BET THEY THINK *TWICE* 'FORE MESSIN' WITH YOU AGAIN.
STILL... TAKE THIS. JUST IN CASE I CAN'T GET HERE *RIGHT AWAY* NEXT TIME.
BUT THIS IS *YOURS*. I CAN'T—
DON'T SWEAT IT, MAN.
I GOT *PLENTY MORE* WHERE THAT CAME FROM.
SEE YOU 'ROUND, ARUNE. AND DON'T FORGET—THIS IS *OUR* NEIGHBORHOOD. SPREAD THE WORD.
OKAY... I WILL.
NYU
OH... AND BE CAREFUL. THERE WAS *ANOTHER ONE* WITH THEM—A REALLY BIG SCARY-LOOKING GUY.
BIG SCARY-LOOKIN' GUY?
OH...
SECOND TIME AROUND
...HELL NO.
AROUND
"HOW DID *YOU* GET HERE?"

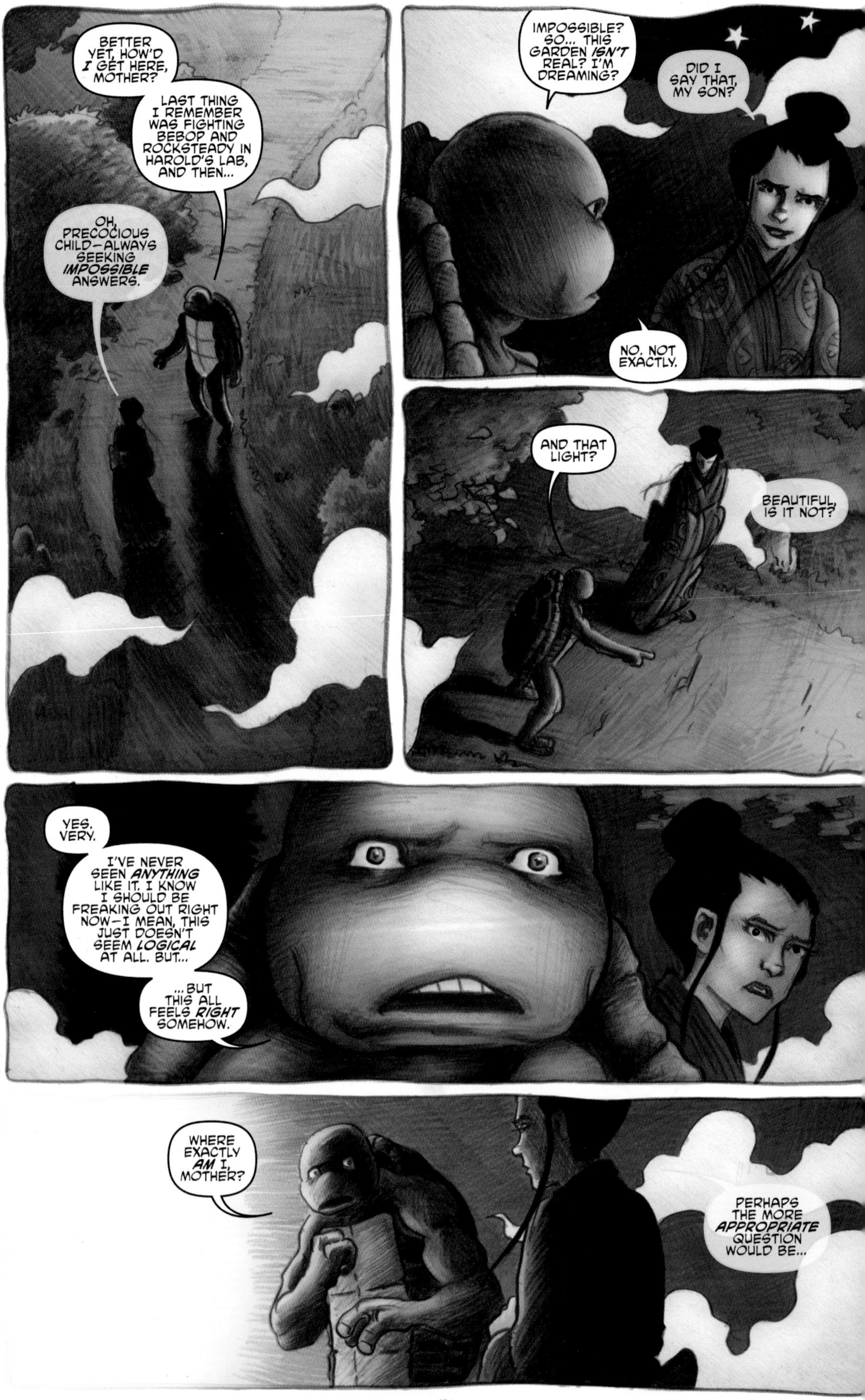
BETTER YET, HOW'D *I* GET HERE, MOTHER?
LAST THING I REMEMBER WAS FIGHTING BEBOP AND ROCKSTEADY IN HAROLD'S LAB, AND THEN...
OH, PRECOCIOUS CHILD—ALWAYS SEEKING *IMPOSSIBLE* ANSWERS.
IMPOSSIBLE? SO... THIS GARDEN *ISN'T* REAL? I'M DREAMING?
DID I SAY THAT, MY SON?
NO. NOT EXACTLY.
AND THAT LIGHT?
BEAUTIFUL, IS IT NOT?
YES. VERY.
I'VE NEVER SEEN *ANYTHING* LIKE IT. I KNOW I SHOULD BE FREAKING OUT RIGHT NOW—I MEAN, THIS JUST DOESN'T SEEM *LOGICAL* AT ALL. BUT...
...BUT THIS ALL FEELS *RIGHT* SOMEHOW.
WHERE EXACTLY *AM* I, MOTHER?
PERHAPS THE MORE *APPROPRIATE* QUESTION WOULD BE...

"...WHERE ARE YOU *GOING?*"

I'M HAVING A HARD TIME *BUYING* THIS, HONEYCUTT.

FRANKLY, THE SCIENCE SEEMS FAR-FETCHED. ARE YOU *CERTAIN* THIS WORKS?

YES, I AM. THOUGH, ADMITTEDLY, I DO HAVE CONCERNS ABOUT SLAP-DASHING THE COMPONENTS TOGETHER THE WAY WE HAVE, BUT TIME IS MOST DEFINITELY OF THE ESSENCE.

OKAY, LET'S SEE...

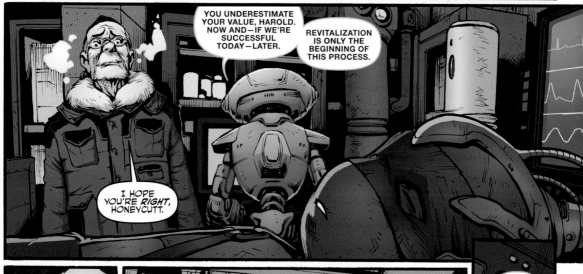

...WOULD YOU HAND ME THAT BLUE CABLE, PLEASE?

HERE. AND IS THERE ANYTHING ELSE I CAN DO?

I FEEL BLASTED *USELESS* RIGHT NOW.

YOU UNDERESTIMATE YOUR VALUE, HAROLD. NOW AND—IF WE'RE SUCCESSFUL TODAY—LATER.

REVITALIZATION IS ONLY THE BEGINNING OF THIS PROCESS.

I HOPE YOU'RE *RIGHT*, HONEYCUTT.

PLEASE BE RIGHT.

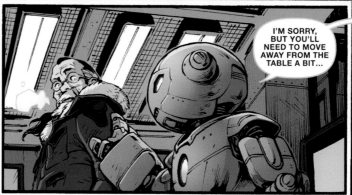

I'M SORRY, BUT YOU'LL NEED TO MOVE AWAY FROM THE TABLE A BIT...

...IT'S TIME.

CLICK

"DO YOU THINK THEY'RE *TOO LATE?*"

19

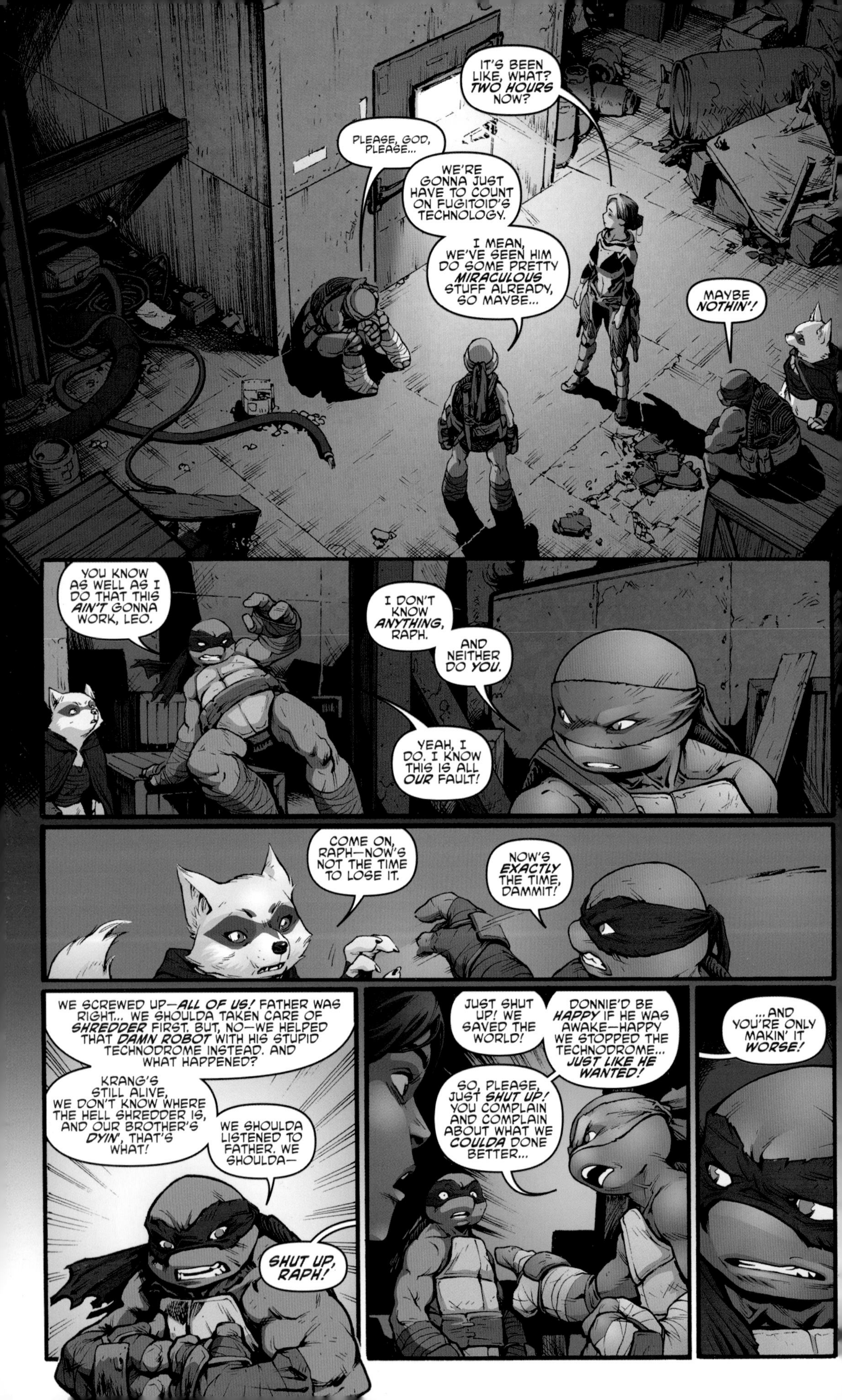
IT'S BEEN LIKE, WHAT? TWO HOURS NOW?
PLEASE, GOD, PLEASE...
WE'RE GONNA JUST HAVE TO COUNT ON FUGITOID'S TECHNOLOGY.
I MEAN, WE'VE SEEN HIM DO SOME PRETTY MIRACULOUS STUFF ALREADY, SO MAYBE...
MAYBE NOTHIN'!
YOU KNOW AS WELL AS I DO THAT THIS AIN'T GONNA WORK, LEO.
I DON'T KNOW ANYTHING, RAPH.
AND NEITHER DO YOU.
YEAH, I DO. I KNOW THIS IS ALL OUR FAULT!
COME ON, RAPH—NOW'S NOT THE TIME TO LOSE IT.
NOW'S EXACTLY THE TIME, DAMMIT!
WE SCREWED UP—ALL OF US! FATHER WAS RIGHT... WE SHOULDA TAKEN CARE OF SHREDDER FIRST. BUT, NO—WE HELPED THAT DAMN ROBOT WITH HIS STUPID TECHNODROME INSTEAD. AND WHAT HAPPENED?
KRANG'S STILL ALIVE, WE DON'T KNOW WHERE THE HELL SHREDDER IS, AND OUR BROTHER'S DYIN', THAT'S WHAT!
WE SHOULDA LISTENED TO FATHER. WE SHOULDA—
SHUT UP, RAPH!
JUST SHUT UP! WE SAVED THE WORLD!
DONNIE'D BE HAPPY IF HE WAS AWAKE—HAPPY WE STOPPED THE TECHNODROME... JUST LIKE HE WANTED!
SO, PLEASE, JUST SHUT UP! YOU COMPLAIN AND COMPLAIN ABOUT WHAT WE COULDA DONE BETTER...
...AND YOU'RE ONLY MAKIN' IT WORSE!

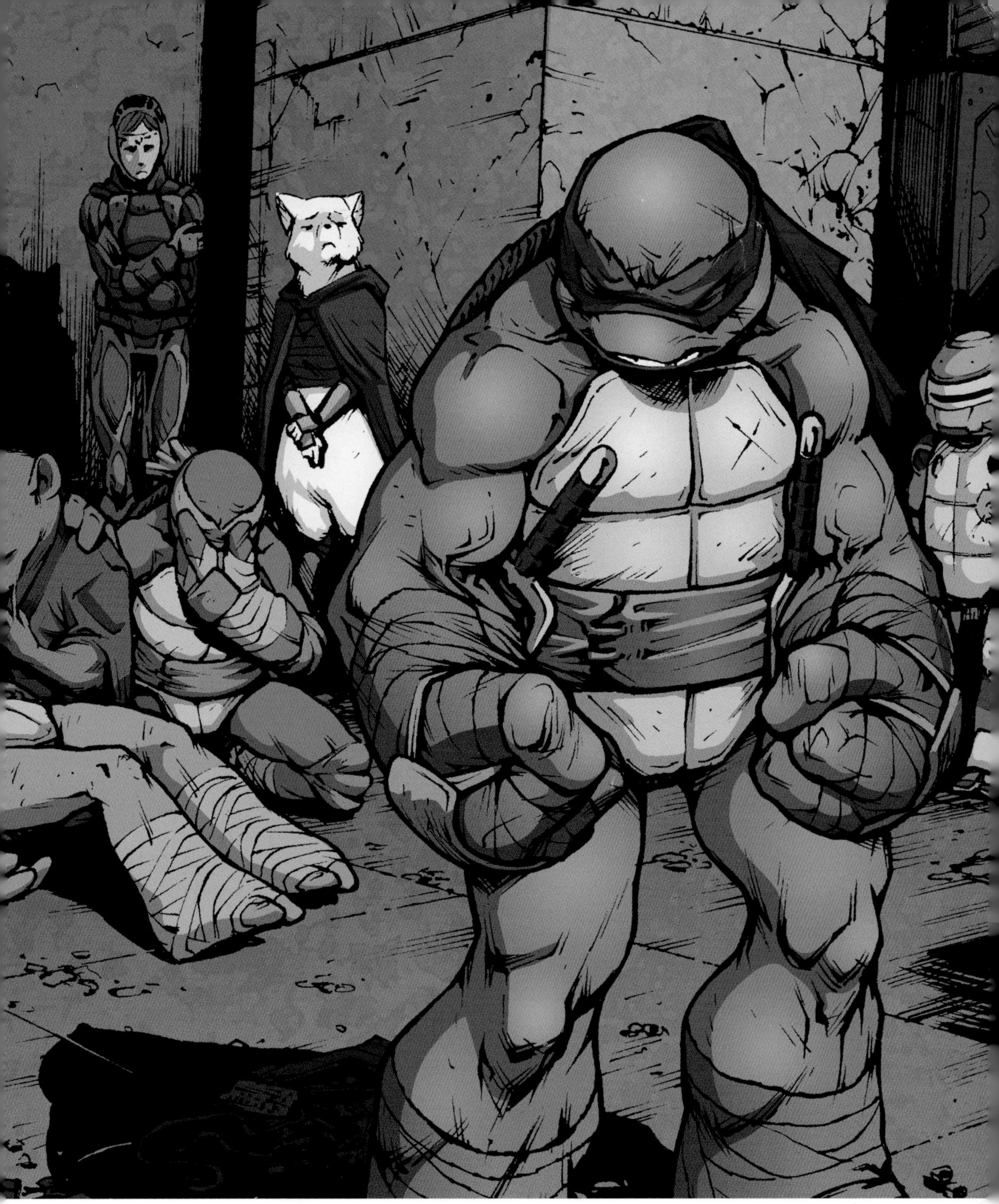

Story by Kevin Eastman, Bobby Curnow, and Tom Waltz • Script by Tom Waltz

Art by Mateus Santolouco

ditional Art by Charles Paul Wilson III (Ch. 1), Dan Duncan (Ch. 3), Sophie Campbell (Ch. 3), and Cory Smith (Ch. 3)

Colors by Ronda Pattison • Letters by Shawn Lee • Series Edits by Bobby Curnow

Cover by Mateus Santolouco

Collection Edits by Justin Eisinger & Alonzo Simon

Production by Tom B. Long

Based on characters created by Peter Laird and Kevin Eastman

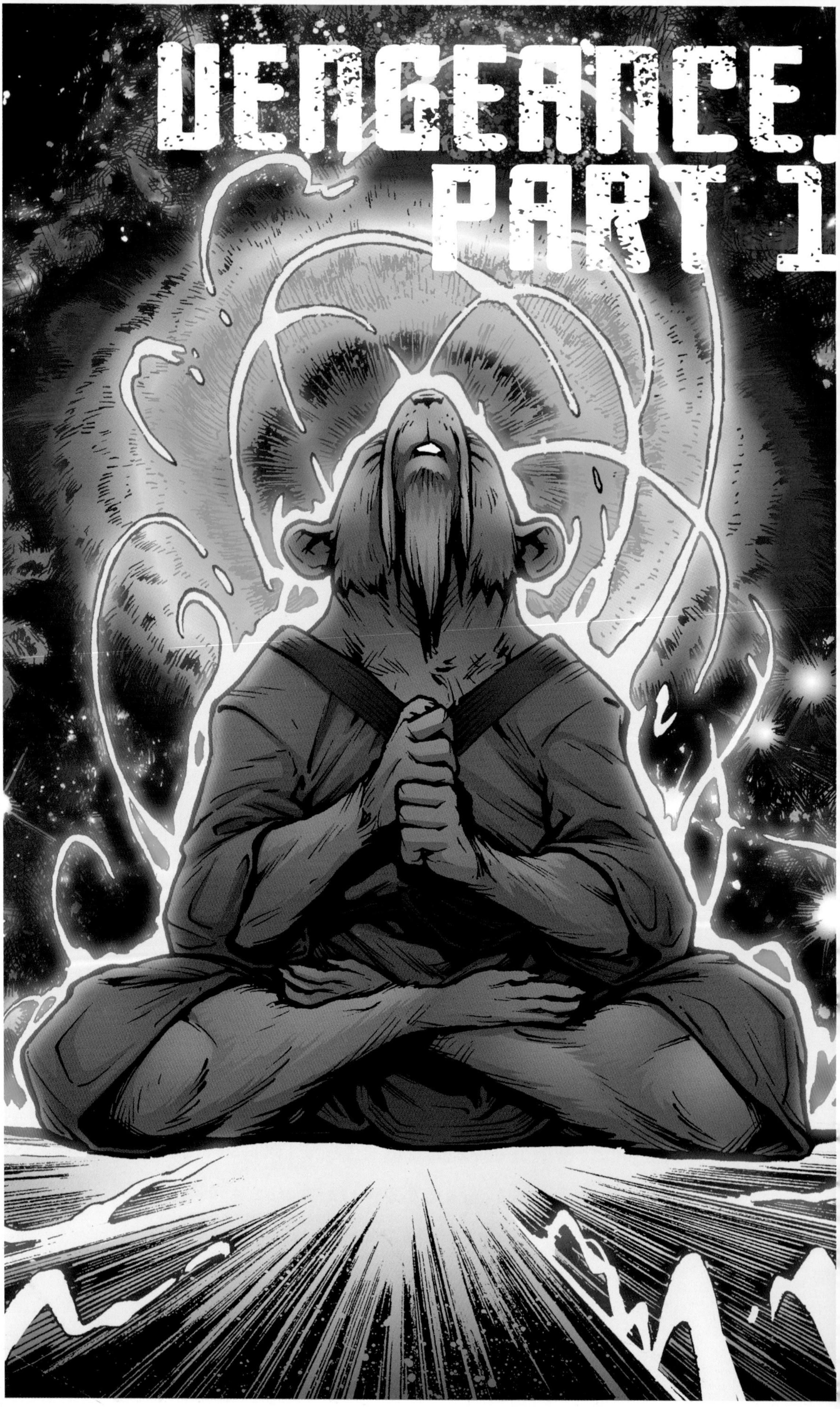
VENGEANCE,
PART 1

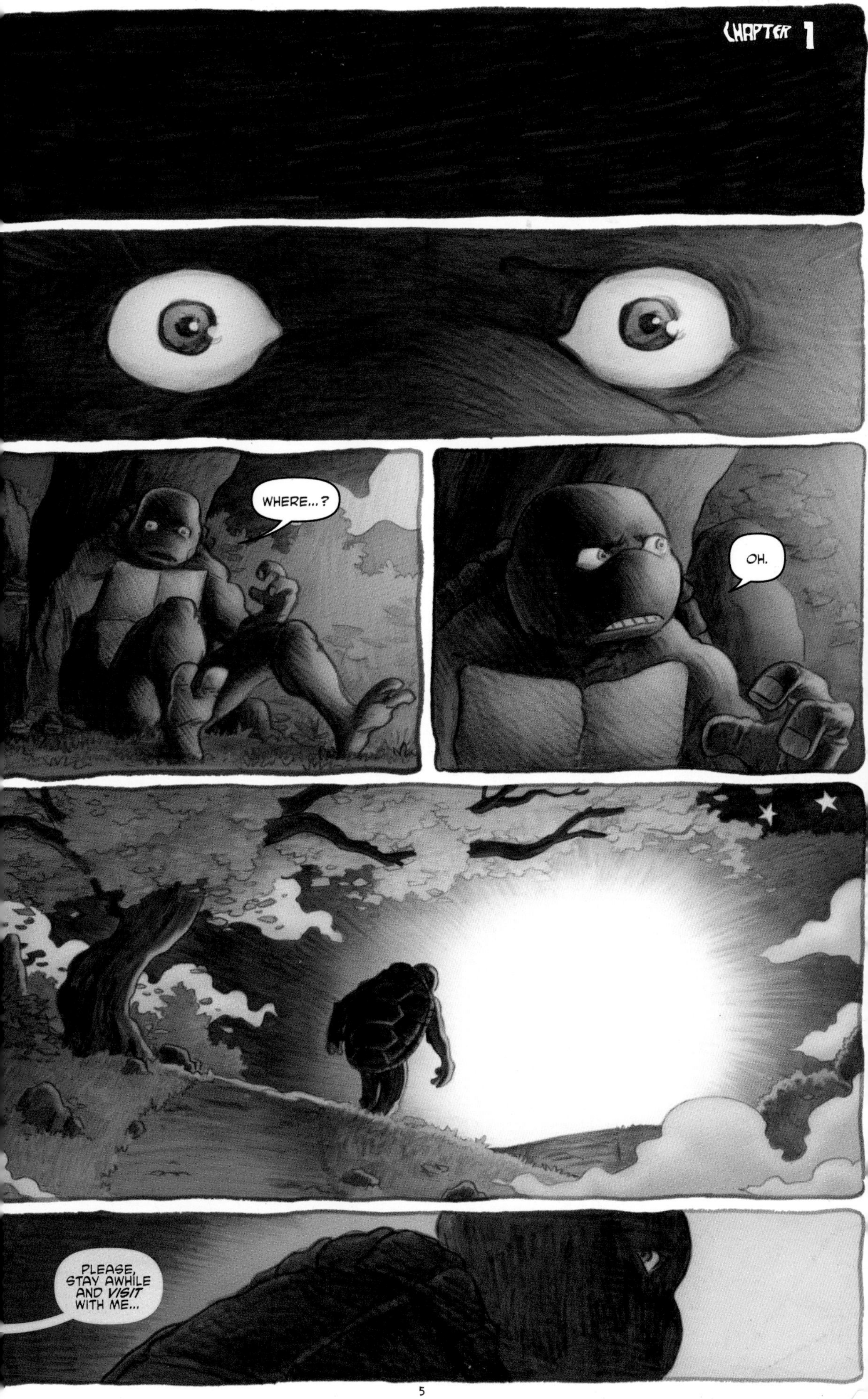
CHAPTER 1
WHERE...?
OH.
PLEASE, STAY AWHILE AND *VISIT* WITH ME...

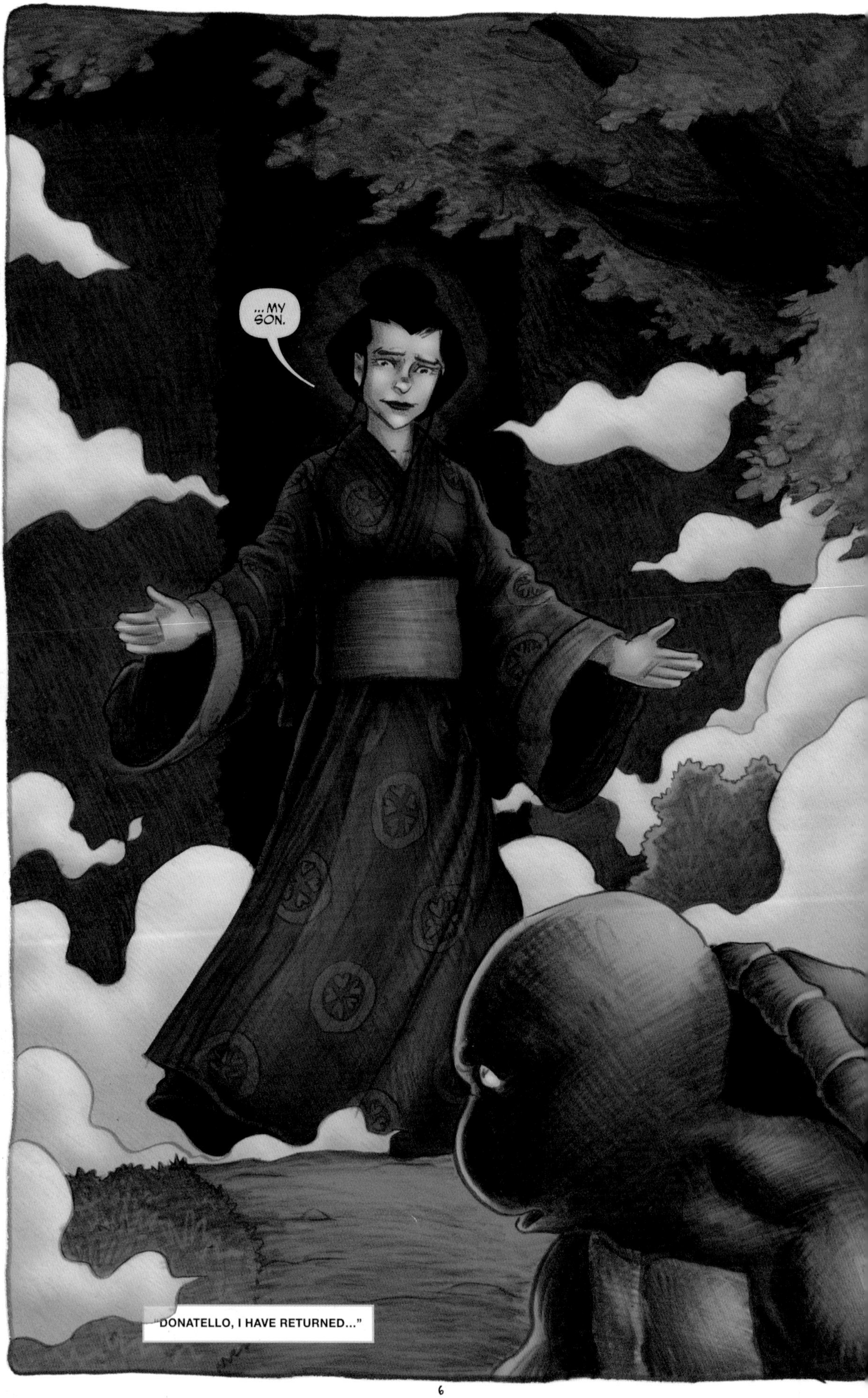
...MY SON.
"DONATELLO, I HAVE RETURNED..."

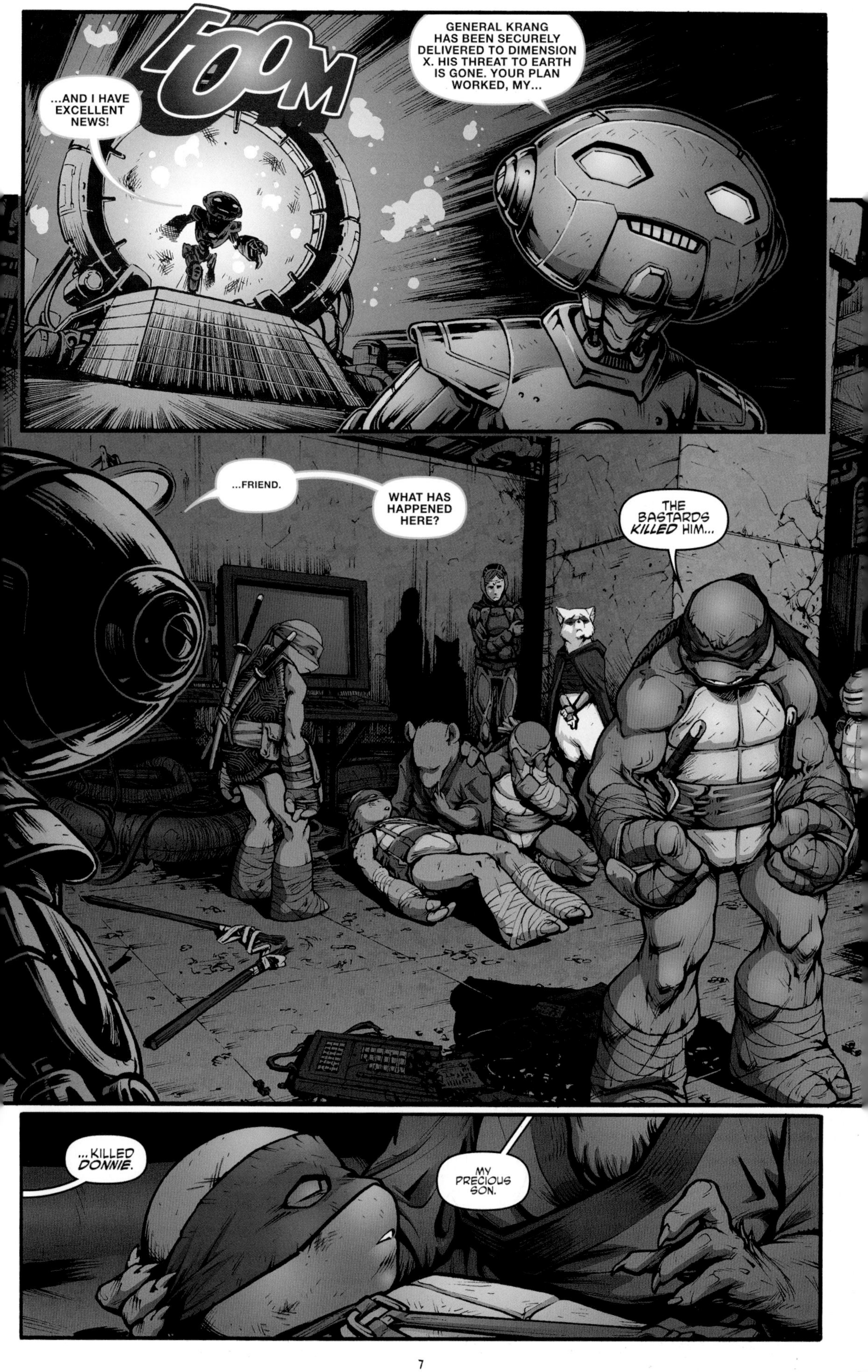
FOOM
...AND I HAVE EXCELLENT NEWS!
GENERAL KRANG HAS BEEN SECURELY DELIVERED TO DIMENSION X. HIS THREAT TO EARTH IS GONE. YOUR PLAN WORKED, MY...
...FRIEND.
WHAT HAS HAPPENED HERE?
THE BASTARDS KILLED HIM...
...KILLED DONNIE.
MY PRECIOUS SON.

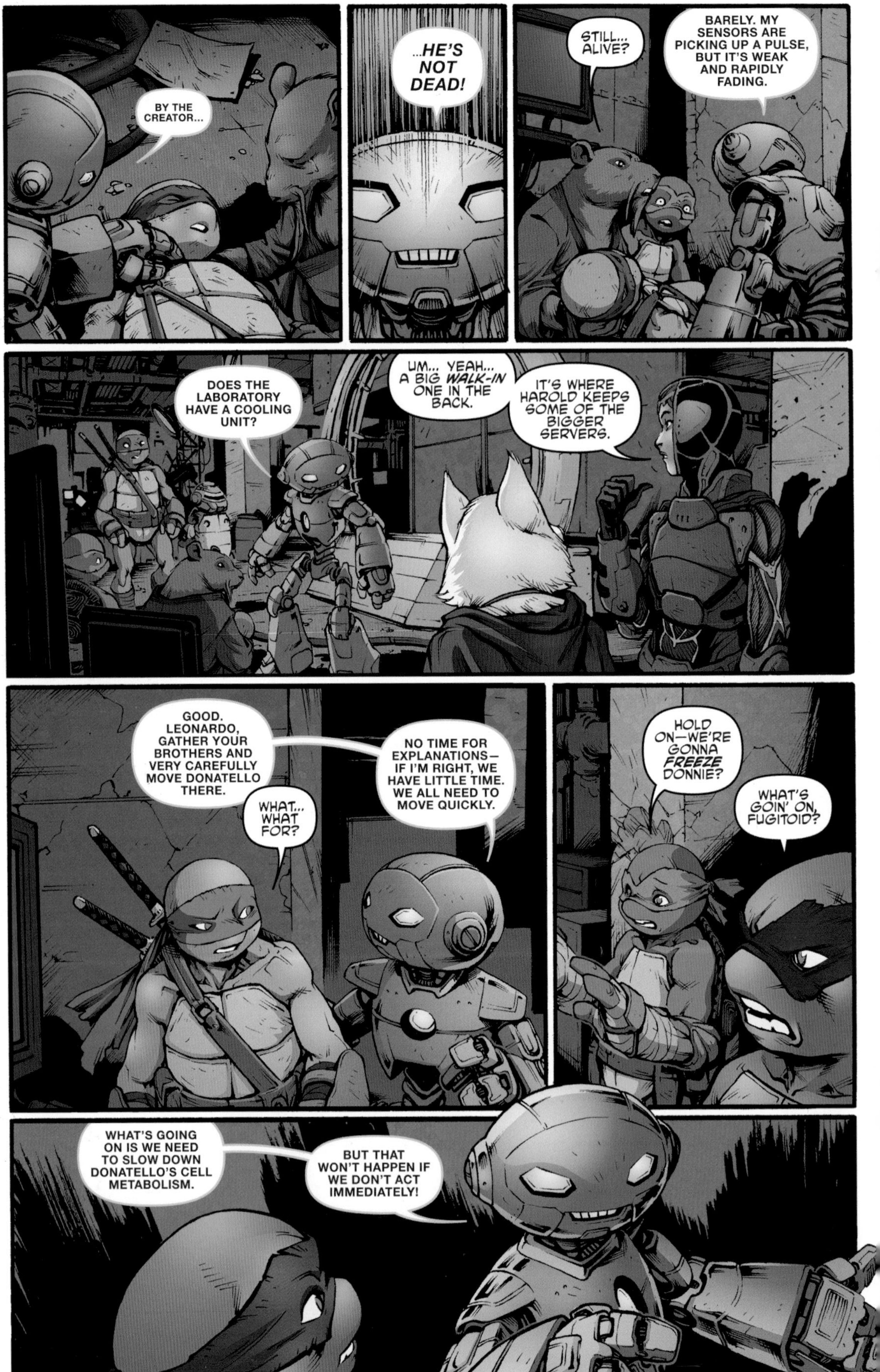
BY THE CREATOR...
...HE'S NOT DEAD!
STILL... ALIVE?
BARELY. MY SENSORS ARE PICKING UP A PULSE, BUT IT'S WEAK AND RAPIDLY FADING.
DOES THE LABORATORY HAVE A COOLING UNIT?
UM... YEAH... A BIG WALK-IN ONE IN THE BACK.
IT'S WHERE HAROLD KEEPS SOME OF THE BIGGER SERVERS.
GOOD. LEONARDO, GATHER YOUR BROTHERS AND VERY CAREFULLY MOVE DONATELLO THERE.
WHAT... WHAT FOR?
NO TIME FOR EXPLANATIONS— IF I'M RIGHT, WE HAVE LITTLE TIME. WE ALL NEED TO MOVE QUICKLY.
HOLD ON—WE'RE GONNA FREEZE DONNIE?
WHAT'S GOIN' ON, FUGITOID?
WHAT'S GOING ON IS WE NEED TO SLOW DOWN DONATELLO'S CELL METABOLISM.
BUT THAT WON'T HAPPEN IF WE DON'T ACT IMMEDIATELY!

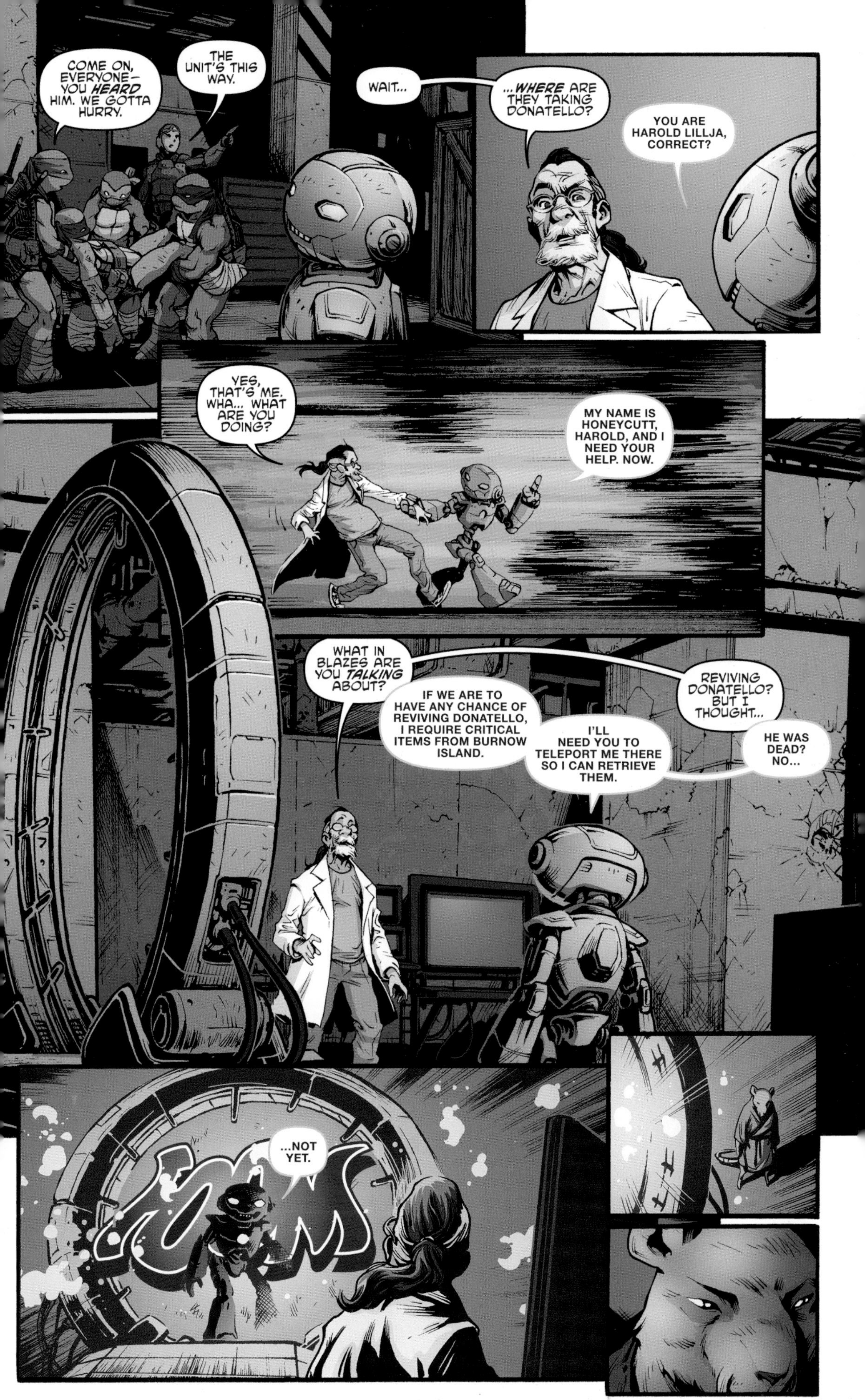
COME ON, EVERYONE— YOU *HEARD* HIM. WE GOTTA HURRY.
THE UNIT'S THIS WAY.
WAIT...
...*WHERE* ARE THEY TAKING DONATELLO?
YOU ARE HAROLD LILLJA, CORRECT?
YES, THAT'S ME. WHA... WHAT ARE YOU DOING?
MY NAME IS HONEYCUTT, HAROLD, AND I NEED YOUR HELP. NOW.
WHAT IN BLAZES ARE YOU *TALKING* ABOUT?
IF WE ARE TO HAVE ANY CHANCE OF REVIVING DONATELLO, I REQUIRE CRITICAL ITEMS FROM BURNOW ISLAND.
I'LL NEED YOU TO TELEPORT ME THERE SO I CAN RETRIEVE THEM.
REVIVING DONATELLO? BUT I THOUGHT...
HE WAS DEAD? NO...
...NOT YET.

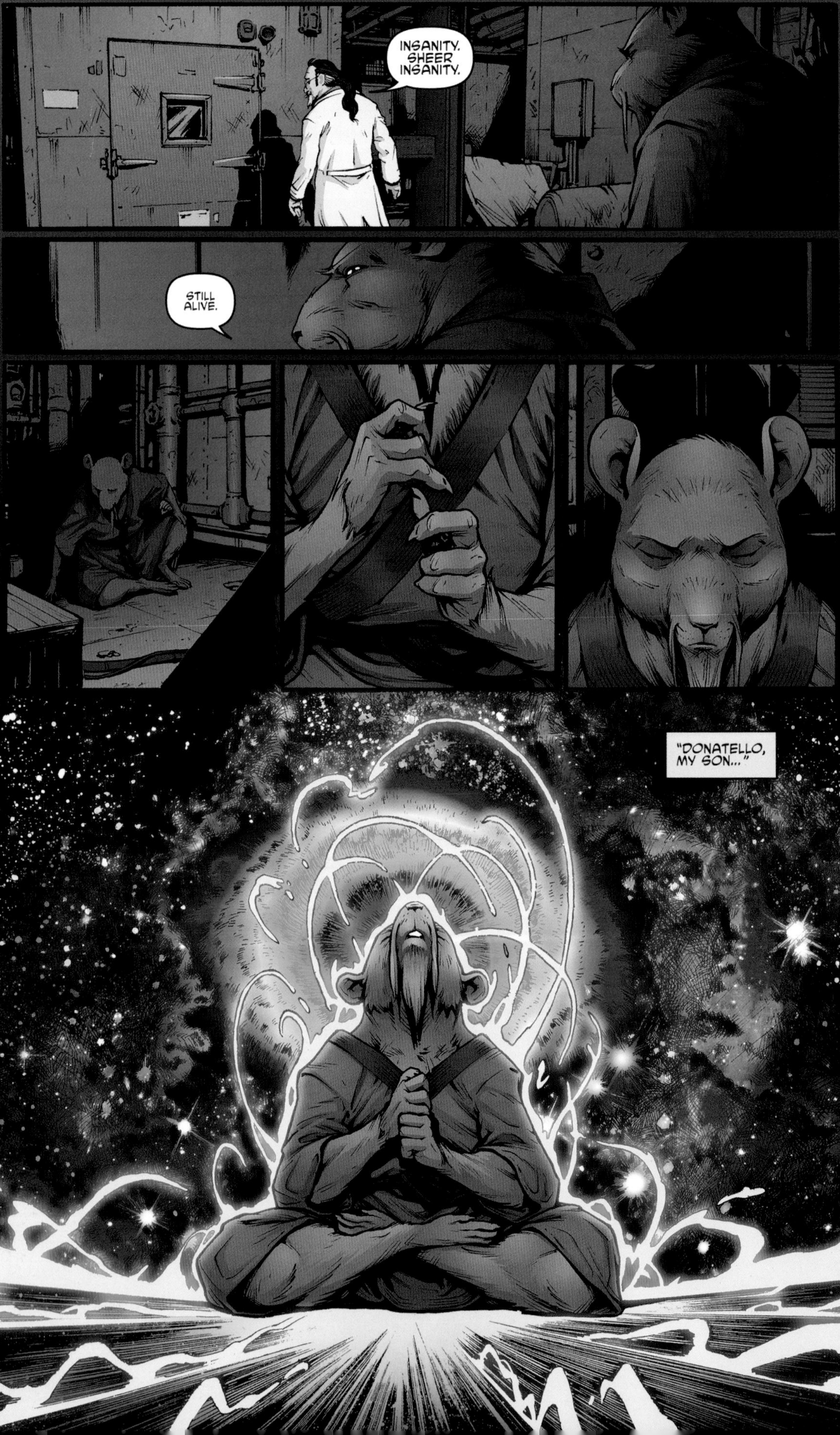
INSANITY. SHEER INSANITY.
STILL ALIVE.
"DONATELLO, MY SON..."

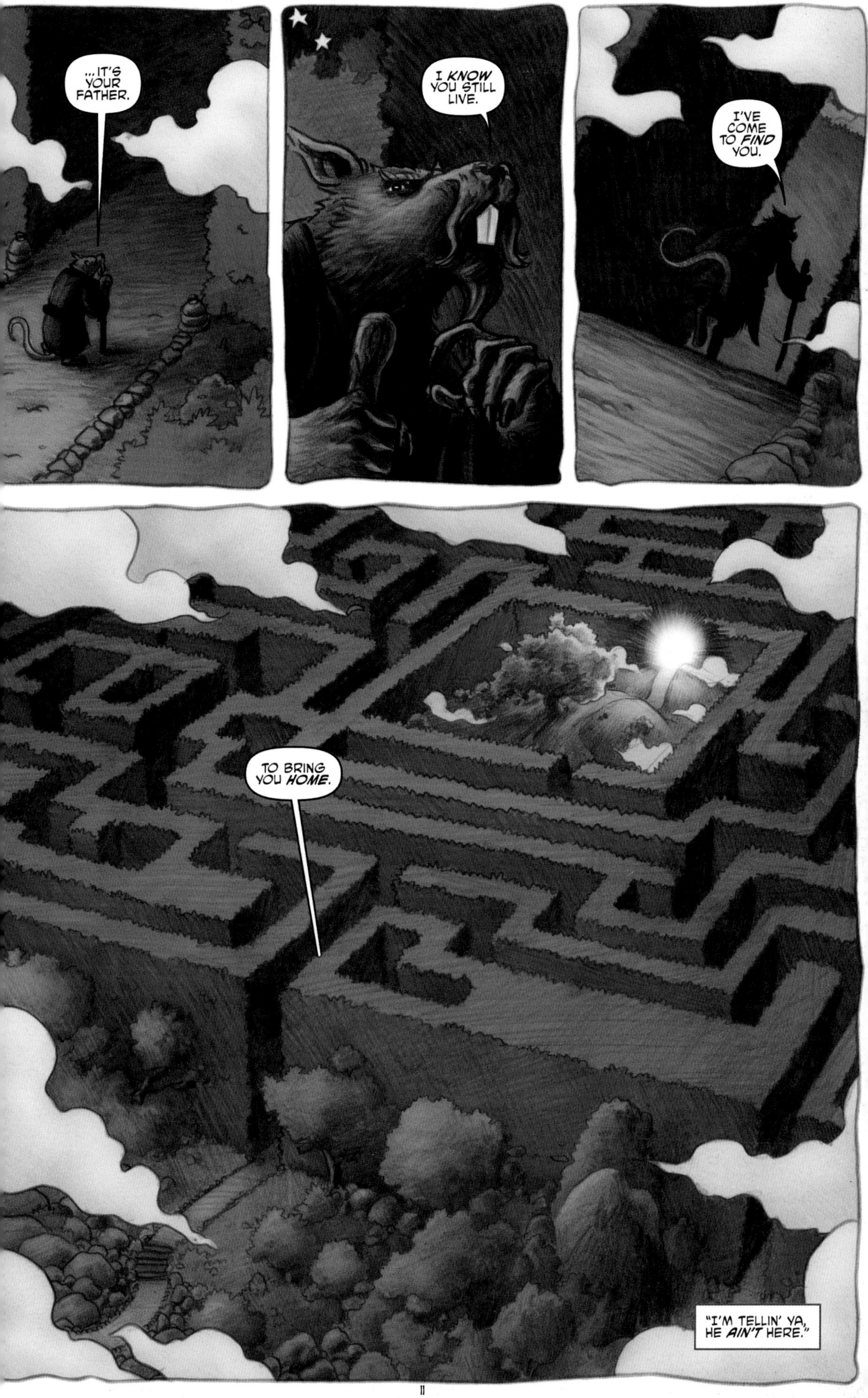
...IT'S YOUR FATHER.
I KNOW YOU STILL LIVE.
I'VE COME TO FIND YOU.
TO BRING YOU HOME.
"I'M TELLIN' YA, HE AIN'T HERE."

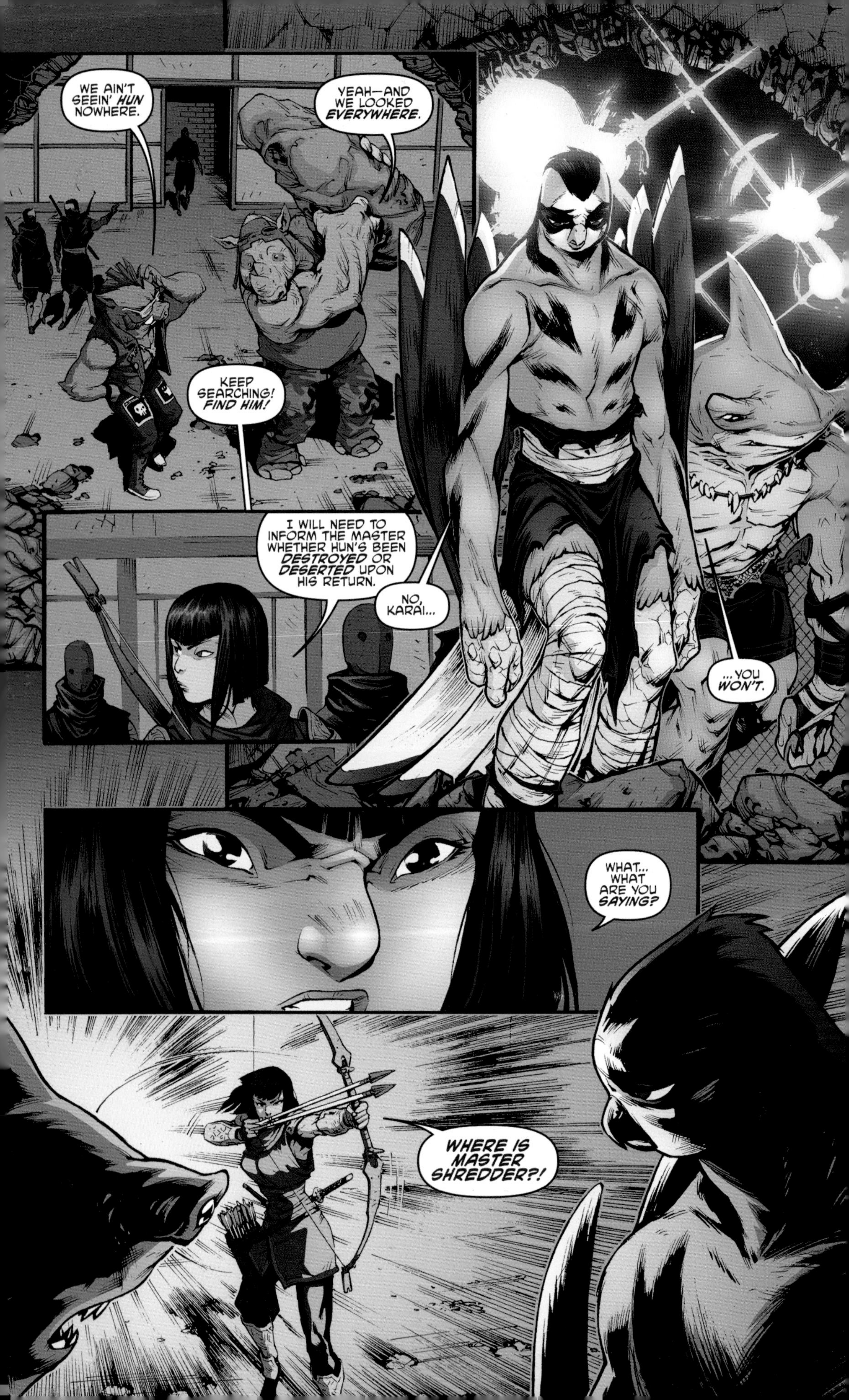
WE AIN'T SEEIN' *HUN* NOWHERE.
YEAH—AND WE LOOKED *EVERYWHERE*.
KEEP SEARCHING! *FIND HIM!*
I WILL NEED TO INFORM THE MASTER WHETHER HUN'S BEEN *DESTROYED* OR *DESERTED* UPON HIS RETURN.
NO, KARAI...
...YOU *WON'T*.
WHAT... WHAT ARE YOU *SAYING?*
WHERE IS MASTER SHREDDER?!

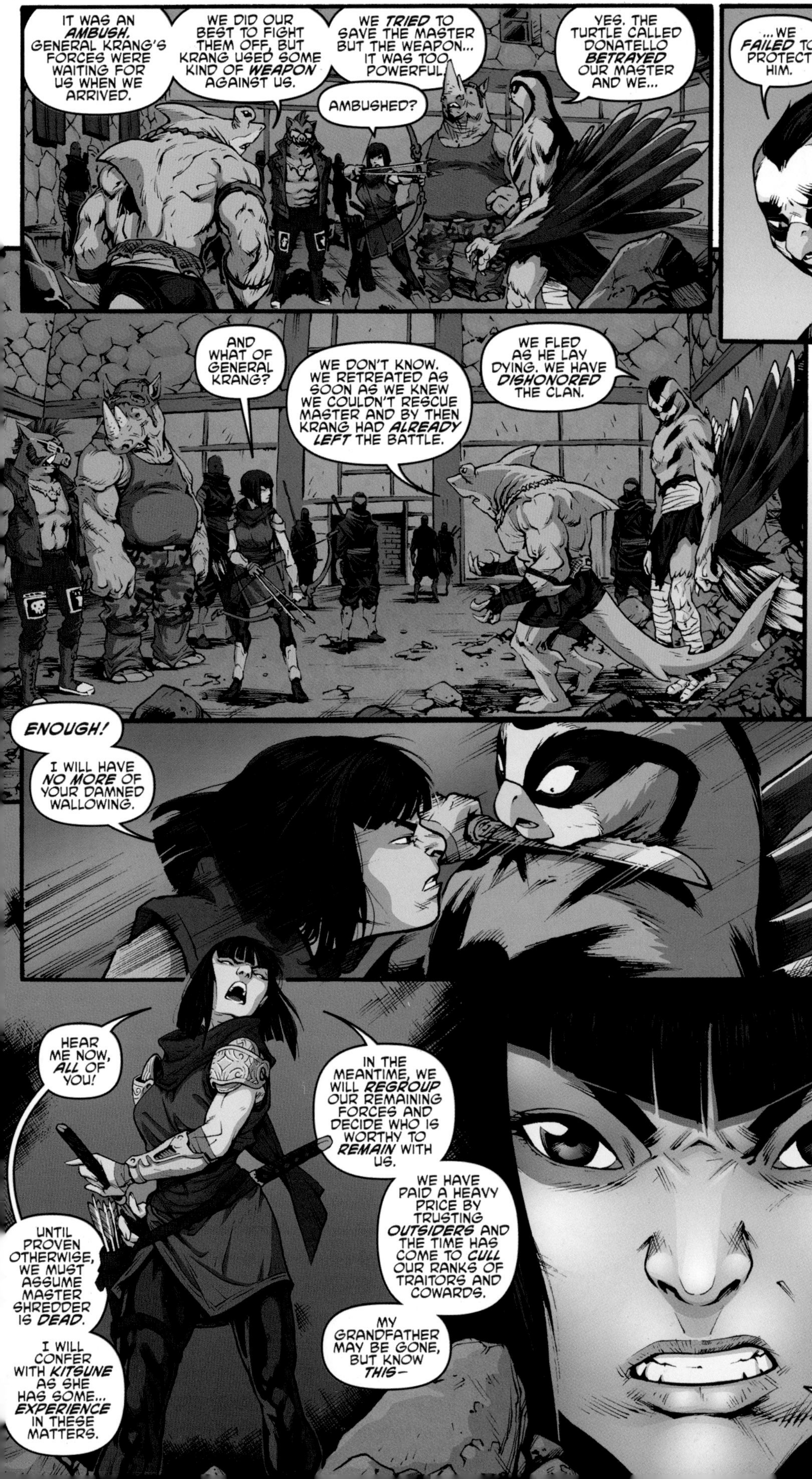
IT WAS AN AMBUSH. GENERAL KRANG'S FORCES WERE WAITING FOR US WHEN WE ARRIVED.
WE DID OUR BEST TO FIGHT THEM OFF, BUT KRANG USED SOME KIND OF WEAPON AGAINST US.
WE TRIED TO SAVE THE MASTER BUT THE WEAPON... IT WAS TOO POWERFUL.
AMBUSHED?
YES. THE TURTLE CALLED DONATELLO BETRAYED OUR MASTER AND WE...
...WE FAILED TO PROTECT HIM.
AND WHAT OF GENERAL KRANG?
WE DON'T KNOW. WE RETREATED AS SOON AS WE KNEW WE COULDN'T RESCUE MASTER AND BY THEN KRANG HAD ALREADY LEFT THE BATTLE.
WE FLED AS HE LAY DYING. WE HAVE DISHONORED THE CLAN.
ENOUGH!
I WILL HAVE NO MORE OF YOUR DAMNED WALLOWING.
HEAR ME NOW, ALL OF YOU!
UNTIL PROVEN OTHERWISE, WE MUST ASSUME MASTER SHREDDER IS DEAD.
I WILL CONFER WITH KITSUNE AS SHE HAS SOME... EXPERIENCE IN THESE MATTERS.
IN THE MEANTIME, WE WILL REGROUP OUR REMAINING FORCES AND DECIDE WHO IS WORTHY TO REMAIN WITH US.
WE HAVE PAID A HEAVY PRICE BY TRUSTING OUTSIDERS AND THE TIME HAS COME TO CULL OUR RANKS OF TRAITORS AND COWARDS.
MY GRANDFATHER MAY BE GONE, BUT KNOW THIS—
—THE FOOT CLAN IS NOT.

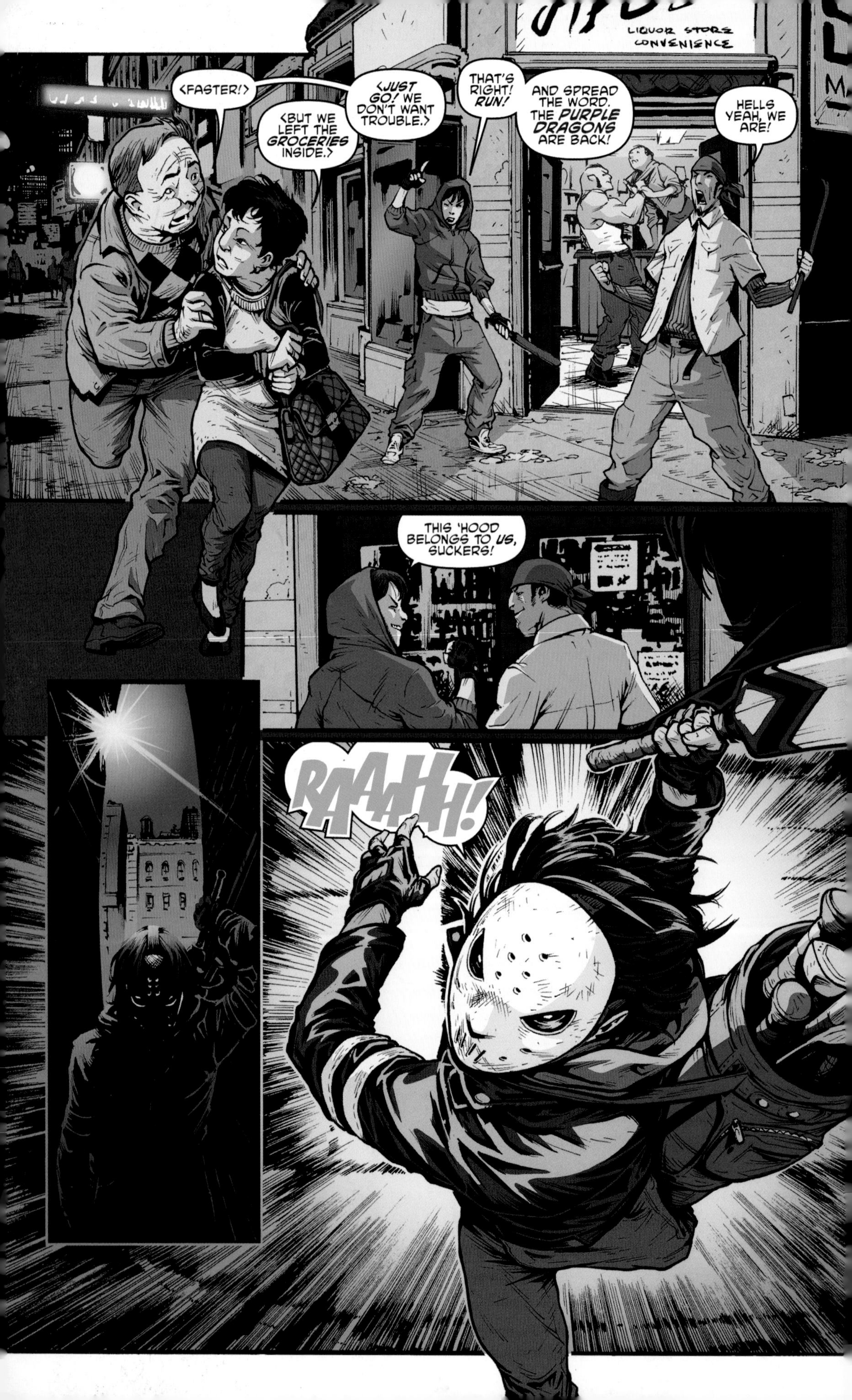
LIQUOR STORE
CONVENIENCE
<FASTER!>
<BUT WE LEFT THE GROCERIES INSIDE.>
<JUST GO! WE DON'T WANT TROUBLE.>
THAT'S RIGHT! RUN!
AND SPREAD THE WORD. THE PURPLE DRAGONS ARE BACK!
HELLS YEAH, WE ARE!
THIS 'HOOD BELONGS TO US, SUCKERS!
RAAAHH!

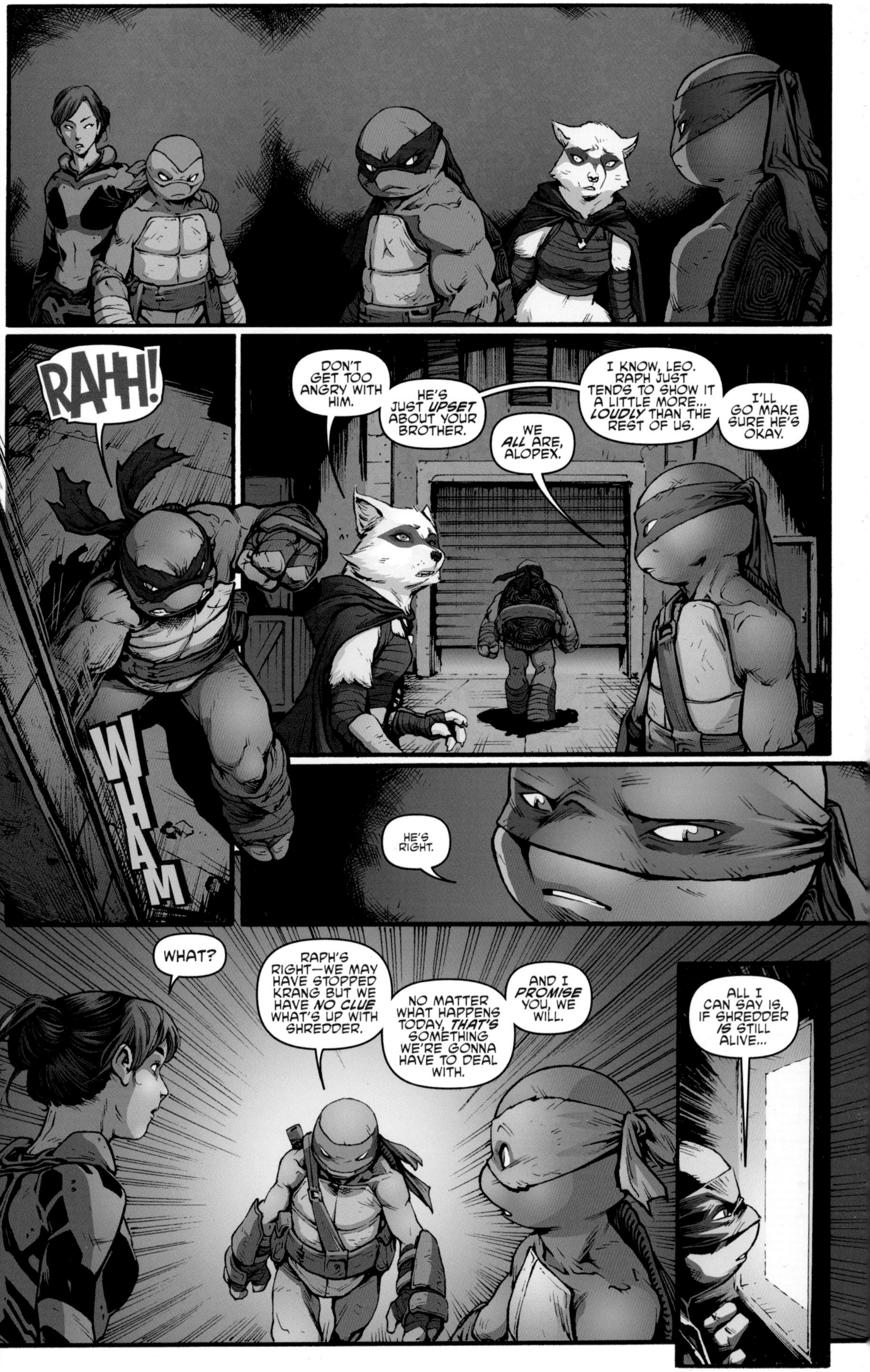
RAHH!
WHAM
DON'T GET TOO ANGRY WITH HIM.
HE'S JUST UPSET ABOUT YOUR BROTHER.
WE ALL ARE, ALOPEX.
I KNOW, LEO. RAPH JUST TENDS TO SHOW IT A LITTLE MORE... LOUDLY THAN THE REST OF US.
I'LL GO MAKE SURE HE'S OKAY.
HE'S RIGHT.
WHAT?
RAPH'S RIGHT—WE MAY HAVE STOPPED KRANG BUT WE HAVE NO CLUE WHAT'S UP WITH SHREDDER.
NO MATTER WHAT HAPPENS TODAY, THAT'S SOMETHING WE'RE GONNA HAVE TO DEAL WITH.
AND I PROMISE YOU, WE WILL.
ALL I CAN SAY IS, IF SHREDDER IS STILL ALIVE...

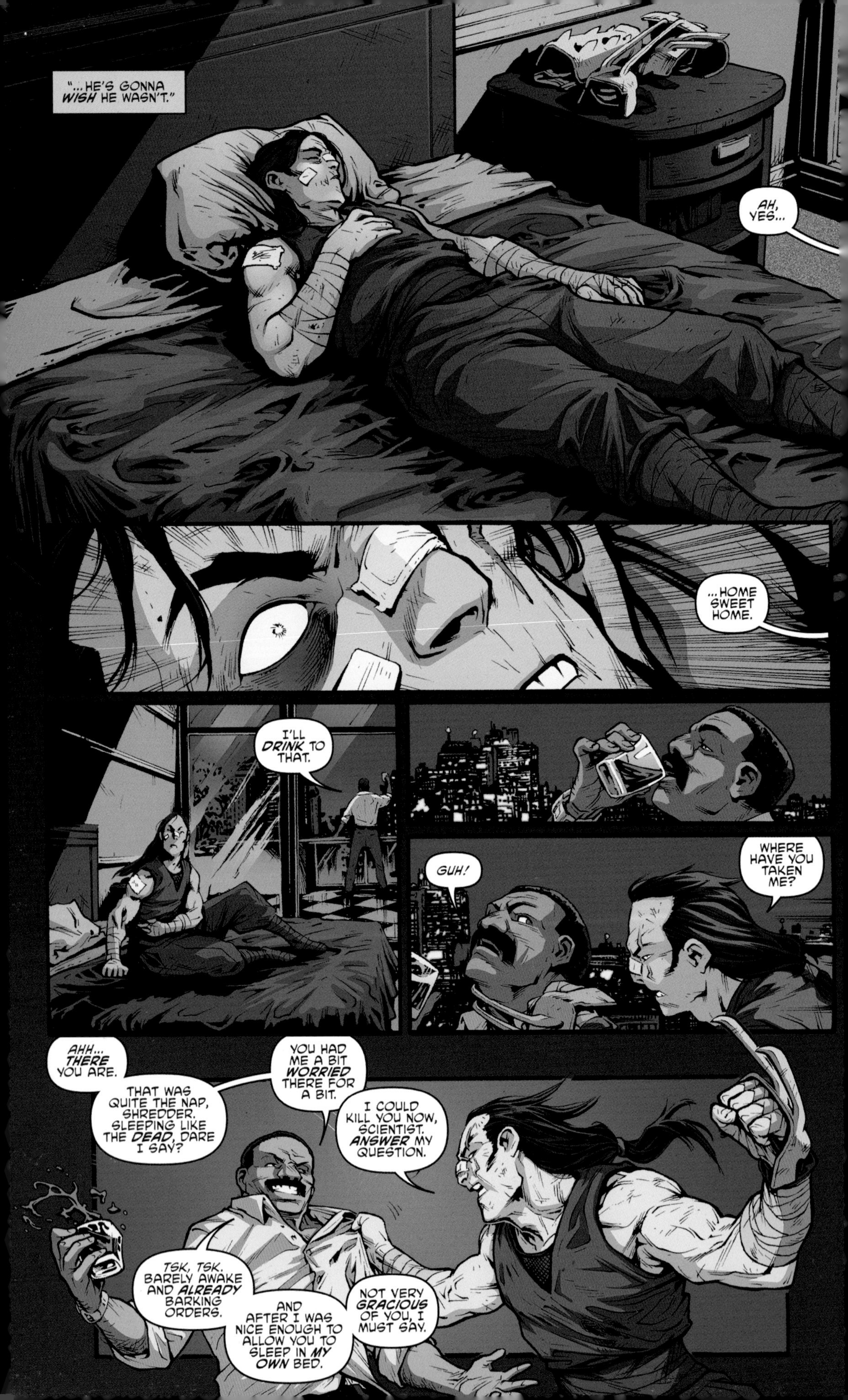
"...HE'S GONNA WISH HE WASN'T."
AH, YES...
...HOME SWEET HOME.
I'LL DRINK TO THAT.
GUH!
WHERE HAVE YOU TAKEN ME?
AHH... THERE YOU ARE.
THAT WAS QUITE THE NAP, SHREDDER. SLEEPING LIKE THE DEAD, DARE I SAY?
YOU HAD ME A BIT WORRIED THERE FOR A BIT.
I COULD KILL YOU NOW, SCIENTIST. ANSWER MY QUESTION.
TSK, TSK. BARELY AWAKE AND ALREADY BARKING ORDERS.
AND AFTER I WAS NICE ENOUGH TO ALLOW YOU TO SLEEP IN MY OWN BED.
NOT VERY GRACIOUS OF YOU, I MUST SAY.

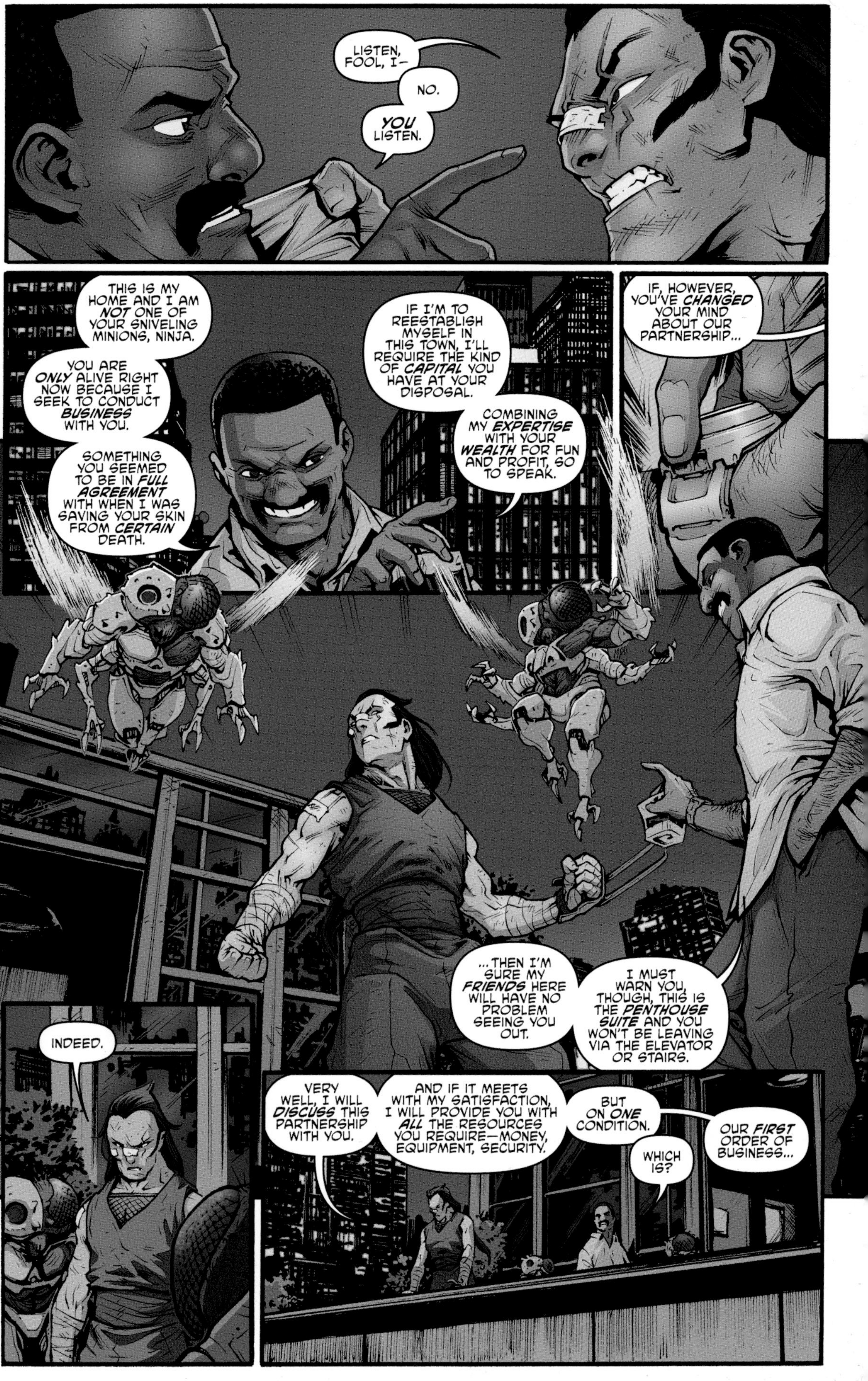

LISTEN, FOOL, I—
NO.
YOU LISTEN.
THIS IS MY HOME AND I AM NOT ONE OF YOUR SNIVELING MINIONS, NINJA.
YOU ARE ONLY ALIVE RIGHT NOW BECAUSE I SEEK TO CONDUCT BUSINESS WITH YOU.
SOMETHING YOU SEEMED TO BE IN FULL AGREEMENT WITH WHEN I WAS SAVING YOUR SKIN FROM CERTAIN DEATH.
IF I'M TO REESTABLISH MYSELF IN THIS TOWN, I'LL REQUIRE THE KIND OF CAPITAL YOU HAVE AT YOUR DISPOSAL.
COMBINING MY EXPERTISE WITH YOUR WEALTH FOR FUN AND PROFIT, SO TO SPEAK.
IF, HOWEVER, YOU'VE CHANGED YOUR MIND ABOUT OUR PARTNERSHIP...
...THEN I'M SURE MY FRIENDS HERE WILL HAVE NO PROBLEM SEEING YOU OUT.
I MUST WARN YOU, THOUGH, THIS IS THE PENTHOUSE SUITE AND YOU WON'T BE LEAVING VIA THE ELEVATOR OR STAIRS.
INDEED.
VERY WELL, I WILL DISCUSS THIS PARTNERSHIP WITH YOU.
AND IF IT MEETS WITH MY SATISFACTION, I WILL PROVIDE YOU WITH ALL THE RESOURCES YOU REQUIRE—MONEY, EQUIPMENT, SECURITY.
BUT ON ONE CONDITION.
WHICH IS?
OUR FIRST ORDER OF BUSINESS...

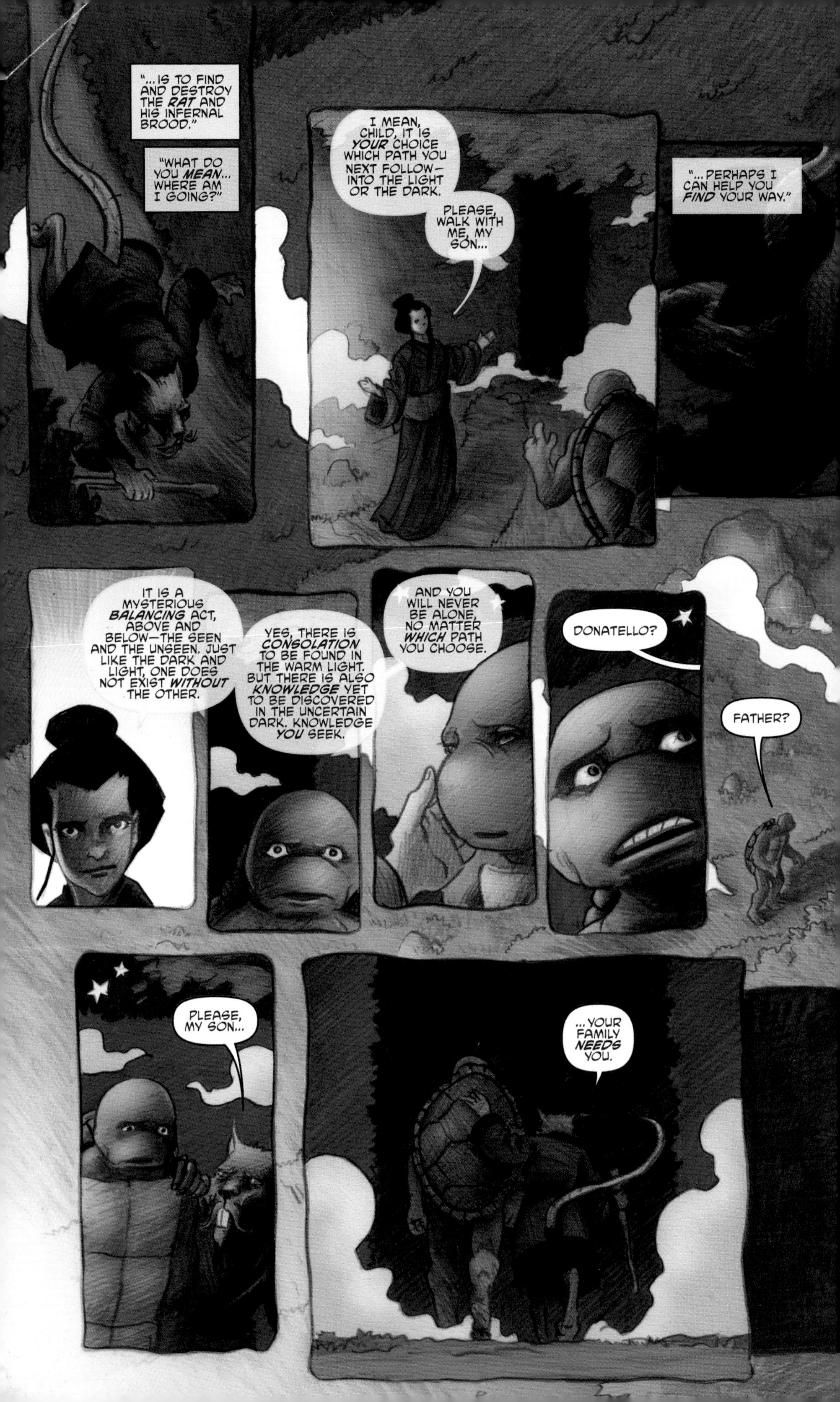

"...IS TO FIND AND DESTROY THE RAT AND HIS INFERNAL BROOD."
"WHAT DO YOU MEAN... WHERE AM I GOING?"
I MEAN, CHILD, IT IS YOUR CHOICE WHICH PATH YOU NEXT FOLLOW—INTO THE LIGHT OR THE DARK.
PLEASE, WALK WITH ME, MY SON...
"...PERHAPS I CAN HELP YOU FIND YOUR WAY."
IT IS A MYSTERIOUS BALANCING ACT, ABOVE AND BELOW—THE SEEN AND THE UNSEEN. JUST LIKE THE DARK AND LIGHT, ONE DOES NOT EXIST WITHOUT THE OTHER.
YES, THERE IS CONSOLATION TO BE FOUND IN THE WARM LIGHT. BUT THERE IS ALSO KNOWLEDGE YET TO BE DISCOVERED IN THE UNCERTAIN DARK. KNOWLEDGE YOU SEEK.
AND YOU WILL NEVER BE ALONE, NO MATTER WHICH PATH YOU CHOOSE.
DONATELLO?
FATHER?
PLEASE, MY SON...
...YOUR FAMILY NEEDS YOU.

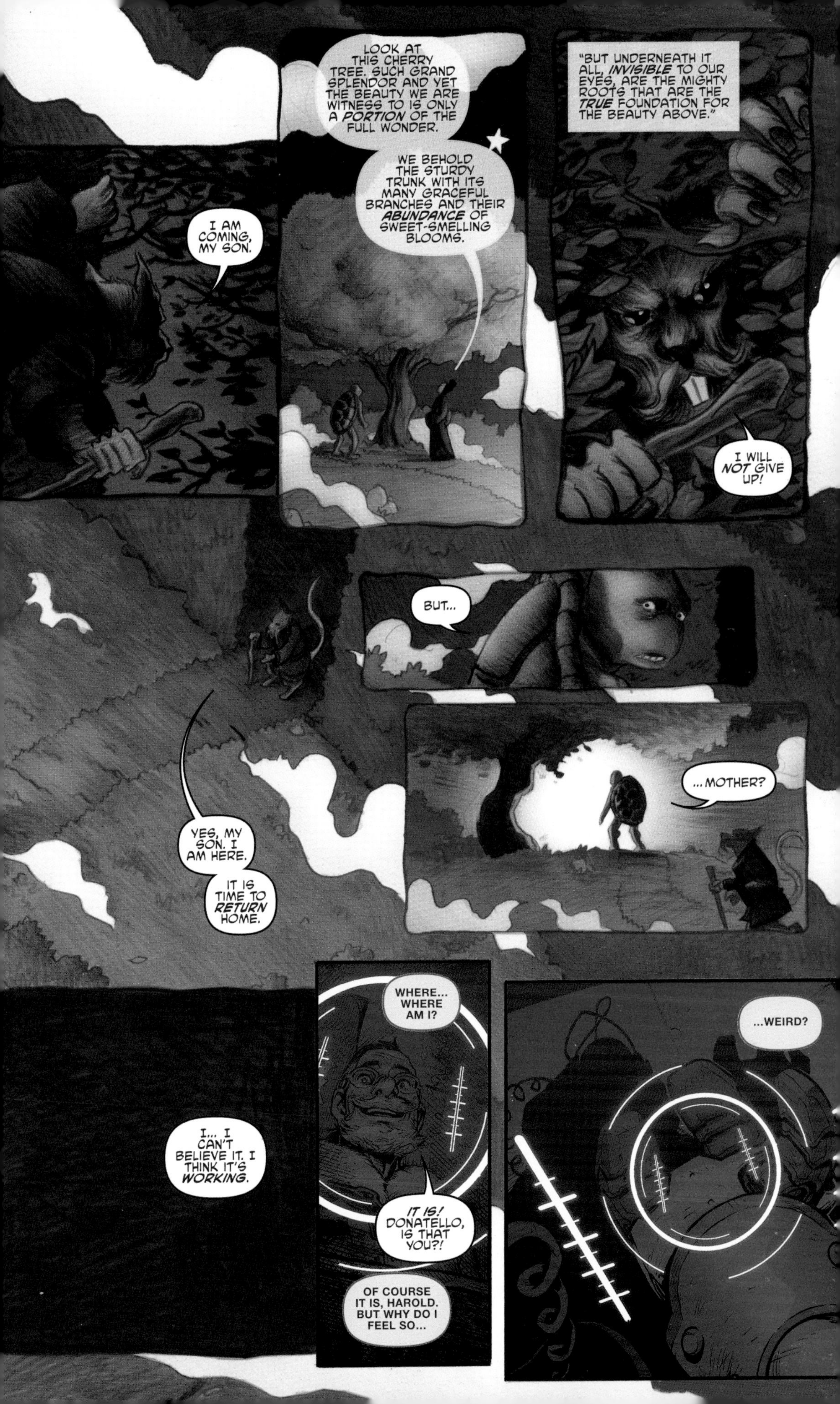
I AM COMING, MY SON.
LOOK AT THIS CHERRY TREE. SUCH GRAND SPLENDOR AND YET THE BEAUTY WE ARE WITNESS TO IS ONLY A PORTION OF THE FULL WONDER.
WE BEHOLD THE STURDY TRUNK WITH ITS MANY GRACEFUL BRANCHES AND THEIR ABUNDANCE OF SWEET-SMELLING BLOOMS.
"BUT UNDERNEATH IT ALL, INVISIBLE TO OUR EYES, ARE THE MIGHTY ROOTS THAT ARE THE TRUE FOUNDATION FOR THE BEAUTY ABOVE."
I WILL NOT GIVE UP!
BUT...
...MOTHER?
YES, MY SON. I AM HERE.
IT IS TIME TO RETURN HOME.
I... I CAN'T BELIEVE IT. I THINK IT'S WORKING.
WHERE... WHERE AM I?
IT IS! DONATELLO, IS THAT YOU?!
OF COURSE IT IS, HAROLD. BUT WHY DO I FEEL SO...
...WEIRD?

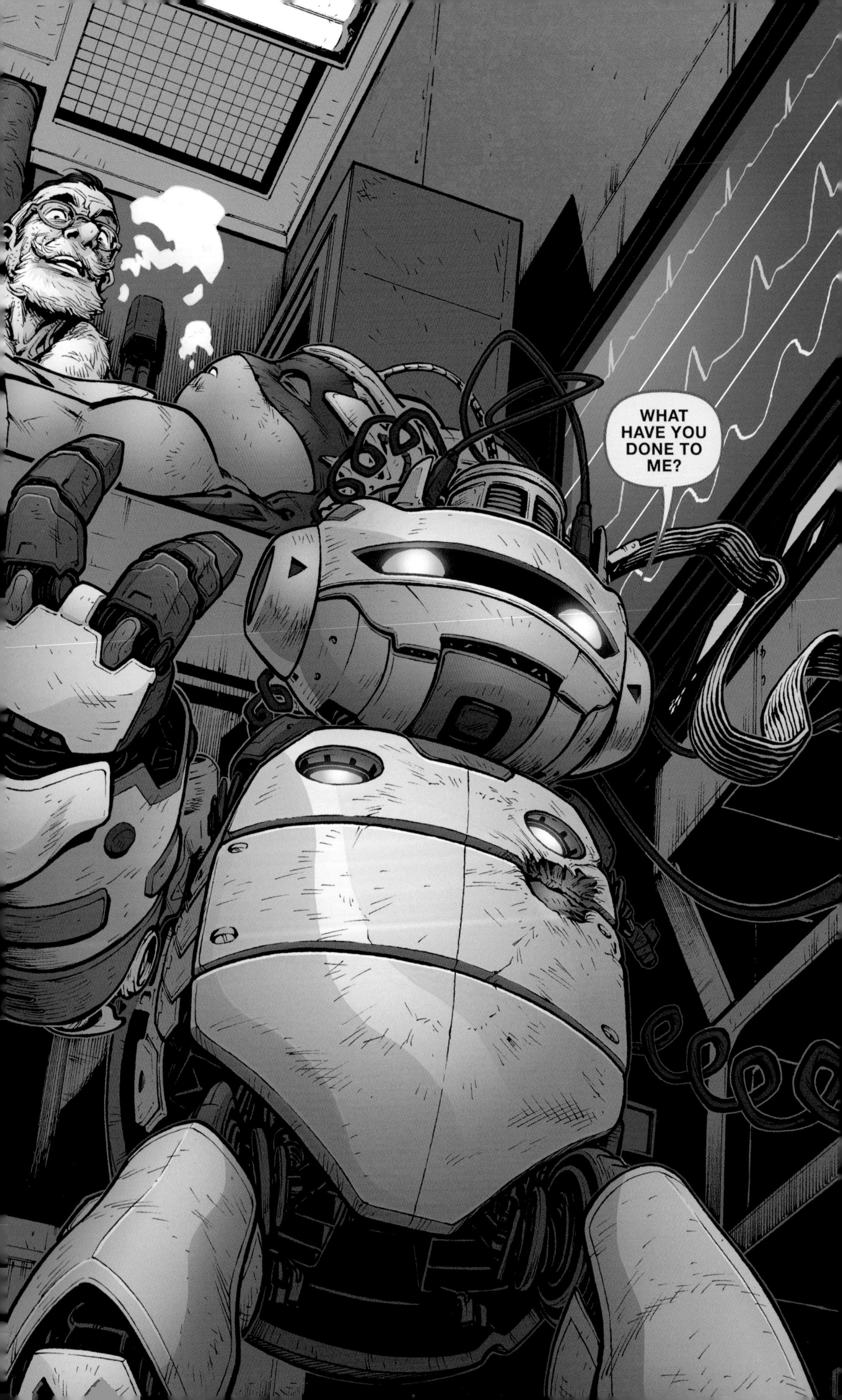
WHAT HAVE YOU DONE TO ME?

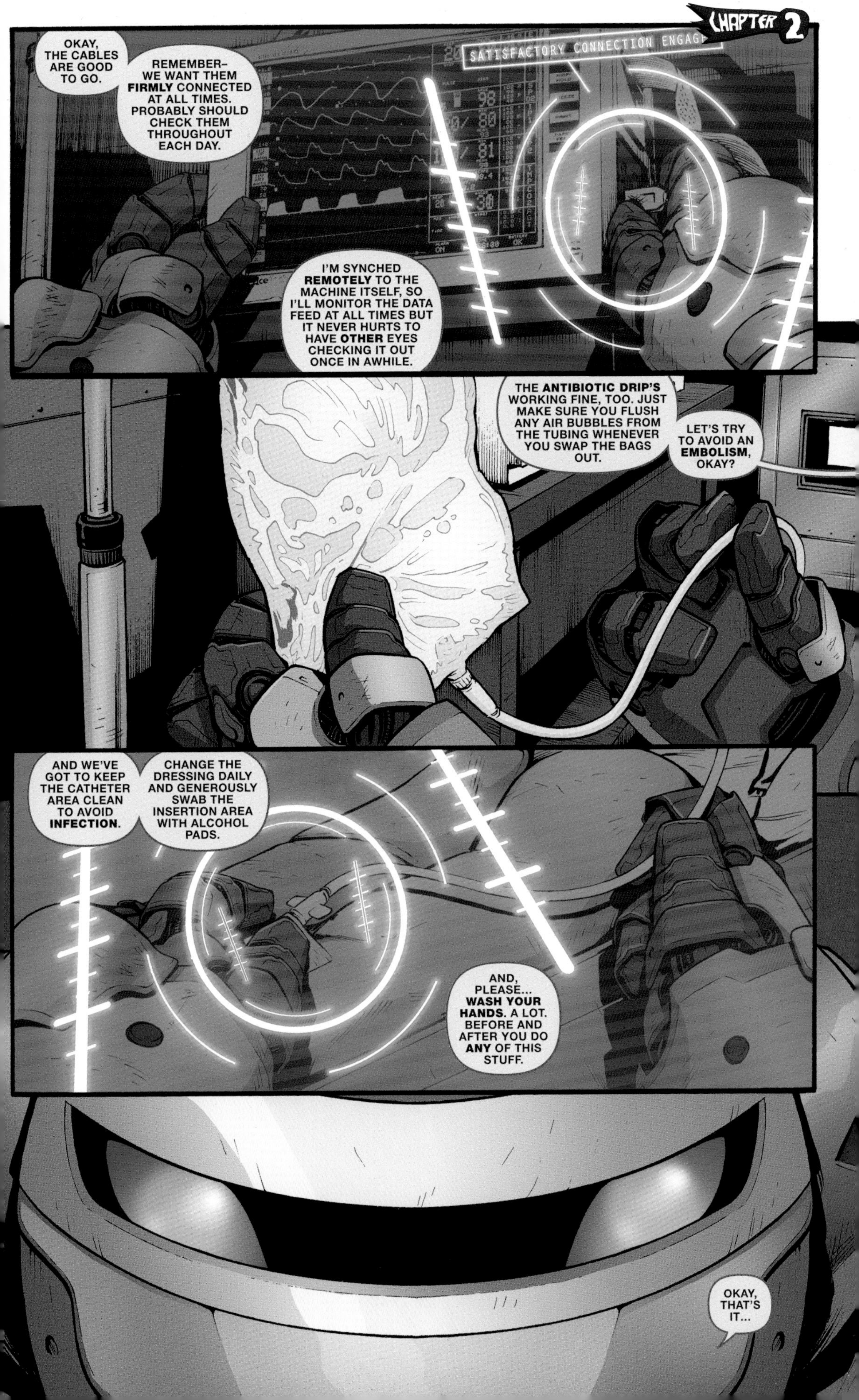

CHAPTER 2
SATISFACTORY CONNECTION ENGAGE
OKAY, THE CABLES ARE GOOD TO GO.
REMEMBER– WE WANT THEM **FIRMLY** CONNECTED AT ALL TIMES. PROBABLY SHOULD CHECK THEM THROUGHOUT EACH DAY.
I'M SYNCHED **REMOTELY** TO THE MACHINE ITSELF, SO I'LL MONITOR THE DATA FEED AT ALL TIMES BUT IT NEVER HURTS TO HAVE **OTHER** EYES CHECKING IT OUT ONCE IN AWHILE.
THE **ANTIBIOTIC DRIP'S** WORKING FINE, TOO. JUST MAKE SURE YOU FLUSH ANY AIR BUBBLES FROM THE TUBING WHENEVER YOU SWAP THE BAGS OUT.
LET'S TRY TO AVOID AN **EMBOLISM**, OKAY?
AND WE'VE GOT TO KEEP THE CATHETER AREA CLEAN TO AVOID **INFECTION**.
CHANGE THE DRESSING DAILY AND GENEROUSLY SWAB THE INSERTION AREA WITH ALCOHOL PADS.
AND, PLEASE... **WASH YOUR HANDS**. A LOT. BEFORE AND AFTER YOU DO **ANY** OF THIS STUFF.
OKAY, THAT'S IT...

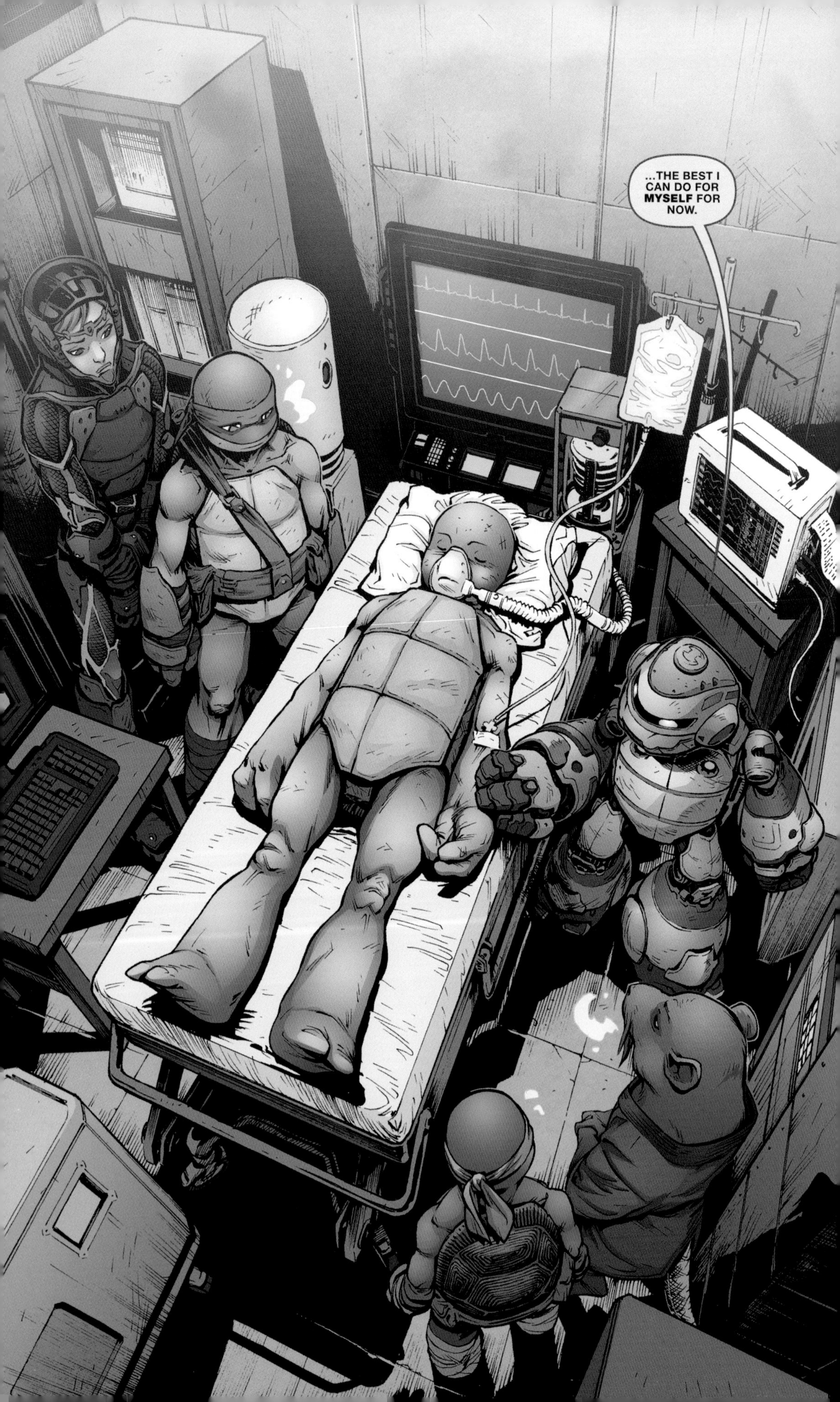
...THE BEST I CAN DO FOR **MYSELF** FOR NOW.

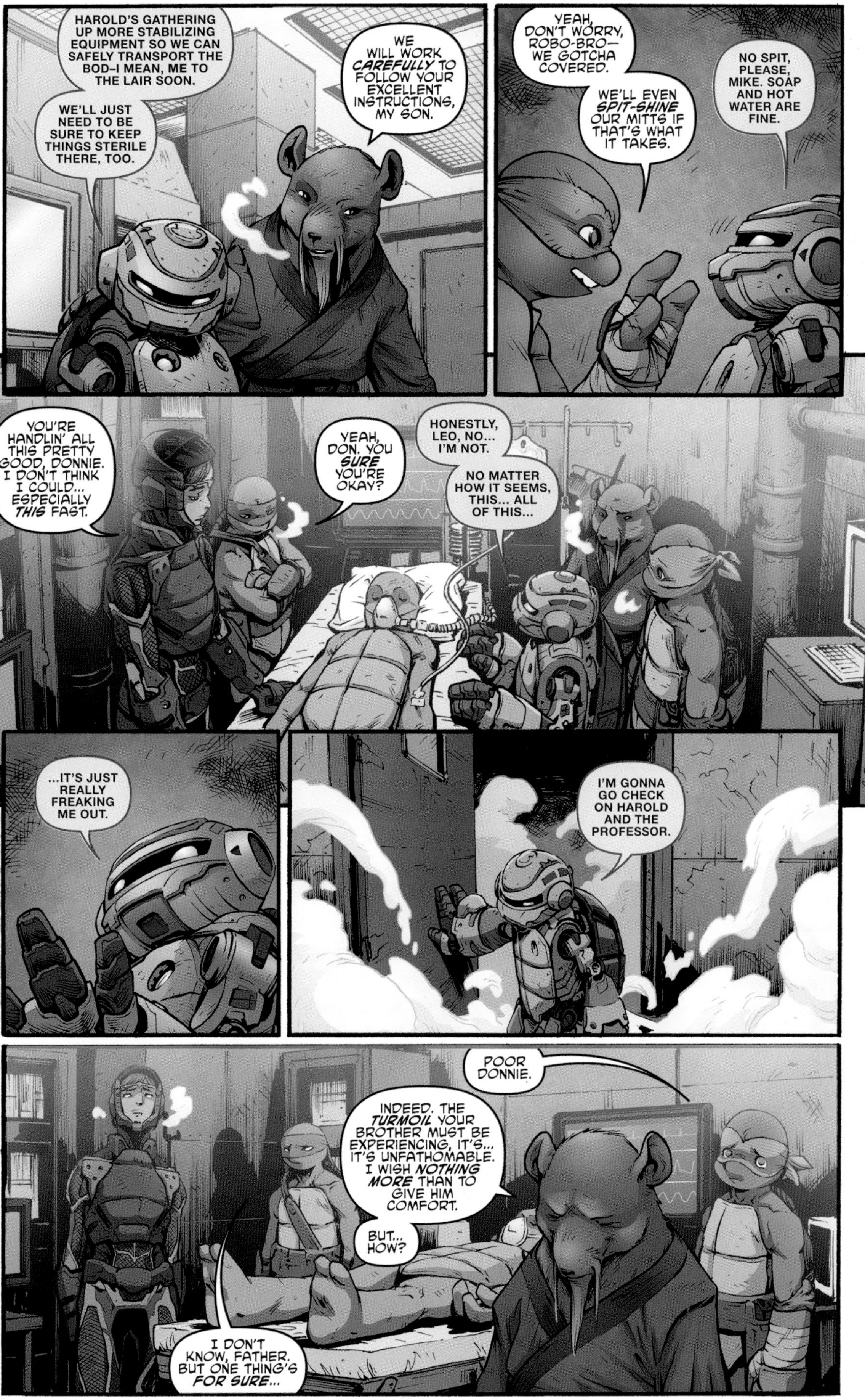
HAROLD'S GATHERING UP MORE STABILIZING EQUIPMENT SO WE CAN SAFELY TRANSPORT THE BOD–I MEAN, ME TO THE LAIR SOON.
WE'LL JUST NEED TO BE SURE TO KEEP THINGS STERILE THERE, TOO.
WE WILL WORK CAREFULLY TO FOLLOW YOUR EXCELLENT INSTRUCTIONS, MY SON.
YEAH, DON'T WORRY, ROBO-BRO– WE GOTCHA COVERED.
WE'LL EVEN SPIT-SHINE OUR MITTS IF THAT'S WHAT IT TAKES.
NO SPIT, PLEASE, MIKE. SOAP AND HOT WATER ARE FINE.
YOU'RE HANDLIN' ALL THIS PRETTY GOOD, DONNIE. I DON'T THINK I COULD... ESPECIALLY THIS FAST.
YEAH, DON. YOU SURE YOU'RE OKAY?
HONESTLY, LEO, NO... I'M NOT.
NO MATTER HOW IT SEEMS, THIS... ALL OF THIS...
...IT'S JUST REALLY FREAKING ME OUT.
I'M GONNA GO CHECK ON HAROLD AND THE PROFESSOR.
POOR DONNIE.
INDEED. THE TURMOIL YOUR BROTHER MUST BE EXPERIENCING, IT'S... IT'S UNFATHOMABLE. I WISH NOTHING MORE THAN TO GIVE HIM COMFORT.
BUT... HOW?
I DON'T KNOW, FATHER. BUT ONE THING'S FOR SURE...

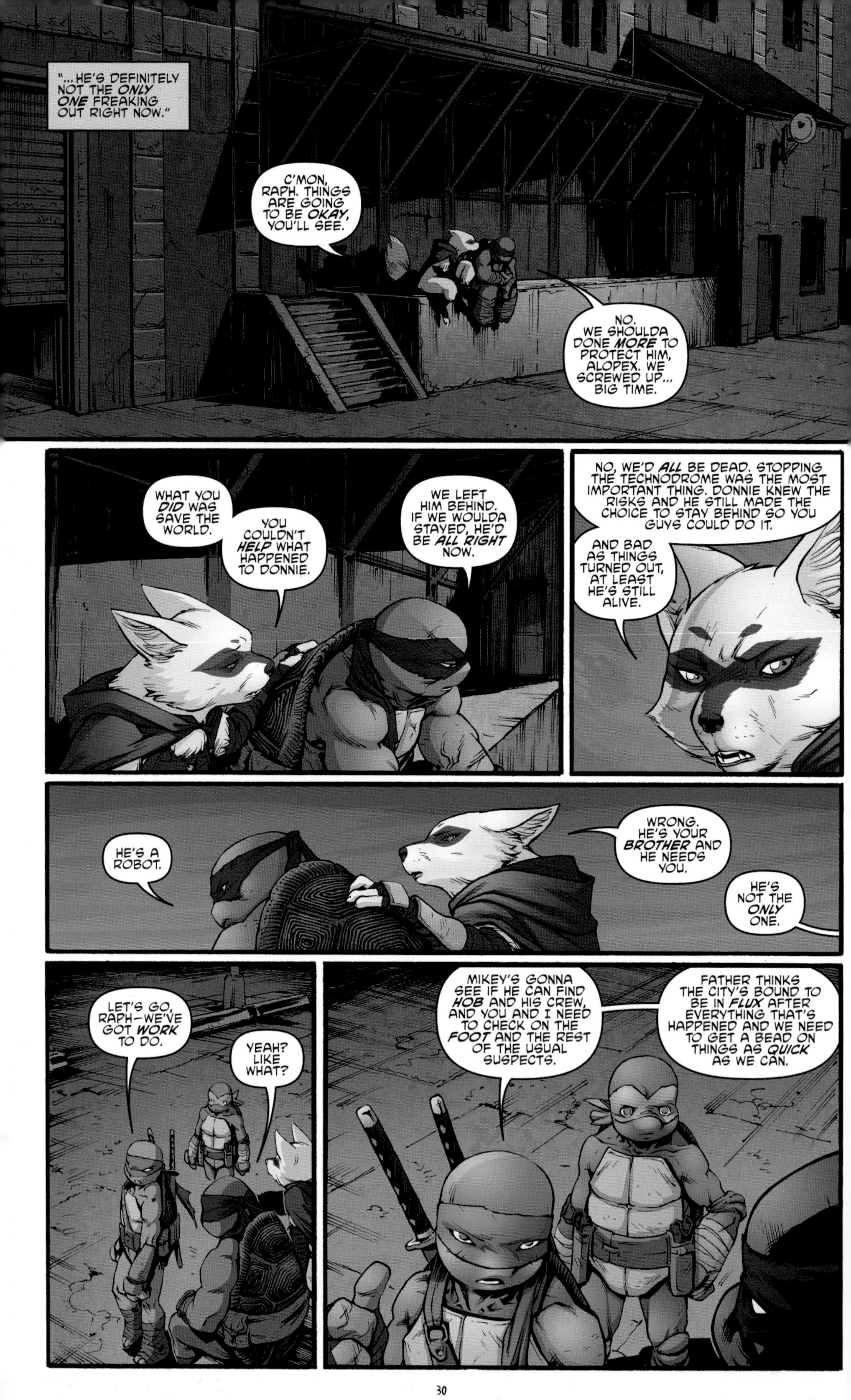
"...HE'S DEFINITELY NOT THE ONLY ONE FREAKING OUT RIGHT NOW."
C'MON, RAPH. THINGS ARE GOING TO BE OKAY, YOU'LL SEE.
NO. WE SHOULDA DONE MORE TO PROTECT HIM, ALOPEX. WE SCREWED UP... BIG TIME.
WHAT YOU DID WAS SAVE THE WORLD.
YOU COULDN'T HELP WHAT HAPPENED TO DONNIE.
WE LEFT HIM BEHIND. IF WE WOULDA STAYED, HE'D BE ALL RIGHT NOW.
NO, WE'D ALL BE DEAD. STOPPING THE TECHNODROME WAS THE MOST IMPORTANT THING. DONNIE KNEW THE RISKS AND HE STILL MADE THE CHOICE TO STAY BEHIND SO YOU GUYS COULD DO IT.
AND BAD AS THINGS TURNED OUT, AT LEAST HE'S STILL ALIVE.
HE'S A ROBOT.
WRONG. HE'S YOUR BROTHER AND HE NEEDS YOU.
HE'S NOT THE ONLY ONE.
LET'S GO, RAPH—WE'VE GOT WORK TO DO.
YEAH? LIKE WHAT?
MIKEY'S GONNA SEE IF HE CAN FIND HOB AND HIS CREW, AND YOU AND I NEED TO CHECK ON THE FOOT AND THE REST OF THE USUAL SUSPECTS.
FATHER THINKS THE CITY'S BOUND TO BE IN FLUX AFTER EVERYTHING THAT'S HAPPENED AND WE NEED TO GET A BEAD ON THINGS AS QUICK AS WE CAN.

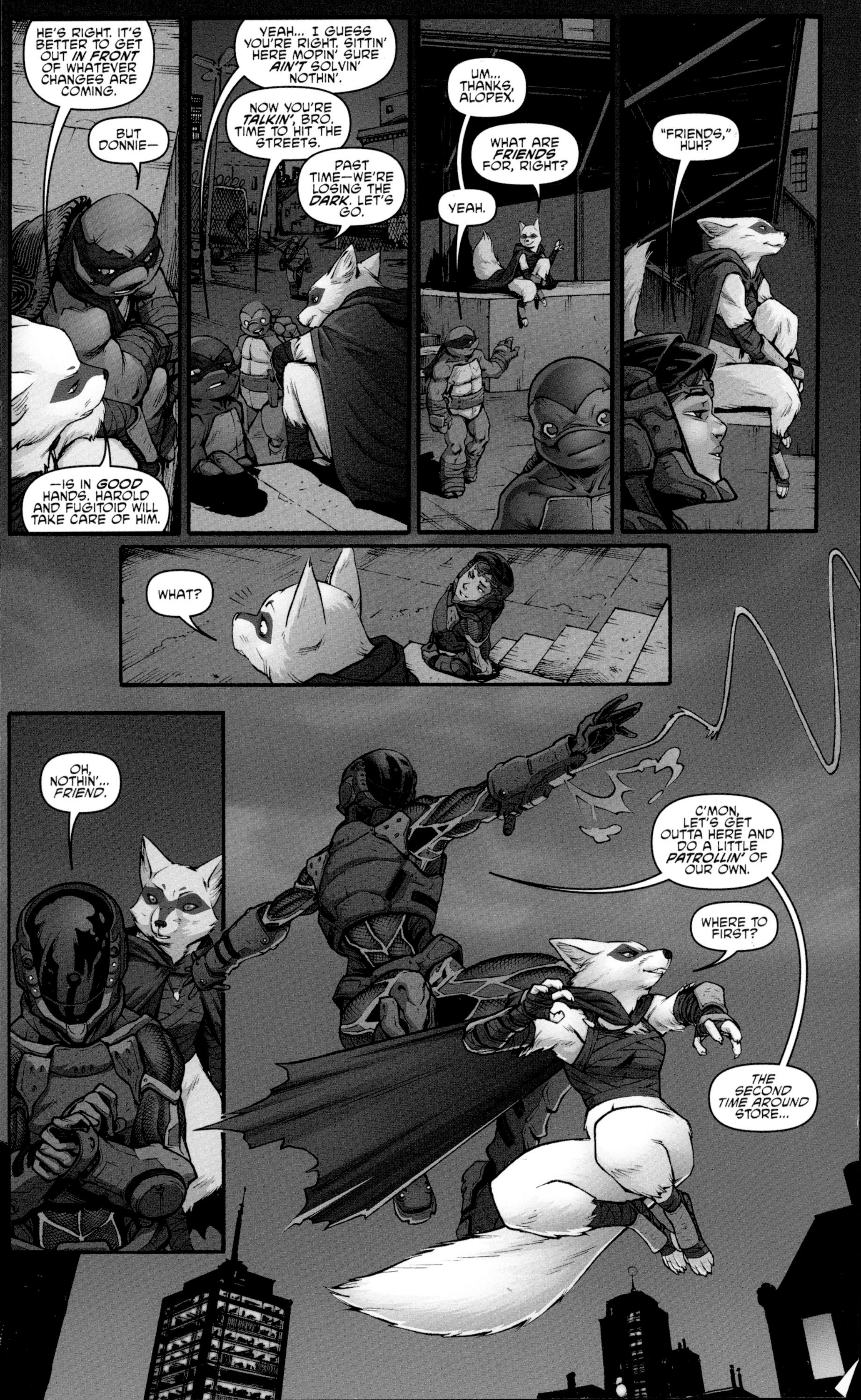

HE'S RIGHT. IT'S BETTER TO GET OUT IN FRONT OF WHATEVER CHANGES ARE COMING.
BUT DONNIE—
—IS IN GOOD HANDS. HAROLD AND FUGITOID WILL TAKE CARE OF HIM.
YEAH... I GUESS YOU'RE RIGHT. SITTIN' HERE MOPIN' SURE AIN'T SOLVIN' NOTHIN'.
NOW YOU'RE TALKIN', BRO. TIME TO HIT THE STREETS.
PAST TIME—WE'RE LOSING THE DARK. LET'S GO.
UM... THANKS, ALOPEX.
WHAT ARE FRIENDS FOR, RIGHT?
YEAH.
"FRIENDS," HUH?
WHAT?
OH, NOTHIN'... FRIEND.
C'MON, LET'S GET OUTTA HERE AND DO A LITTLE PATROLLIN' OF OUR OWN.
WHERE TO FIRST?
THE SECOND TIME AROUND STORE...

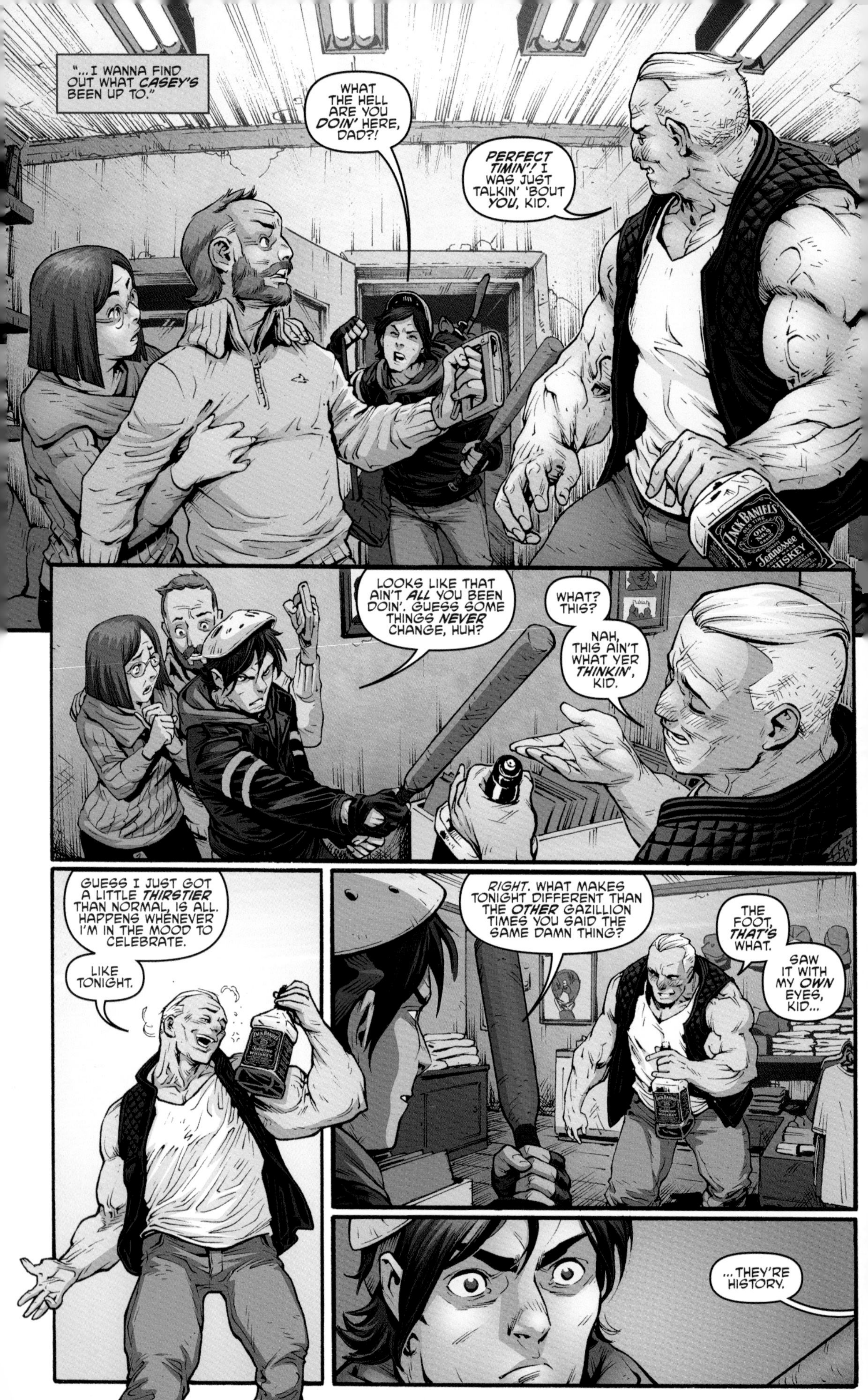
"...I WANNA FIND OUT WHAT CASEY'S BEEN UP TO."
WHAT THE HELL ARE YOU DOIN' HERE, DAD?!
PERFECT TIMIN'! I WAS JUST TALKIN' 'BOUT YOU, KID.
LOOKS LIKE THAT AIN'T ALL YOU BEEN DOIN'. GUESS SOME THINGS NEVER CHANGE, HUH?
WHAT? THIS?
NAH, THIS AIN'T WHAT YER THINKIN', KID.
GUESS I JUST GOT A LITTLE THIRSTIER THAN NORMAL, IS ALL. HAPPENS WHENEVER I'M IN THE MOOD TO CELEBRATE.
LIKE TONIGHT.
RIGHT. WHAT MAKES TONIGHT DIFFERENT THAN THE OTHER GAZILLION TIMES YOU SAID THE SAME DAMN THING?
THE FOOT, THAT'S WHAT.
SAW IT WITH MY OWN EYES, KID...
...THEY'RE HISTORY.

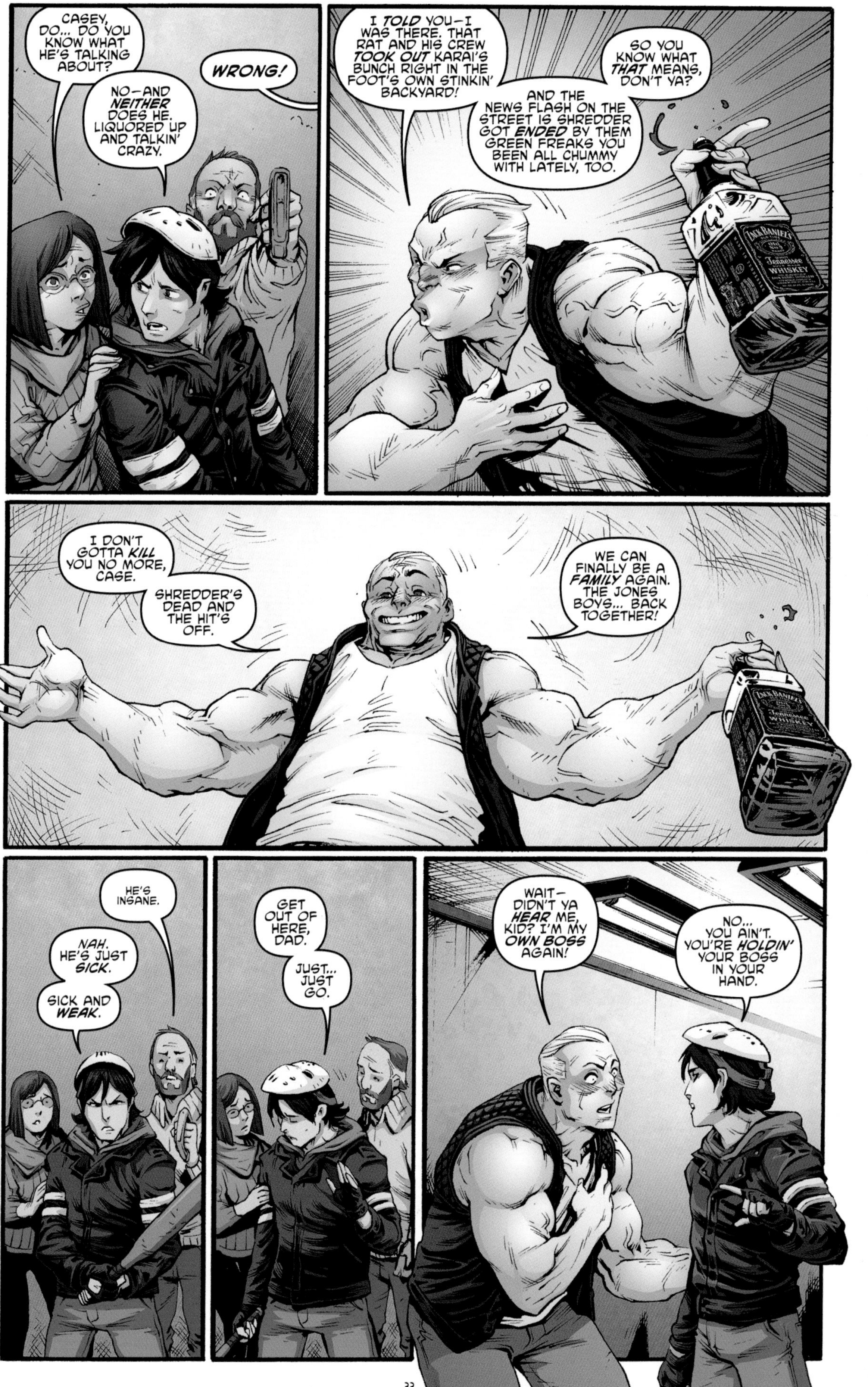
CASEY, DO... DO YOU KNOW WHAT HE'S TALKING ABOUT?
NO—AND NEITHER DOES HE. LIQUORED UP AND TALKIN' CRAZY.
WRONG!
I TOLD YOU—I WAS THERE. THAT RAT AND HIS CREW TOOK OUT KARAI'S BUNCH RIGHT IN THE FOOT'S OWN STINKIN' BACKYARD!
AND THE NEWS FLASH ON THE STREET IS SHREDDER GOT ENDED BY THEM GREEN FREAKS YOU BEEN ALL CHUMMY WITH LATELY, TOO.
SO YOU KNOW WHAT THAT MEANS, DON'T YA?
I DON'T GOTTA KILL YOU NO MORE, CASE.
SHREDDER'S DEAD AND THE HIT'S OFF.
WE CAN FINALLY BE A FAMILY AGAIN. THE JONES BOYS... BACK TOGETHER!
HE'S INSANE.
NAH. HE'S JUST SICK.
SICK AND WEAK.
GET OUT OF HERE, DAD.
JUST... JUST GO.
WAIT—DIDN'T YA HEAR ME, KID? I'M MY OWN BOSS AGAIN!
NO... YOU AIN'T. YOU'RE HOLDIN' YOUR BOSS IN YOUR HAND.

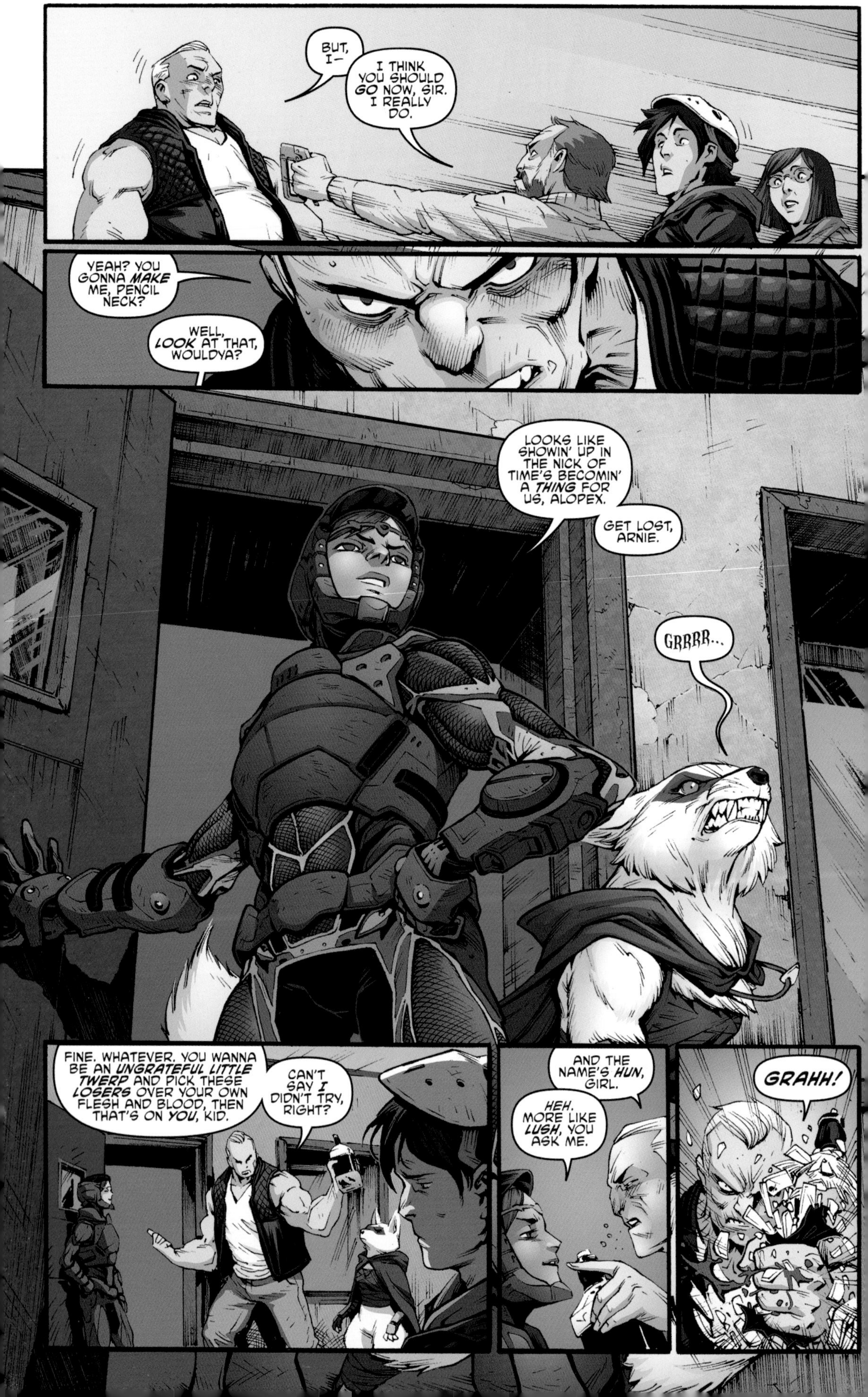

BUT, I—
I THINK YOU SHOULD GO NOW, SIR. I REALLY DO.
YEAH? YOU GONNA MAKE ME, PENCIL NECK?
WELL, LOOK AT THAT, WOULDYA?
LOOKS LIKE SHOWIN' UP IN THE NICK OF TIME'S BECOMIN' A THING FOR US, ALOPEX.
GET LOST, ARNIE.
GRRRR...
FINE. WHATEVER. YOU WANNA BE AN UNGRATEFUL LITTLE TWERP AND PICK THESE LOSERS OVER YOUR OWN FLESH AND BLOOD, THEN THAT'S ON YOU, KID.
CAN'T SAY I DIDN'T TRY, RIGHT?
AND THE NAME'S HUN, GIRL.
HEH. MORE LIKE LUSH, YOU ASK ME.
GRAHH!

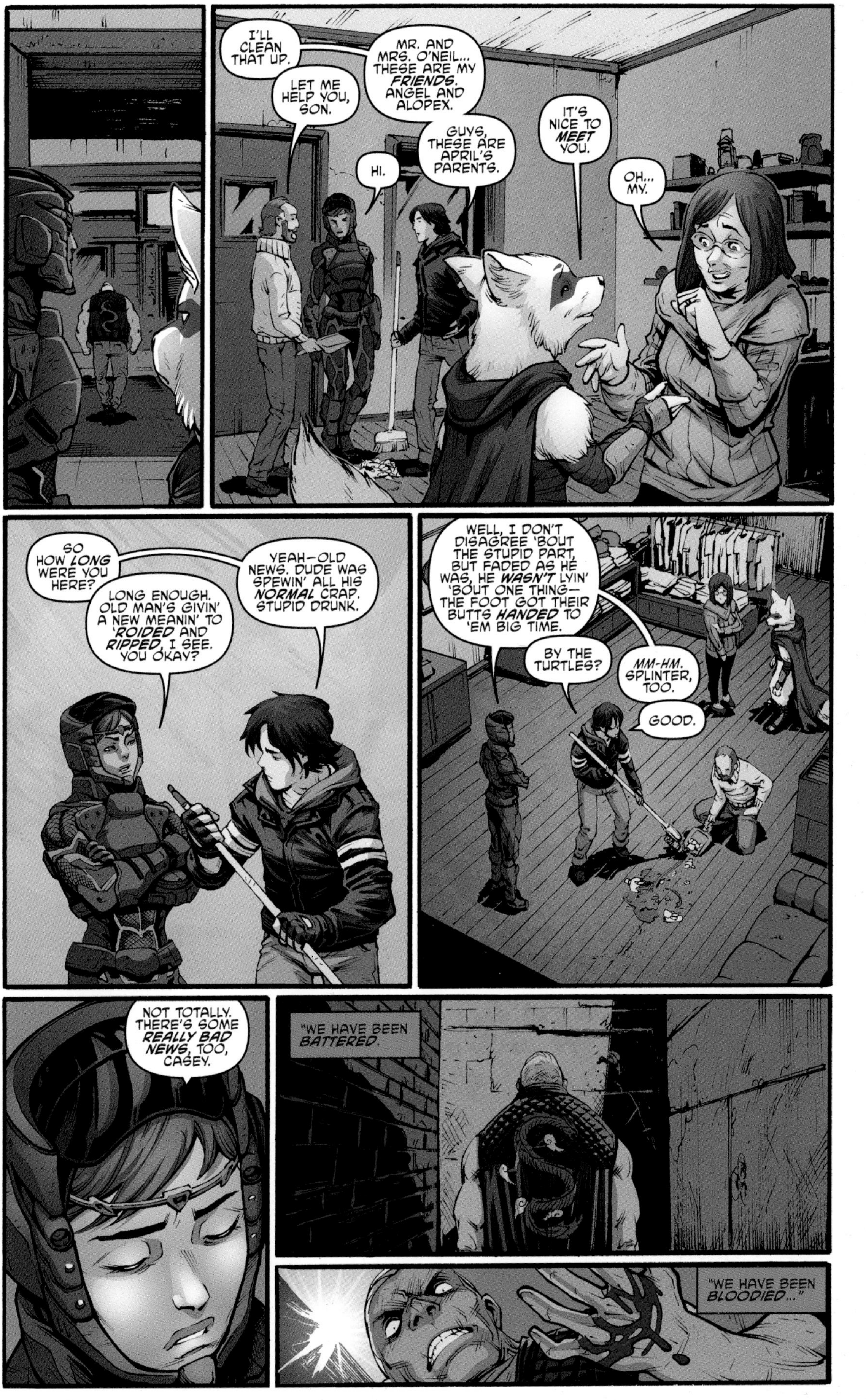
I'LL CLEAN THAT UP.
LET ME HELP YOU, SON.
MR. AND MRS. O'NEIL... THESE ARE MY *FRIENDS*. ANGEL AND ALOPEX.
HI.
GUYS, THESE ARE APRIL'S PARENTS.
IT'S NICE TO *MEET* YOU.
OH... MY.
SO HOW *LONG* WERE YOU HERE?
LONG ENOUGH. OLD MAN'S GIVIN' A NEW MEANIN' TO *'ROIDED* AND *RIPPED*, I SEE. YOU OKAY?
YEAH—OLD NEWS. DUDE WAS SPEWIN' ALL HIS *NORMAL* CRAP. STUPID DRUNK.
WELL, I DON'T DISAGREE 'BOUT THE STUPID PART, BUT FADED AS HE WAS, HE *WASN'T* LYIN' 'BOUT ONE THING— THE FOOT GOT THEIR BUTTS *HANDED* TO 'EM BIG TIME.
BY THE TURTLES?
MM-HM. SPLINTER, TOO.
GOOD.
NOT TOTALLY. THERE'S SOME *REALLY BAD NEWS*, TOO, CASEY.
"WE HAVE BEEN *BATTERED*.
"WE HAVE BEEN *BLOODIED*..."

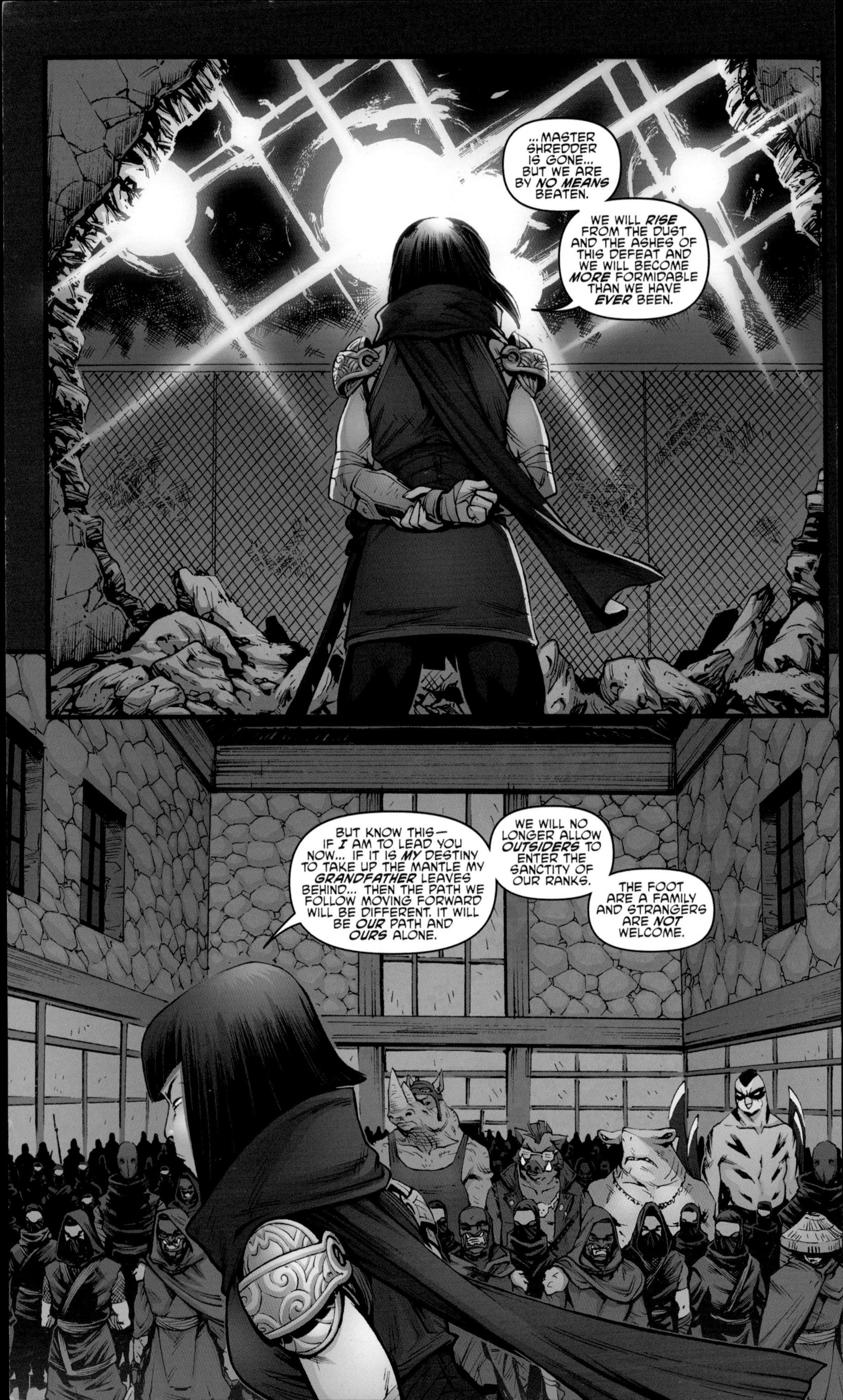
...MASTER SHREDDER IS GONE... BUT WE ARE BY NO MEANS BEATEN.
WE WILL RISE FROM THE DUST AND THE ASHES OF THIS DEFEAT AND WE WILL BECOME MORE FORMIDABLE THAN WE HAVE EVER BEEN.
BUT KNOW THIS— IF I AM TO LEAD YOU NOW... IF IT IS MY DESTINY TO TAKE UP THE MANTLE MY GRANDFATHER LEAVES BEHIND... THEN THE PATH WE FOLLOW MOVING FORWARD WILL BE DIFFERENT. IT WILL BE OUR PATH AND OURS ALONE.
WE WILL NO LONGER ALLOW OUTSIDERS TO ENTER THE SANCTITY OF OUR RANKS.
THE FOOT ARE A FAMILY AND STRANGERS ARE NOT WELCOME.

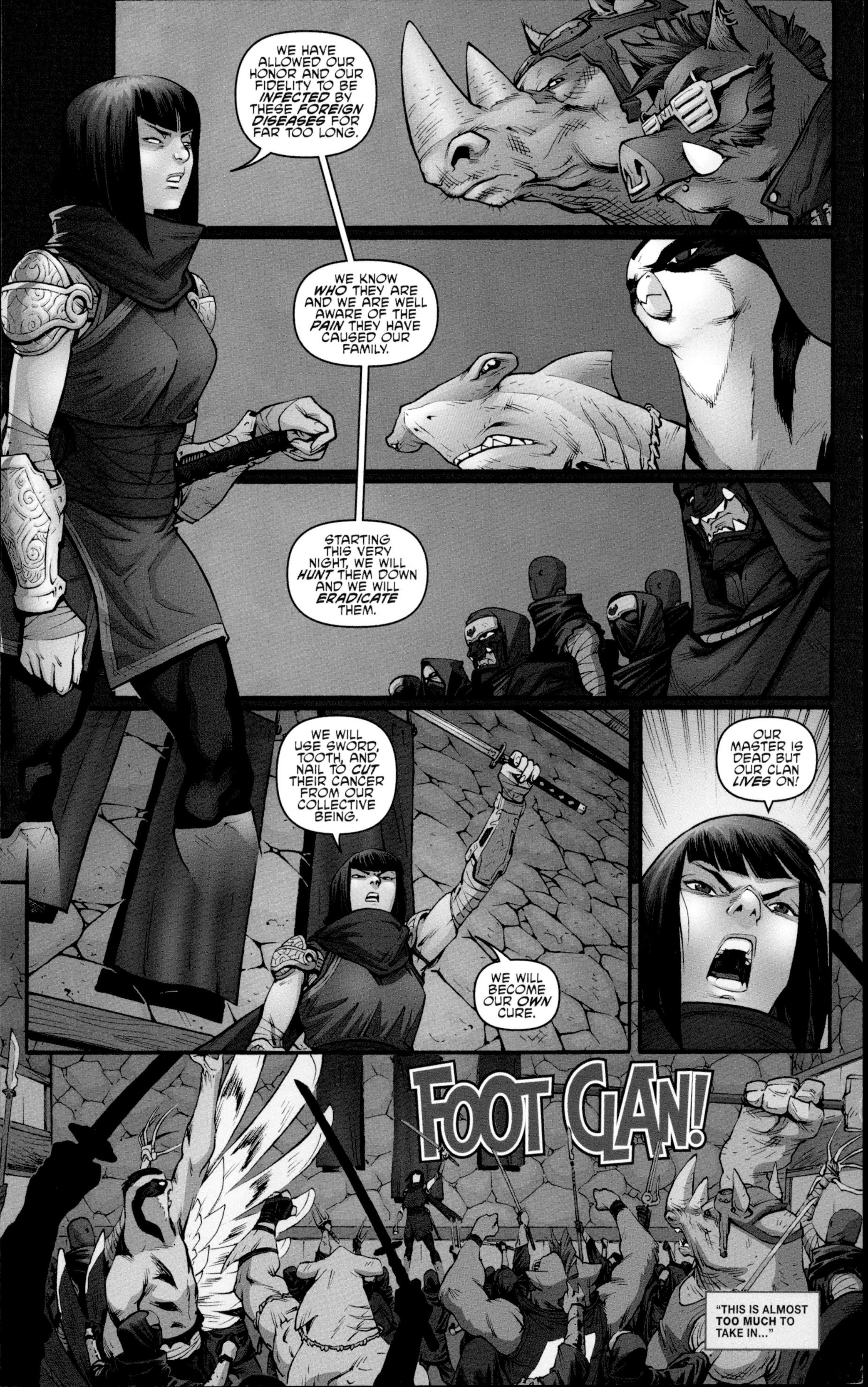
WE HAVE ALLOWED OUR HONOR AND OUR FIDELITY TO BE INFECTED BY THESE FOREIGN DISEASES FOR FAR TOO LONG.
WE KNOW WHO THEY ARE AND WE ARE WELL AWARE OF THE PAIN THEY HAVE CAUSED OUR FAMILY.
STARTING THIS VERY NIGHT, WE WILL HUNT THEM DOWN AND WE WILL ERADICATE THEM.
WE WILL USE SWORD, TOOTH, AND NAIL TO CUT THEIR CANCER FROM OUR COLLECTIVE BEING.
WE WILL BECOME OUR OWN CURE.
OUR MASTER IS DEAD BUT OUR CLAN LIVES ON!
FOOT CLAN!
"THIS IS ALMOST TOO MUCH TO TAKE IN..."

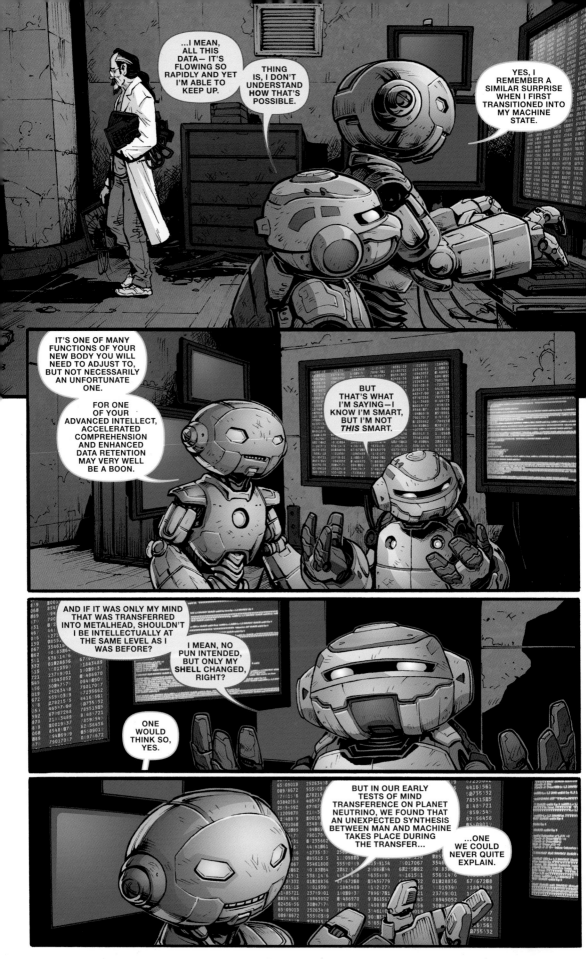

...I MEAN, ALL THIS DATA— IT'S FLOWING SO RAPIDLY AND YET I'M ABLE TO KEEP UP.

THING IS, I DON'T UNDERSTAND *HOW* THAT'S POSSIBLE.

YES, I REMEMBER A SIMILAR SURPRISE WHEN I FIRST TRANSITIONED INTO MY MACHINE STATE.

IT'S ONE OF MANY FUNCTIONS OF YOUR NEW BODY YOU WILL NEED TO ADJUST TO, BUT NOT NECESSARILY AN UNFORTUNATE ONE.

FOR ONE OF YOUR ADVANCED INTELLECT, ACCELERATED COMPREHENSION AND ENHANCED DATA RETENTION MAY VERY WELL BE A BOON.

BUT THAT'S WHAT I'M SAYING— I KNOW I'M SMART, BUT I'M NOT *THIS* SMART.

AND IF IT WAS ONLY MY MIND THAT WAS TRANSFERRED INTO METALHEAD, SHOULDN'T I BE INTELLECTUALLY AT THE SAME LEVEL AS I WAS BEFORE?

I MEAN, NO PUN INTENDED, BUT ONLY MY *SHELL* CHANGED, RIGHT?

ONE WOULD THINK SO, YES.

BUT IN OUR EARLY TESTS OF MIND TRANSFERENCE ON PLANET NEUTRINO, WE FOUND THAT AN UNEXPECTED SYNTHESIS BETWEEN MAN AND MACHINE TAKES PLACE DURING THE TRANSFER...

...ONE WE COULD NEVER QUITE EXPLAIN.

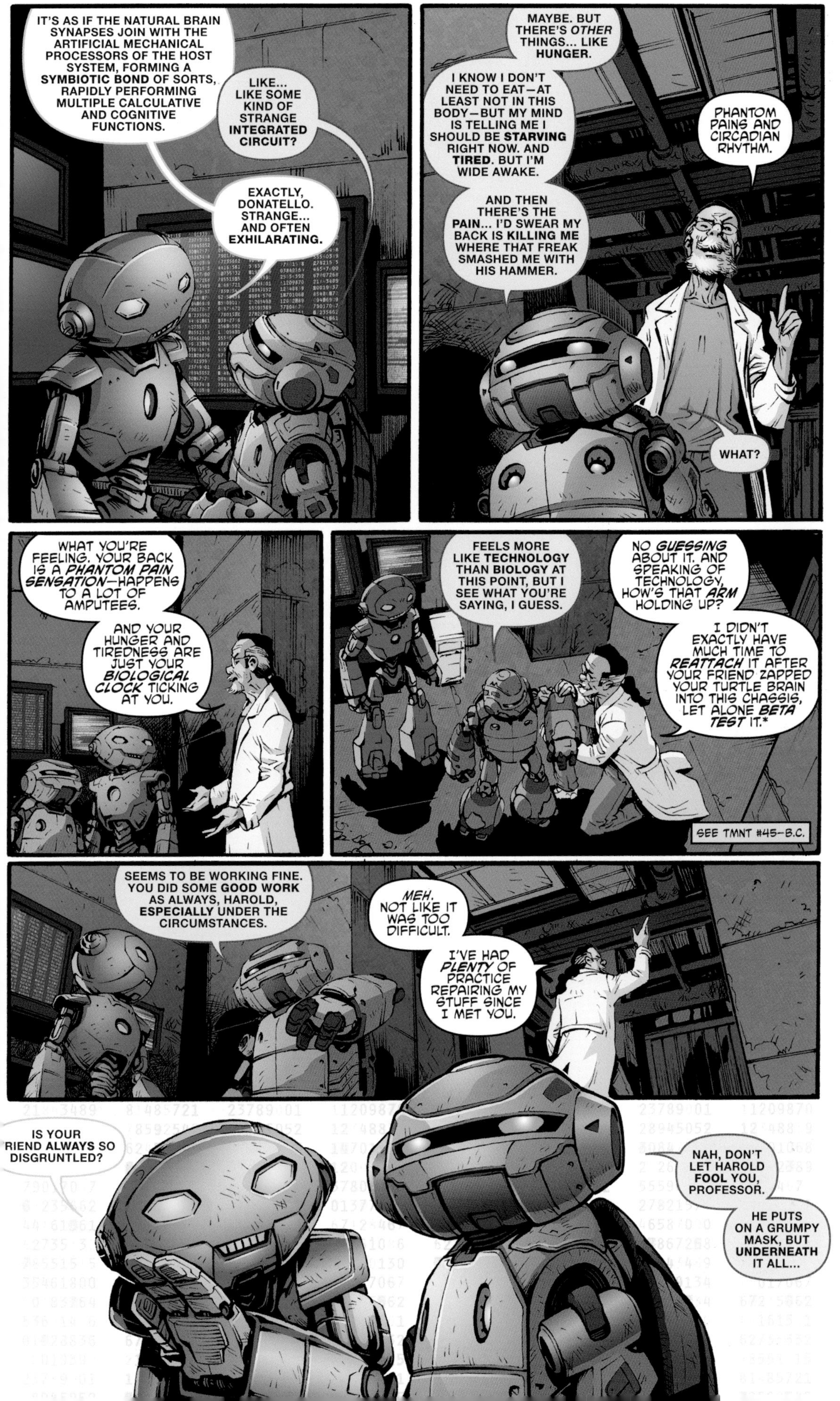

IT'S AS IF THE NATURAL BRAIN SYNAPSES JOIN WITH THE ARTIFICIAL MECHANICAL PROCESSORS OF THE HOST SYSTEM, FORMING A SYMBIOTIC BOND OF SORTS, RAPIDLY PERFORMING MULTIPLE CALCULATIVE AND COGNITIVE FUNCTIONS.
LIKE... LIKE SOME KIND OF STRANGE INTEGRATED CIRCUIT?
EXACTLY, DONATELLO. STRANGE... AND OFTEN EXHILARATING.
MAYBE. BUT THERE'S OTHER THINGS... LIKE HUNGER.
I KNOW I DON'T NEED TO EAT—AT LEAST NOT IN THIS BODY—BUT MY MIND IS TELLING ME I SHOULD BE STARVING RIGHT NOW. AND TIRED. BUT I'M WIDE AWAKE.
AND THEN THERE'S THE PAIN... I'D SWEAR MY BACK IS KILLING ME WHERE THAT FREAK SMASHED ME WITH HIS HAMMER.
PHANTOM PAINS AND CIRCADIAN RHYTHM.
WHAT?
WHAT YOU'RE FEELING. YOUR BACK IS A PHANTOM PAIN SENSATION—HAPPENS TO A LOT OF AMPUTEES.
AND YOUR HUNGER AND TIREDNESS ARE JUST YOUR BIOLOGICAL CLOCK TICKING AT YOU.
FEELS MORE LIKE TECHNOLOGY THAN BIOLOGY AT THIS POINT, BUT I SEE WHAT YOU'RE SAYING, I GUESS.
NO GUESSING ABOUT IT. AND SPEAKING OF TECHNOLOGY, HOW'S THAT ARM HOLDING UP?
I DIDN'T EXACTLY HAVE MUCH TIME TO REATTACH IT AFTER YOUR FRIEND ZAPPED YOUR TURTLE BRAIN INTO THIS CHASSIS, LET ALONE BETA TEST IT.*
SEE TMNT #45—B.C.
SEEMS TO BE WORKING FINE. YOU DID SOME GOOD WORK AS ALWAYS, HAROLD, ESPECIALLY UNDER THE CIRCUMSTANCES.
MEH. NOT LIKE IT WAS TOO DIFFICULT.
I'VE HAD PLENTY OF PRACTICE REPAIRING MY STUFF SINCE I MET YOU.
IS YOUR RIEND ALWAYS SO DISGRUNTLED?
NAH, DON'T LET HAROLD FOOL YOU, PROFESSOR.
HE PUTS ON A GRUMPY MASK, BUT UNDERNEATH IT ALL...

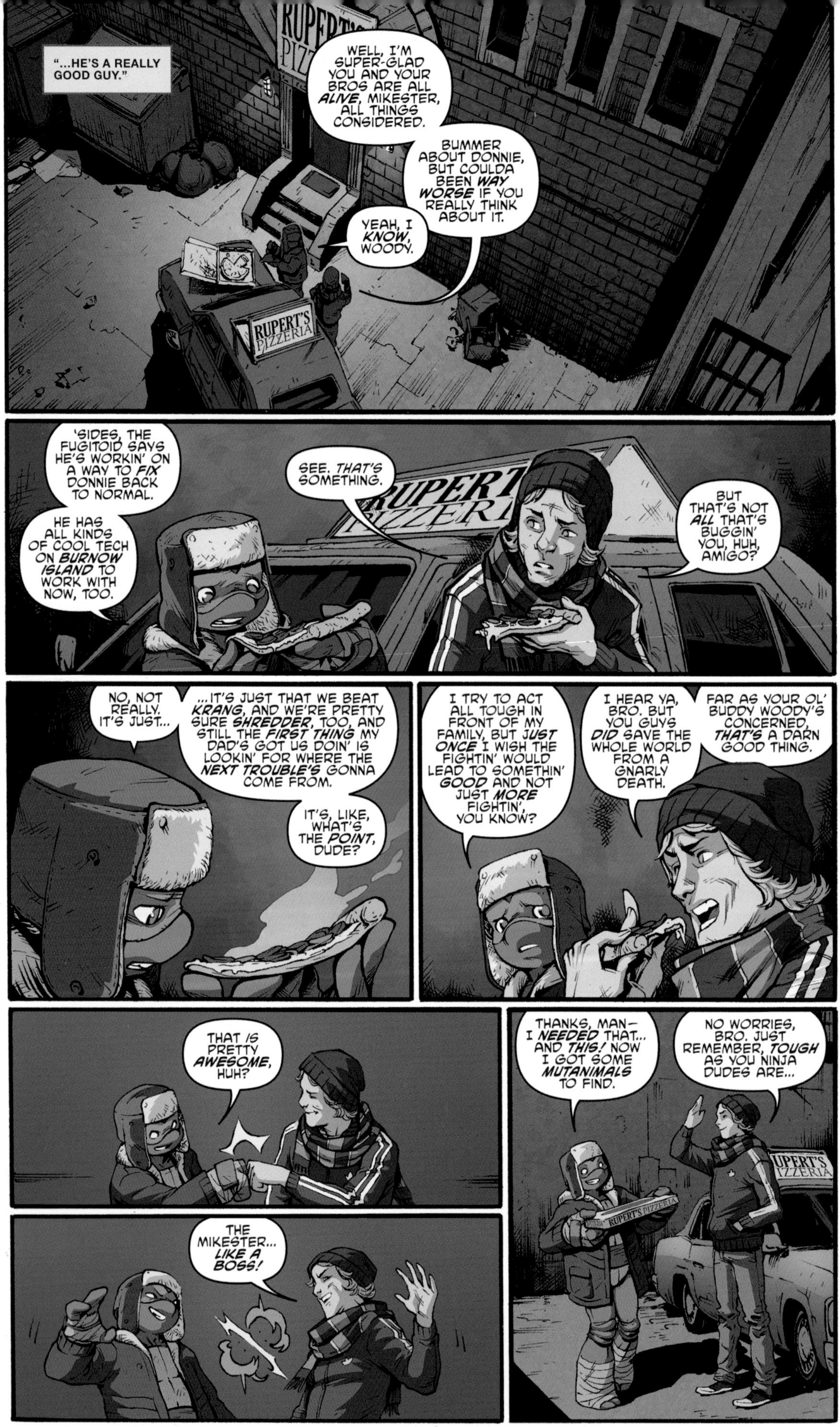

"...HE'S A REALLY GOOD GUY."
RUPERT'S PIZZ
WELL, I'M SUPER-GLAD YOU AND YOUR BROS ARE ALL ALIVE, MIKESTER, ALL THINGS CONSIDERED.
BUMMER ABOUT DONNIE, BUT COULDA BEEN WAY WORSE IF YOU REALLY THINK ABOUT IT.
YEAH, I KNOW, WOODY.
RUPERT'S PIZZERIA
'SIDES, THE FUGITOID SAYS HE'S WORKIN' ON A WAY TO FIX DONNIE BACK TO NORMAL.
HE HAS ALL KINDS OF COOL TECH ON BURNOW ISLAND TO WORK WITH NOW, TOO.
SEE. THAT'S SOMETHING.
BUT THAT'S NOT ALL THAT'S BUGGIN' YOU, HUH, AMIGO?
NO, NOT REALLY. IT'S JUST...
...IT'S JUST THAT WE BEAT KRANG, AND WE'RE PRETTY SURE SHREDDER, TOO, AND STILL THE FIRST THING MY DAD'S GOT US DOIN' IS LOOKIN' FOR WHERE THE NEXT TROUBLE'S GONNA COME FROM.
IT'S, LIKE, WHAT'S THE POINT, DUDE?
I TRY TO ACT ALL TOUGH IN FRONT OF MY FAMILY, BUT JUST ONCE I WISH THE FIGHTIN' WOULD LEAD TO SOMETHIN' GOOD AND NOT JUST MORE FIGHTIN', YOU KNOW?
I HEAR YA, BRO. BUT YOU GUYS DID SAVE THE WHOLE WORLD FROM A GNARLY DEATH.
FAR AS YOUR OL' BUDDY WOODY'S CONCERNED, THAT'S A DARN GOOD THING.
THAT IS PRETTY AWESOME, HUH?
THE MIKESTER... LIKE A BOSS!
THANKS, MAN-- I NEEDED THAT... AND THIS! NOW I GOT SOME MUTANIMALS TO FIND.
NO WORRIES, BRO. JUST REMEMBER, TOUGH AS YOU NINJA DUDES ARE...
RUPERT'S PIZZERIA
RUPERT'S PIZZERIA

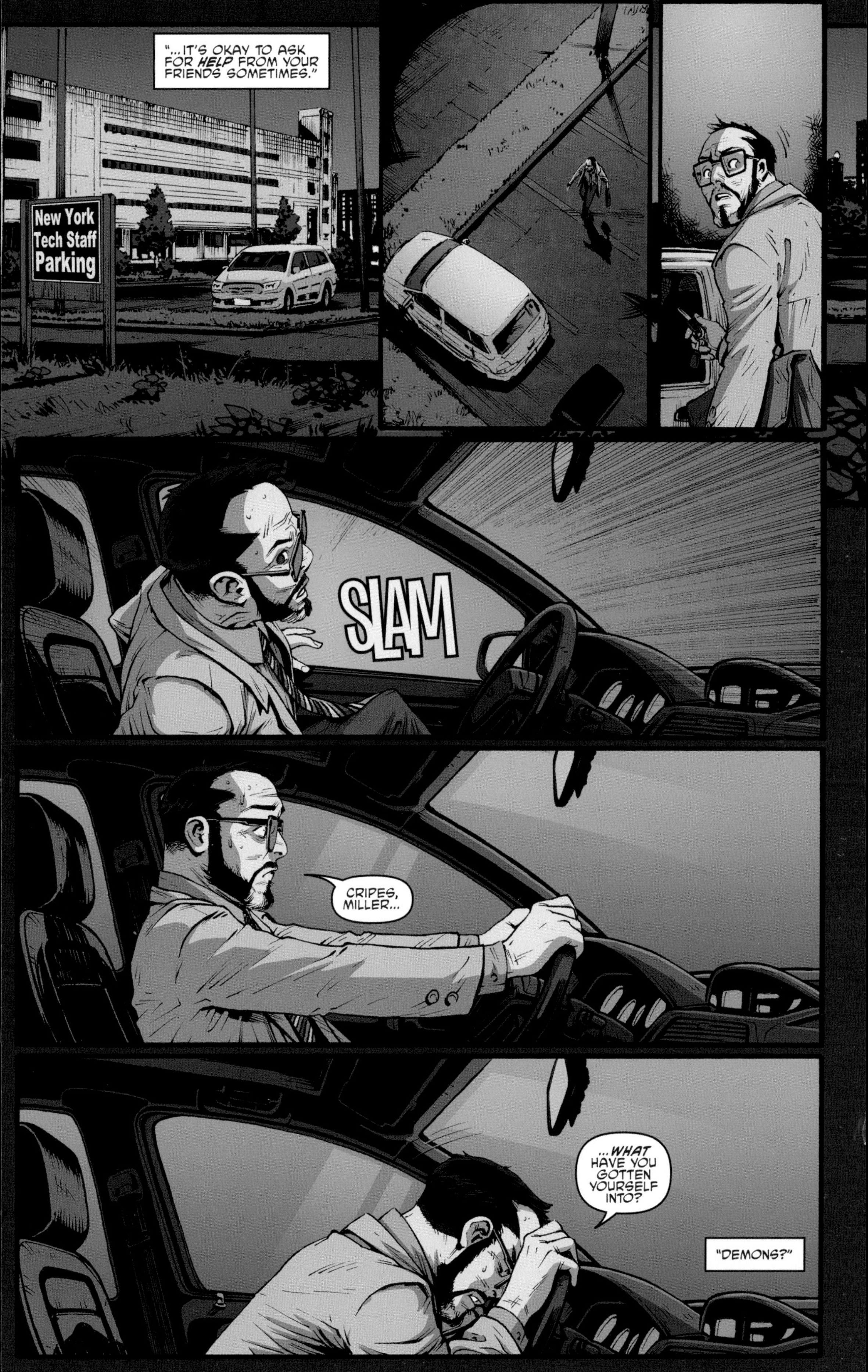
"...IT'S OKAY TO ASK FOR HELP FROM YOUR FRIENDS SOMETIMES."
New York Tech Staff Parking
SLAM
CRIPES, MILLER...
...WHAT HAVE YOU GOTTEN YOURSELF INTO?
"DEMONS?"

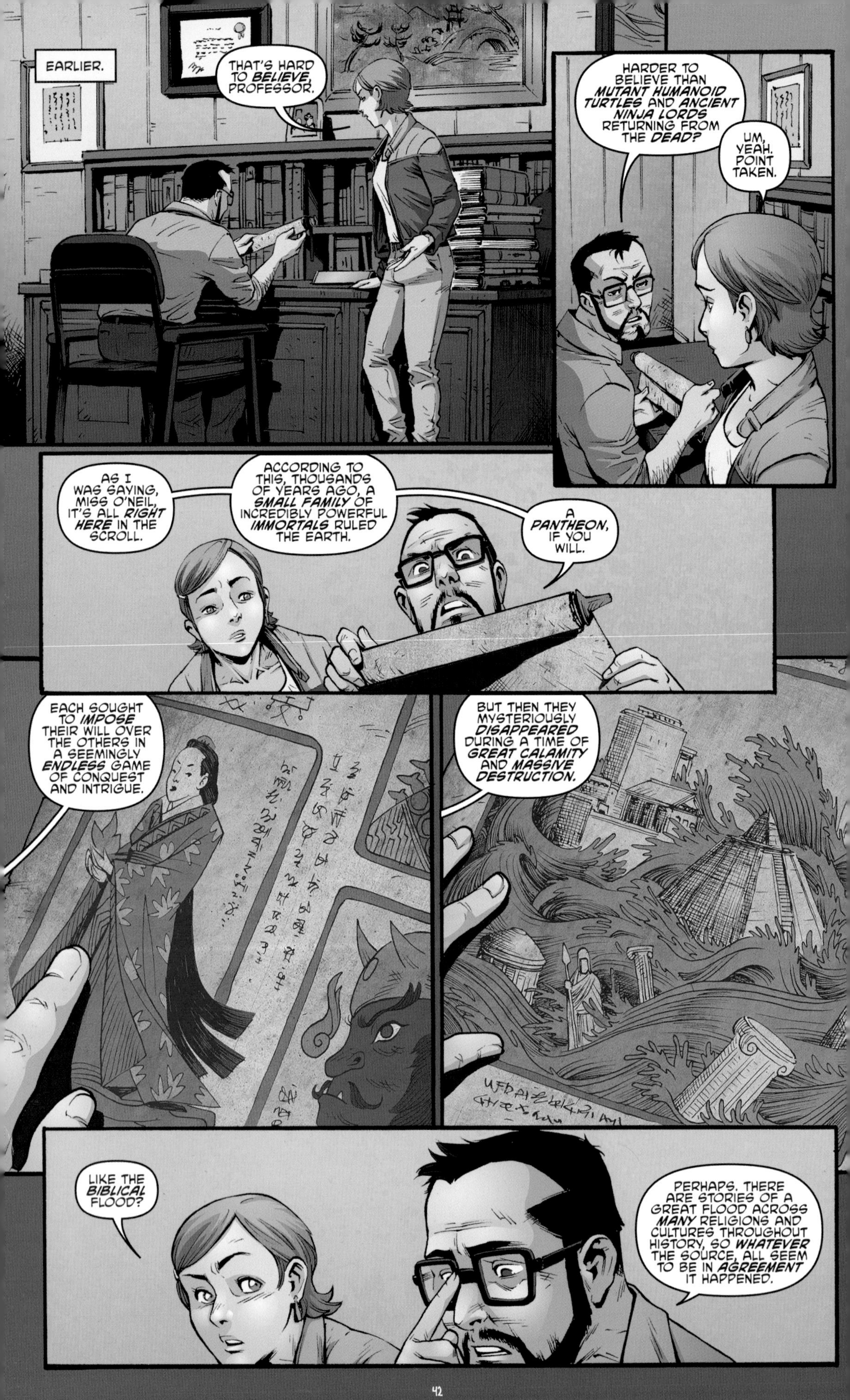
EARLIER.
THAT'S HARD TO BELIEVE, PROFESSOR.
HARDER TO BELIEVE THAN MUTANT HUMANOID TURTLES AND ANCIENT NINJA LORDS RETURNING FROM THE DEAD?
UM, YEAH. POINT TAKEN.
AS I WAS SAYING, MISS O'NEIL, IT'S ALL RIGHT HERE IN THE SCROLL.
ACCORDING TO THIS, THOUSANDS OF YEARS AGO, A SMALL FAMILY OF INCREDIBLY POWERFUL IMMORTALS RULED THE EARTH.
A PANTHEON, IF YOU WILL.
EACH SOUGHT TO IMPOSE THEIR WILL OVER THE OTHERS IN A SEEMINGLY ENDLESS GAME OF CONQUEST AND INTRIGUE.
BUT THEN THEY MYSTERIOUSLY DISAPPEARED DURING A TIME OF GREAT CALAMITY AND MASSIVE DESTRUCTION.
LIKE THE BIBLICAL FLOOD?
PERHAPS. THERE ARE STORIES OF A GREAT FLOOD ACROSS MANY RELIGIONS AND CULTURES THROUGHOUT HISTORY, SO WHATEVER THE SOURCE, ALL SEEM TO BE IN AGREEMENT IT HAPPENED.

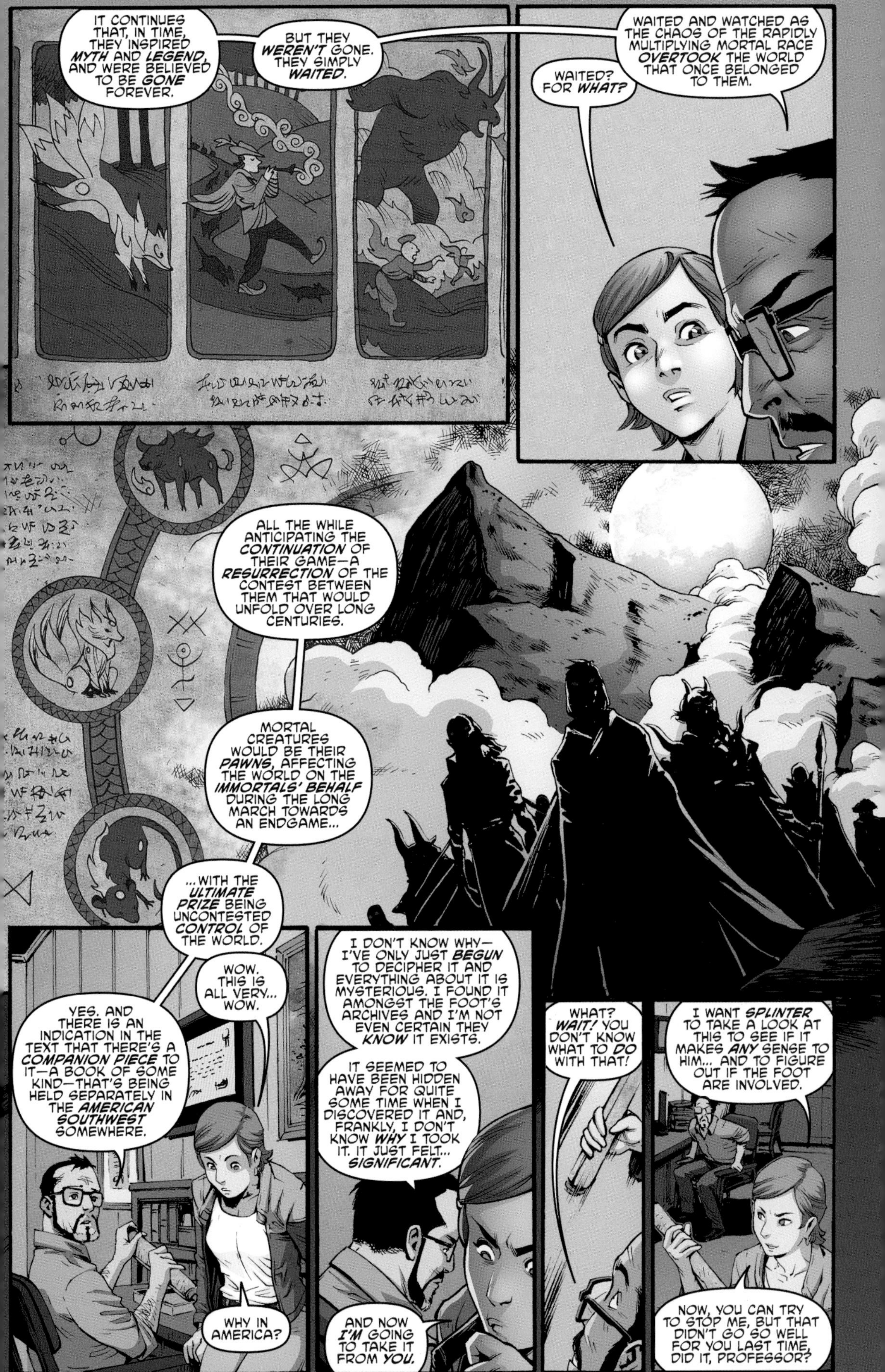
IT CONTINUES THAT, IN TIME, THEY INSPIRED MYTH AND LEGEND, AND WERE BELIEVED TO BE GONE FOREVER.
BUT THEY WEREN'T GONE. THEY SIMPLY WAITED.
WAITED AND WATCHED AS THE CHAOS OF THE RAPIDLY MULTIPLYING MORTAL RACE OVERTOOK THE WORLD THAT ONCE BELONGED TO THEM.
WAITED? FOR WHAT?
ALL THE WHILE ANTICIPATING THE CONTINUATION OF THEIR GAME—A RESURRECTION OF THE CONTEST BETWEEN THEM THAT WOULD UNFOLD OVER LONG CENTURIES.
MORTAL CREATURES WOULD BE THEIR PAWNS, AFFECTING THE WORLD ON THE IMMORTALS' BEHALF DURING THE LONG MARCH TOWARDS AN ENDGAME...
...WITH THE ULTIMATE PRIZE BEING UNCONTESTED CONTROL OF THE WORLD.
WOW. THIS IS ALL VERY... WOW.
YES. AND THERE IS AN INDICATION IN THE TEXT THAT THERE'S A COMPANION PIECE TO IT—A BOOK OF SOME KIND—THAT'S BEING HELD SEPARATELY IN THE AMERICAN SOUTHWEST SOMEWHERE.
WHY IN AMERICA?
I DON'T KNOW WHY—I'VE ONLY JUST BEGUN TO DECIPHER IT AND EVERYTHING ABOUT IT IS MYSTERIOUS. I FOUND IT AMONGST THE FOOT'S ARCHIVES AND I'M NOT EVEN CERTAIN THEY KNOW IT EXISTS.
IT SEEMED TO HAVE BEEN HIDDEN AWAY FOR QUITE SOME TIME WHEN I DISCOVERED IT AND, FRANKLY, I DON'T KNOW WHY I TOOK IT. IT JUST FELT... SIGNIFICANT.
AND NOW I'M GOING TO TAKE IT FROM YOU.
WHAT? WAIT! YOU DON'T KNOW WHAT TO DO WITH THAT!
I WANT SPLINTER TO TAKE A LOOK AT THIS TO SEE IF IT MAKES ANY SENSE TO HIM... AND TO FIGURE OUT IF THE FOOT ARE INVOLVED.
NOW, YOU CAN TRY TO STOP ME, BUT THAT DIDN'T GO SO WELL FOR YOU LAST TIME, DID IT, PROFESSOR?

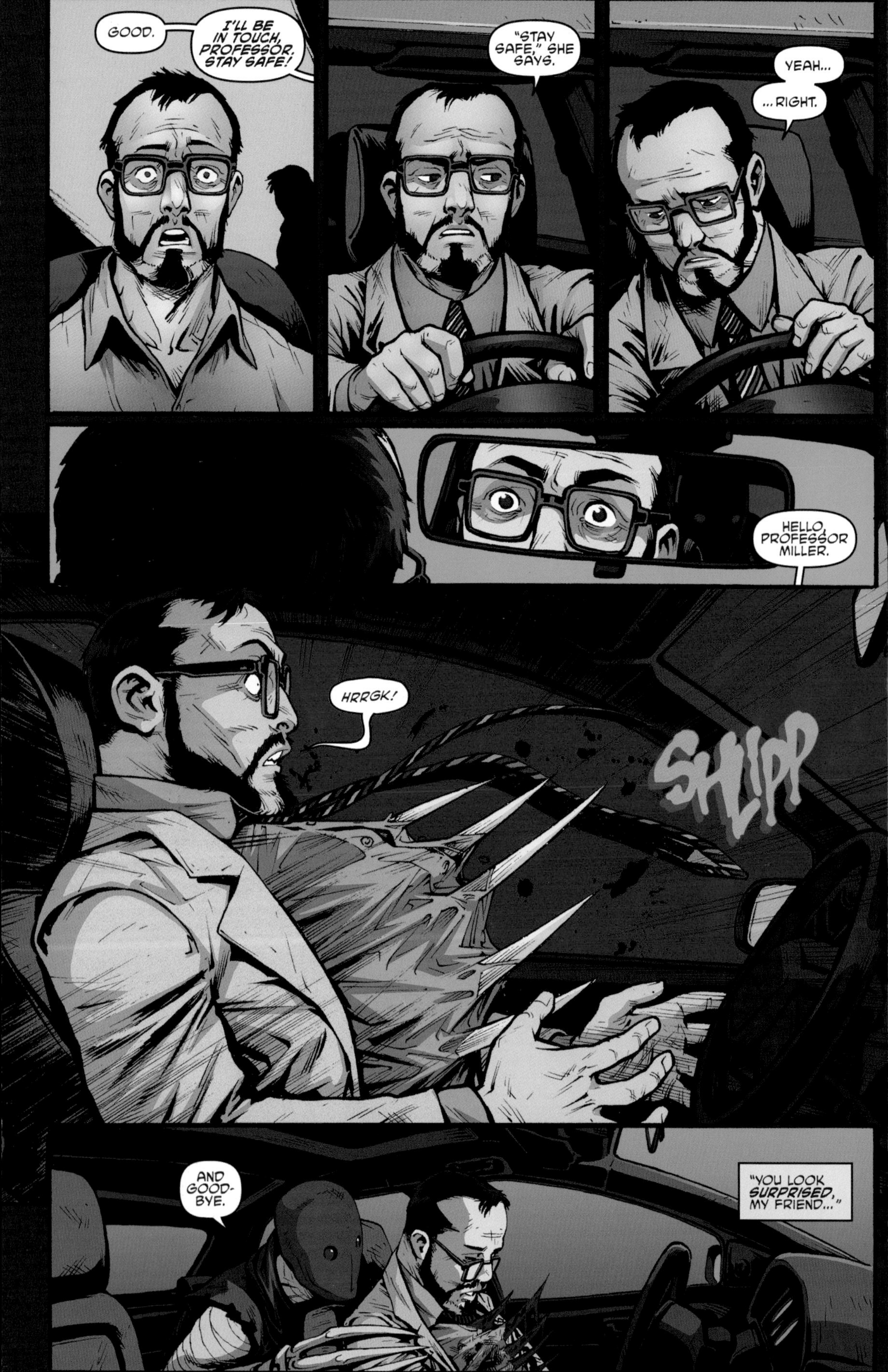
GOOD.
I'LL BE IN TOUCH, PROFESSOR. STAY SAFE!
"STAY SAFE," SHE SAYS.
YEAH...
...RIGHT.
HELLO, PROFESSOR MILLER.
HRRGK!
SHLIPP
AND GOOD-BYE.
"YOU LOOK SURPRISED, MY FRIEND..."

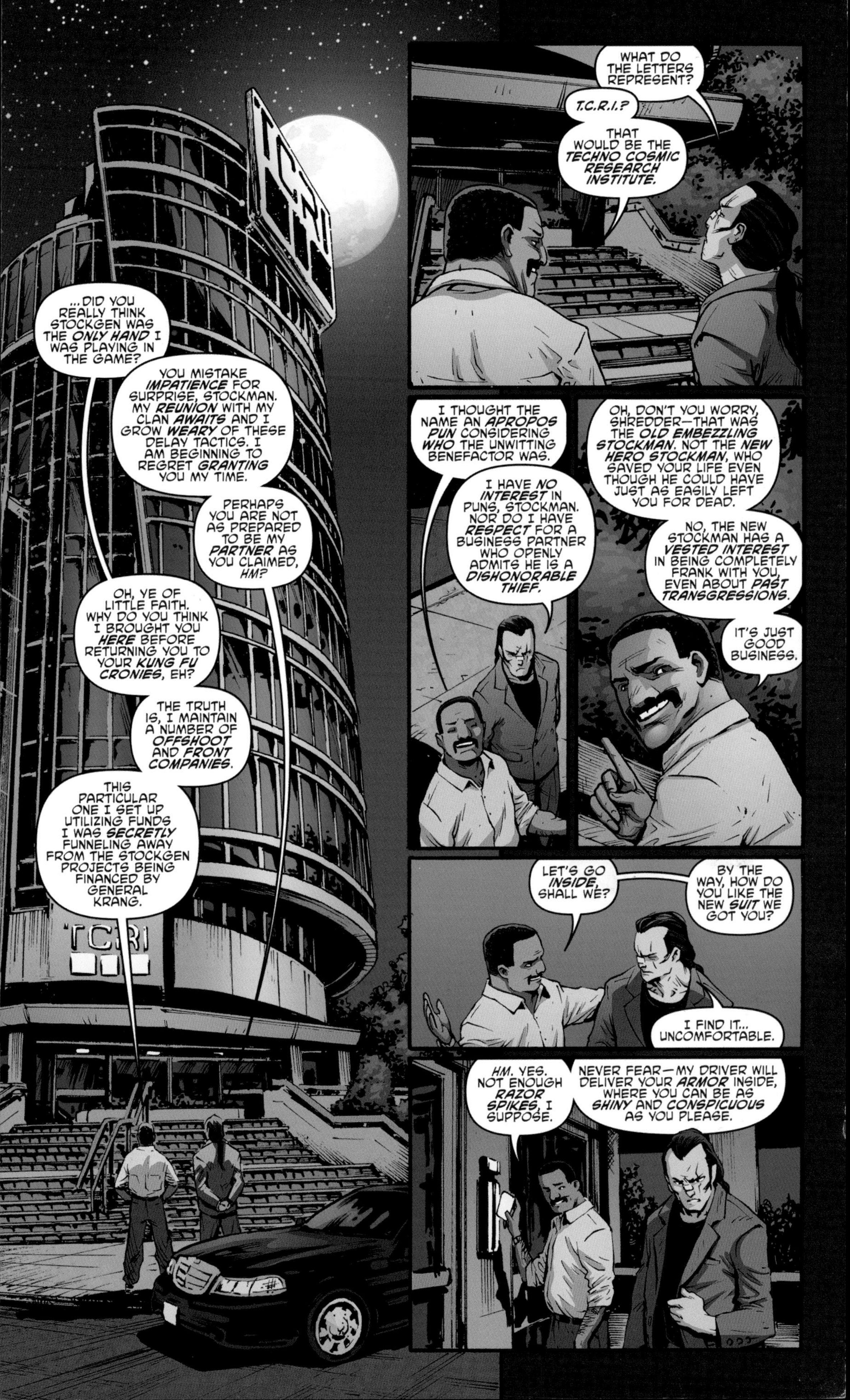
...DID YOU REALLY THINK STOCKGEN WAS THE ONLY HAND I WAS PLAYING IN THE GAME?
YOU MISTAKE IMPATIENCE FOR SURPRISE, STOCKMAN. MY REUNION WITH MY CLAN AWAITS AND I GROW WEARY OF THESE DELAY TACTICS. I AM BEGINNING TO REGRET GRANTING YOU MY TIME.
PERHAPS YOU ARE NOT AS PREPARED TO BE MY PARTNER AS YOU CLAIMED, HM?
OH, YE OF LITTLE FAITH. WHY DO YOU THINK I BROUGHT YOU HERE BEFORE RETURNING YOU TO YOUR KUNG FU CRONIES, EH?
THE TRUTH IS, I MAINTAIN A NUMBER OF OFFSHOOT AND FRONT COMPANIES.
THIS PARTICULAR ONE I SET UP UTILIZING FUNDS I WAS SECRETLY FUNNELING AWAY FROM THE STOCKGEN PROJECTS BEING FINANCED BY GENERAL KRANG.
TCRI
WHAT DO THE LETTERS REPRESENT?
T.C.R.I.?
THAT WOULD BE THE TECHNO COSMIC RESEARCH INSTITUTE.
I THOUGHT THE NAME AN APROPOS PUN CONSIDERING WHO THE UNWITTING BENEFACTOR WAS.
I HAVE NO INTEREST IN PUNS, STOCKMAN. NOR DO I HAVE RESPECT FOR A BUSINESS PARTNER WHO OPENLY ADMITS HE IS A DISHONORABLE THIEF.
OH, DON'T YOU WORRY, SHREDDER—THAT WAS THE OLD EMBEZZLING STOCKMAN. NOT THE NEW HERO STOCKMAN, WHO SAVED YOUR LIFE EVEN THOUGH HE COULD HAVE JUST AS EASILY LEFT YOU FOR DEAD.
NO, THE NEW STOCKMAN HAS A VESTED INTEREST IN BEING COMPLETELY FRANK WITH YOU, EVEN ABOUT PAST TRANSGRESSIONS.
IT'S JUST GOOD BUSINESS.
LET'S GO INSIDE, SHALL WE?
BY THE WAY, HOW DO YOU LIKE THE NEW SUIT WE GOT YOU?
I FIND IT... UNCOMFORTABLE.
HM. YES. NOT ENOUGH RAZOR SPIKES, I SUPPOSE.
NEVER FEAR—MY DRIVER WILL DELIVER YOUR ARMOR INSIDE, WHERE YOU CAN BE AS SHINY AND CONSPICUOUS AS YOU PLEASE.

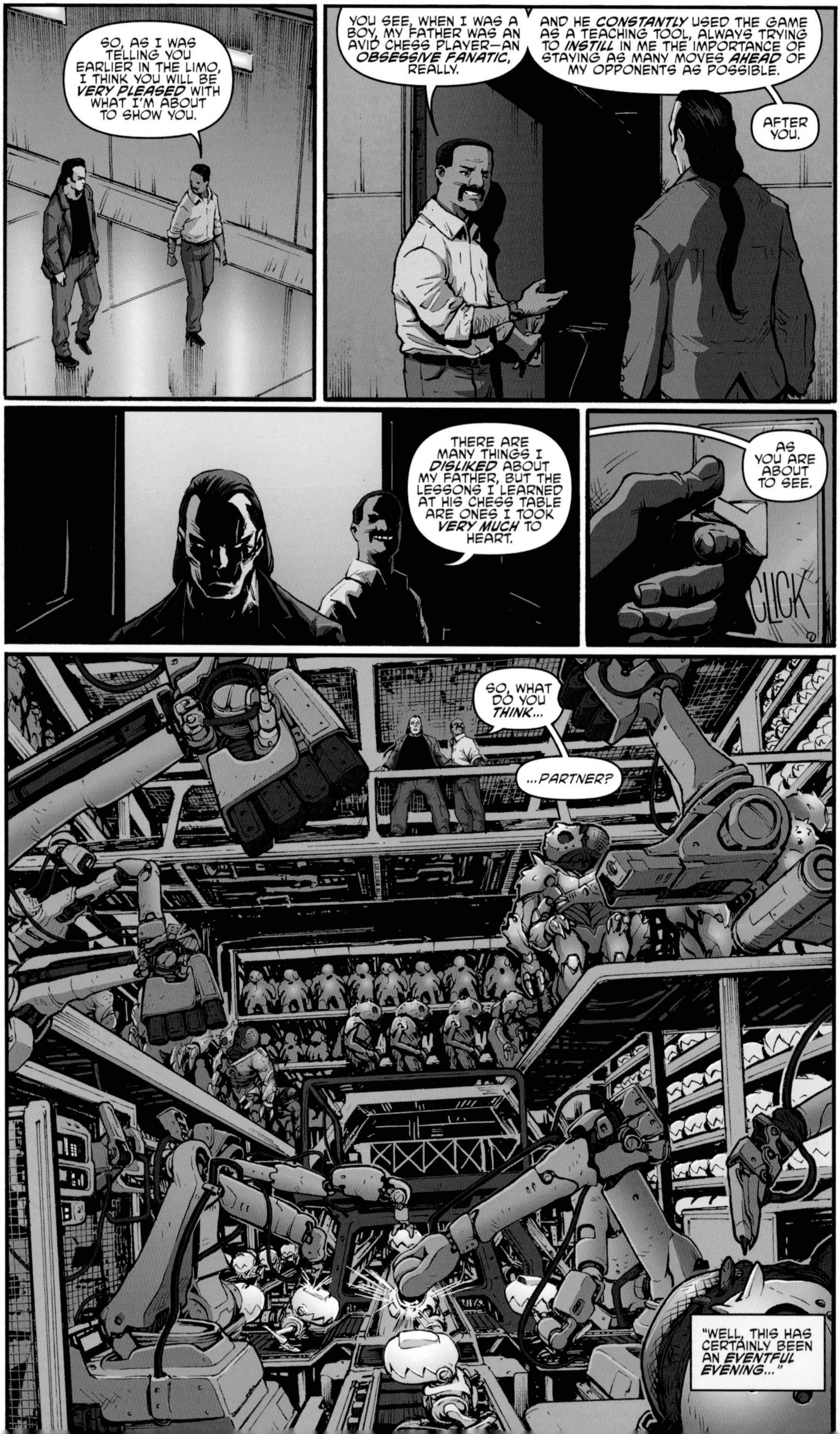

SO, AS I WAS TELLING YOU EARLIER IN THE LIMO, I THINK YOU WILL BE VERY PLEASED WITH WHAT I'M ABOUT TO SHOW YOU.
YOU SEE, WHEN I WAS A BOY, MY FATHER WAS AN AVID CHESS PLAYER—AN OBSESSIVE FANATIC, REALLY.
AND HE CONSTANTLY USED THE GAME AS A TEACHING TOOL, ALWAYS TRYING TO INSTILL IN ME THE IMPORTANCE OF STAYING AS MANY MOVES AHEAD OF MY OPPONENTS AS POSSIBLE.
AFTER YOU.
THERE ARE MANY THINGS I DISLIKED ABOUT MY FATHER, BUT THE LESSONS I LEARNED AT HIS CHESS TABLE ARE ONES I TOOK VERY MUCH TO HEART.
AS YOU ARE ABOUT TO SEE.
CLICK
SO, WHAT DO YOU THINK...
...PARTNER?
"WELL, THIS HAS CERTAINLY BEEN AN EVENTFUL EVENING..."

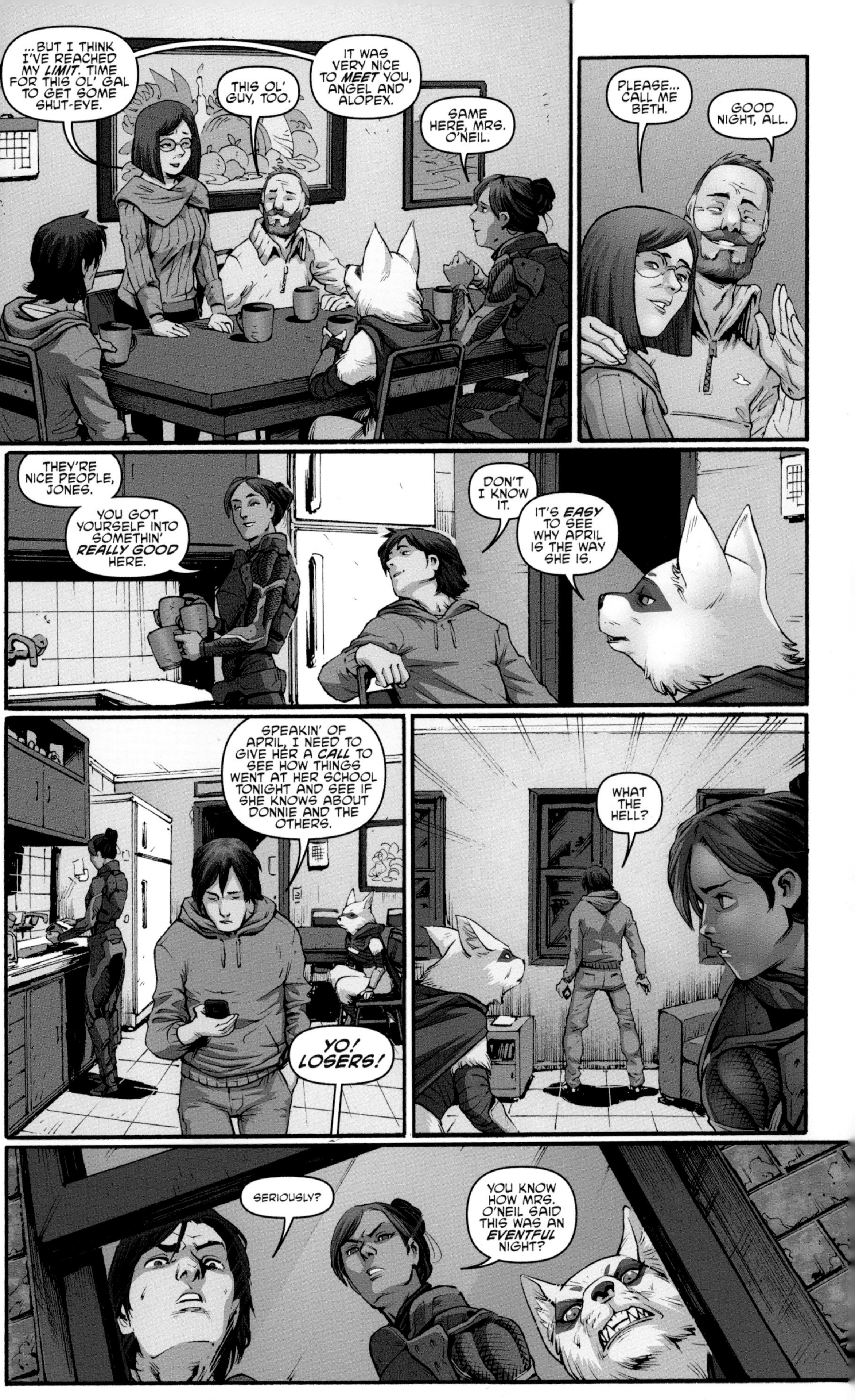
...BUT I THINK I'VE REACHED MY LIMIT. TIME FOR THIS OL' GAL TO GET SOME SHUT-EYE.
THIS OL' GUY, TOO.
IT WAS VERY NICE TO MEET YOU, ANGEL AND ALOPEX.
SAME HERE, MRS. O'NEIL.
PLEASE... CALL ME BETH.
GOOD NIGHT, ALL.
THEY'RE NICE PEOPLE, JONES.
YOU GOT YOURSELF INTO SOMETHIN' REALLY GOOD HERE.
DON'T I KNOW IT.
IT'S EASY TO SEE WHY APRIL IS THE WAY SHE IS.
SPEAKIN' OF APRIL, I NEED TO GIVE HER A CALL TO SEE HOW THINGS WENT AT HER SCHOOL TONIGHT AND SEE IF SHE KNOWS ABOUT DONNIE AND THE OTHERS.
YO! LOSERS!
WHAT THE HELL?
SERIOUSLY?
YOU KNOW HOW MRS. O'NEIL SAID THIS WAS AN EVENTFUL NIGHT?

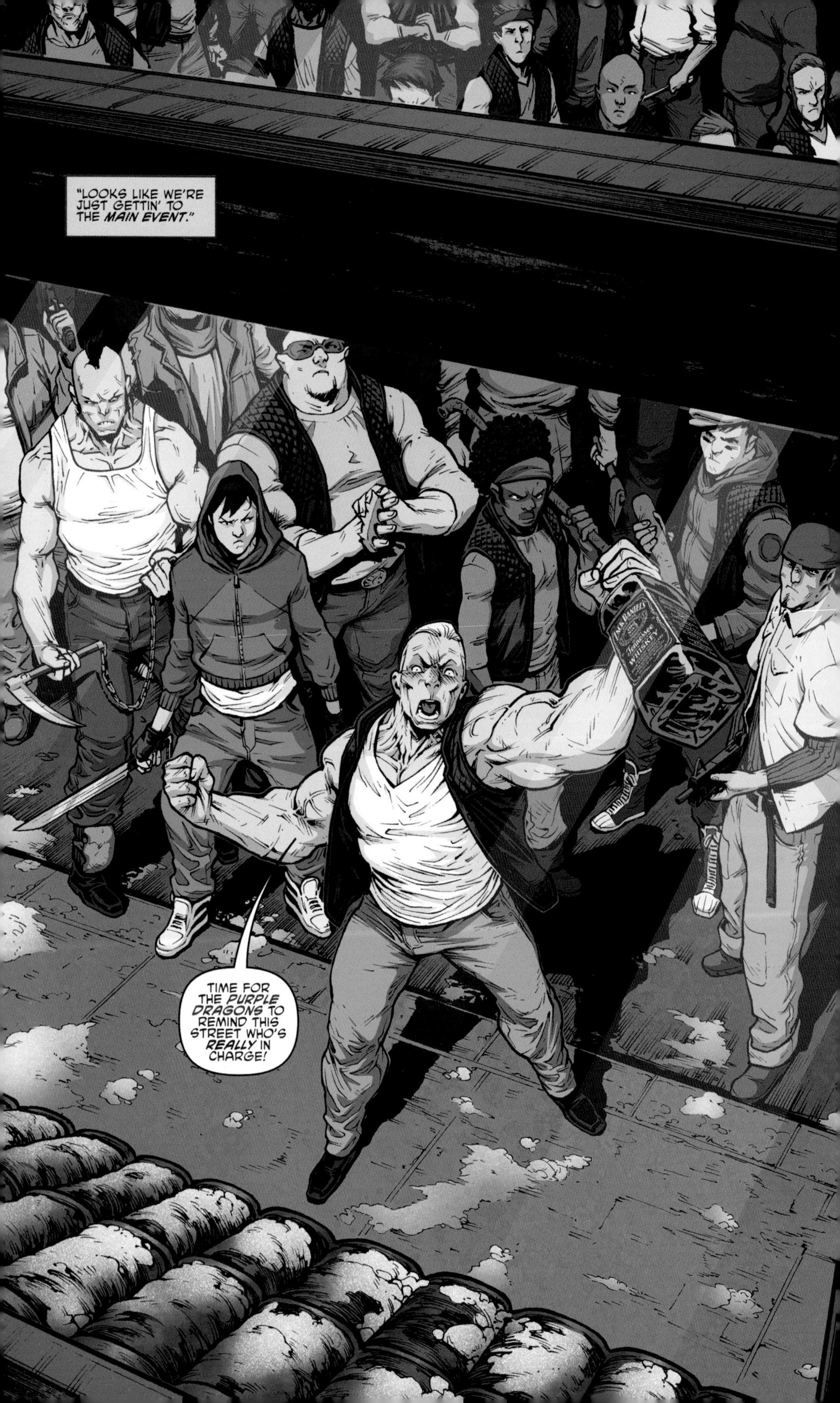
"LOOKS LIKE WE'RE JUST GETTIN' TO THE *MAIN EVENT*."
TIME FOR THE *PURPLE DRAGONS* TO REMIND THIS STREET WHO'S *REALLY* IN CHARGE!

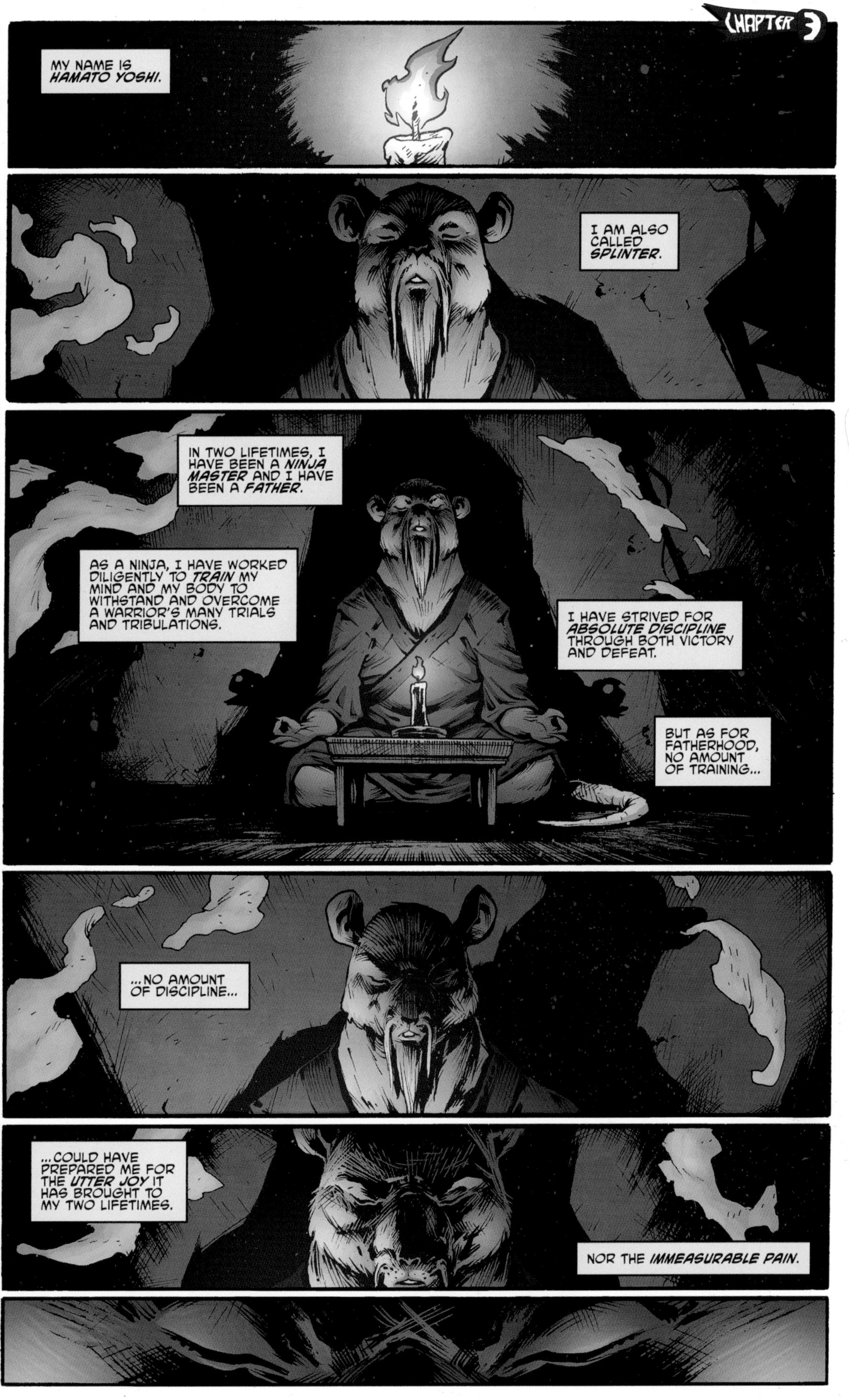
CHAPTER 3
MY NAME IS HAMATO YOSHI.
I AM ALSO CALLED SPLINTER.
IN TWO LIFETIMES, I HAVE BEEN A NINJA MASTER AND I HAVE BEEN A FATHER.
AS A NINJA, I HAVE WORKED DILIGENTLY TO TRAIN MY MIND AND MY BODY TO WITHSTAND AND OVERCOME A WARRIOR'S MANY TRIALS AND TRIBULATIONS.
I HAVE STRIVED FOR ABSOLUTE DISCIPLINE THROUGH BOTH VICTORY AND DEFEAT.
BUT AS FOR FATHERHOOD, NO AMOUNT OF TRAINING...
...NO AMOUNT OF DISCIPLINE...
...COULD HAVE PREPARED ME FOR THE UTTER JOY IT HAS BROUGHT TO MY TWO LIFETIMES.
NOR THE IMMEASURABLE PAIN.

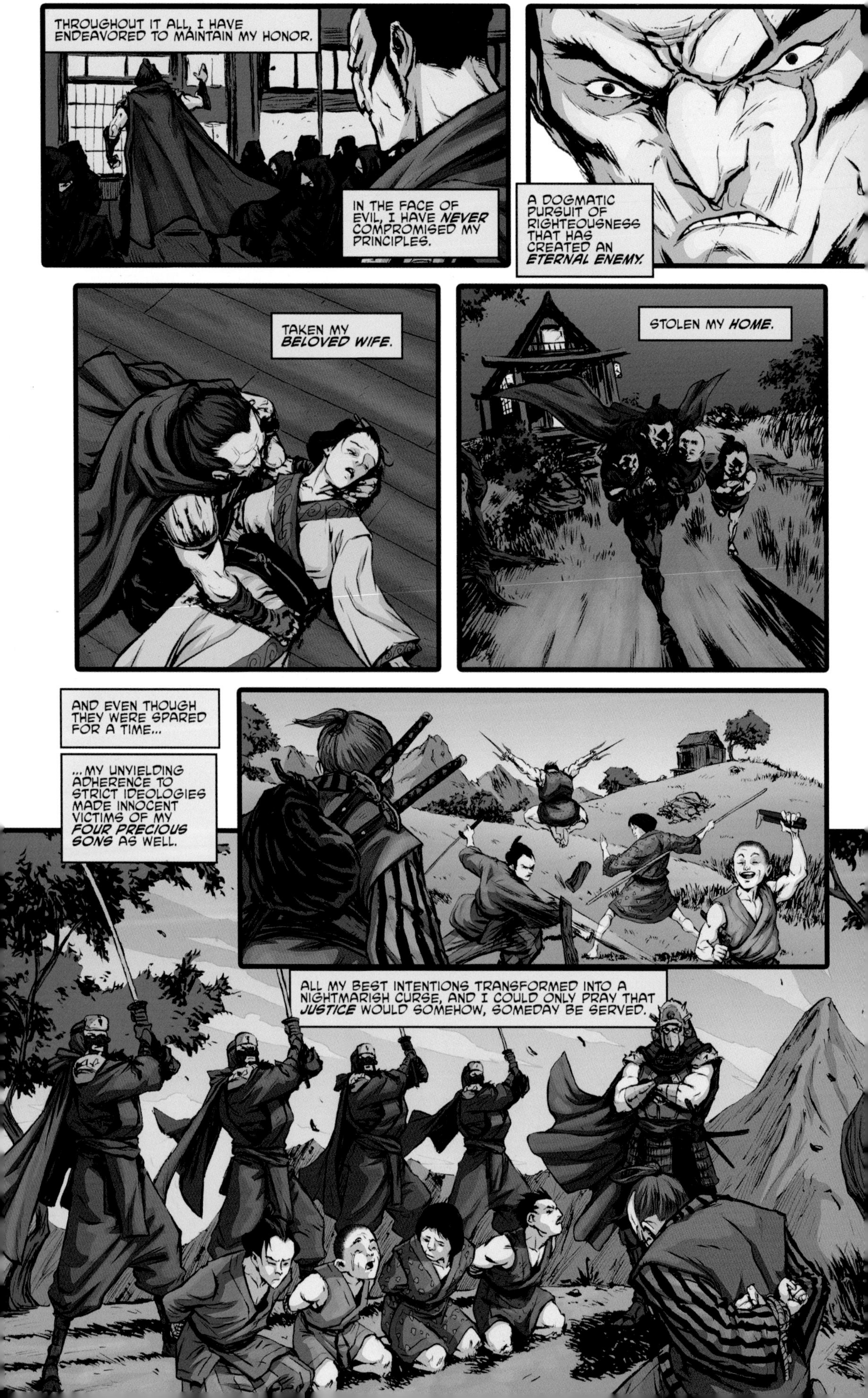
THROUGHOUT IT ALL, I HAVE ENDEAVORED TO MAINTAIN MY HONOR.
IN THE FACE OF EVIL, I HAVE NEVER COMPROMISED MY PRINCIPLES.
A DOGMATIC PURSUIT OF RIGHTEOUSNESS THAT HAS CREATED AN ETERNAL ENEMY.
TAKEN MY BELOVED WIFE.
STOLEN MY HOME.
AND EVEN THOUGH THEY WERE SPARED FOR A TIME...
...MY UNYIELDING ADHERENCE TO STRICT IDEOLOGIES MADE INNOCENT VICTIMS OF MY FOUR PRECIOUS SONS AS WELL.
ALL MY BEST INTENTIONS TRANSFORMED INTO A NIGHTMARISH CURSE, AND I COULD ONLY PRAY THAT JUSTICE WOULD SOMEHOW, SOMEDAY BE SERVED.

AMAZINGLY, THE UNIVERSE *ANSWERED* MY PRAYERS, THOUGH IN A MOST MYSTERIOUS FASHION.

MY BEAUTIFUL SONS AND I HAD BEEN *RETURNED* FROM OUR UNTIMELY DEATHS...

...NEWLY FORMED AND TRAPPED IN A *FAR FUTURE* TIME AND PLACE.

BUT FATE AND DESTINY WOULD *NOT* BE DENIED, AND WE SOON FOUND OURSELVES FREE AND METAMORPHOSED EVER CLOSER TO THE HUMANITY WE HAD LOST CENTURIES BEFORE.

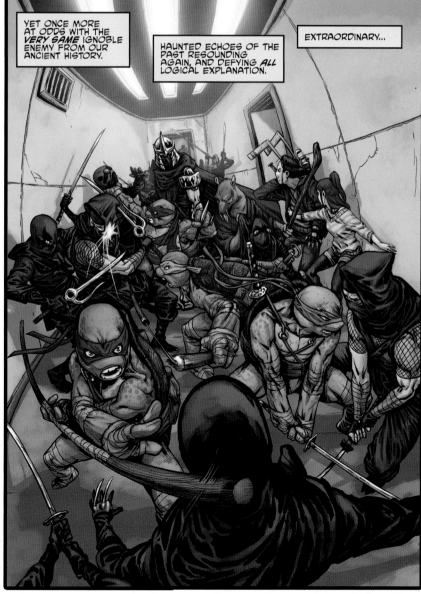

YET ONCE MORE AT ODDS WITH THE *VERY SAME* IGNOBLE ENEMY FROM OUR ANCIENT HISTORY.

HAUNTED ECHOES OF THE PAST RESOUNDING AGAIN, AND DEFYING *ALL* LOGICAL EXPLANATION.

EXTRAORDINARY...

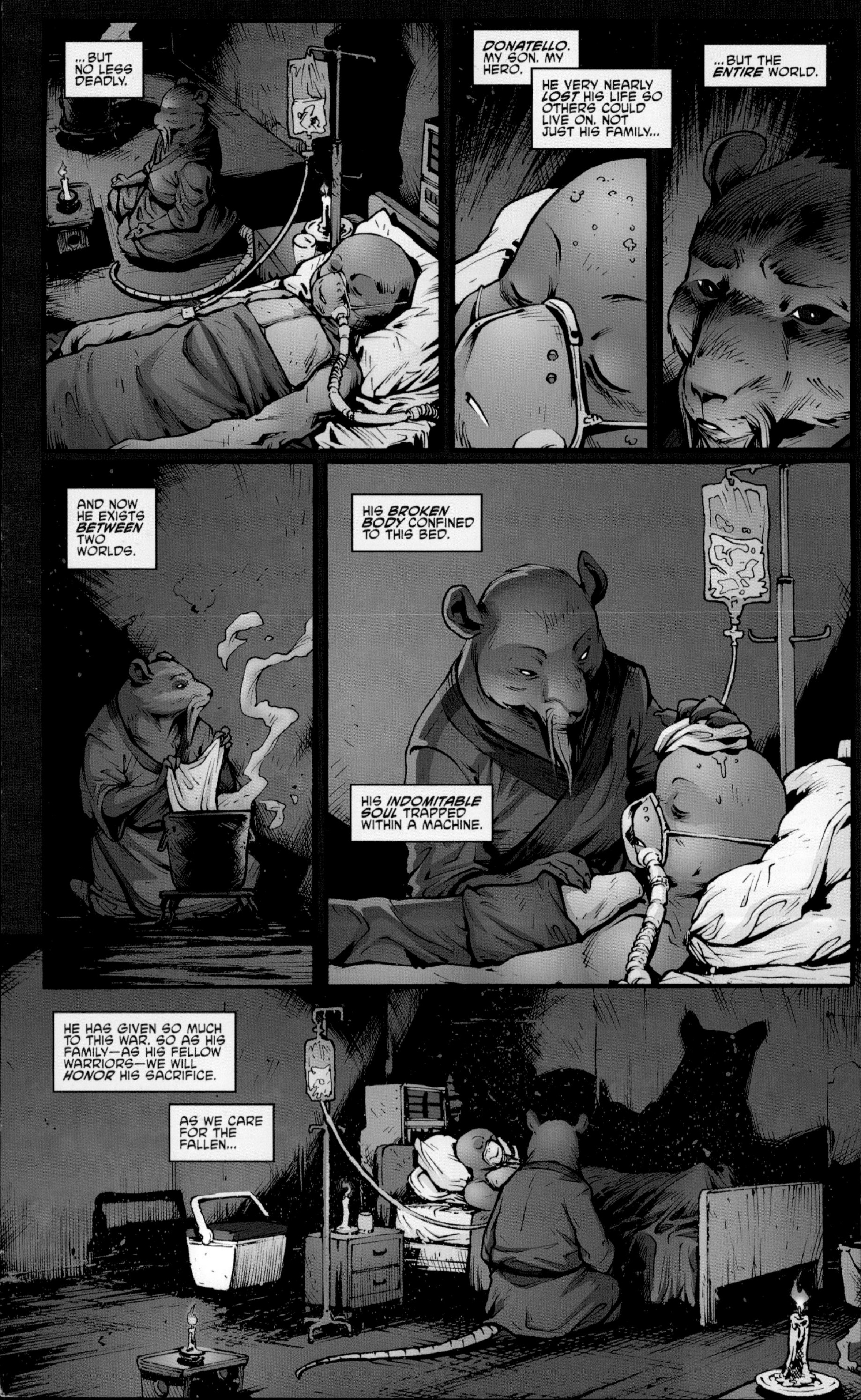
...BUT NO LESS DEADLY.
DONATELLO. MY SON. MY HERO.
HE VERY NEARLY LOST HIS LIFE SO OTHERS COULD LIVE ON. NOT JUST HIS FAMILY...
...BUT THE ENTIRE WORLD.
AND NOW HE EXISTS BETWEEN TWO WORLDS.
HIS BROKEN BODY CONFINED TO THIS BED.
HIS INDOMITABLE SOUL TRAPPED WITHIN A MACHINE.
HE HAS GIVEN SO MUCH TO THIS WAR. SO AS HIS FAMILY—AS HIS FELLOW WARRIORS—WE WILL HONOR HIS SACRIFICE.
AS WE CARE FOR THE FALLEN...

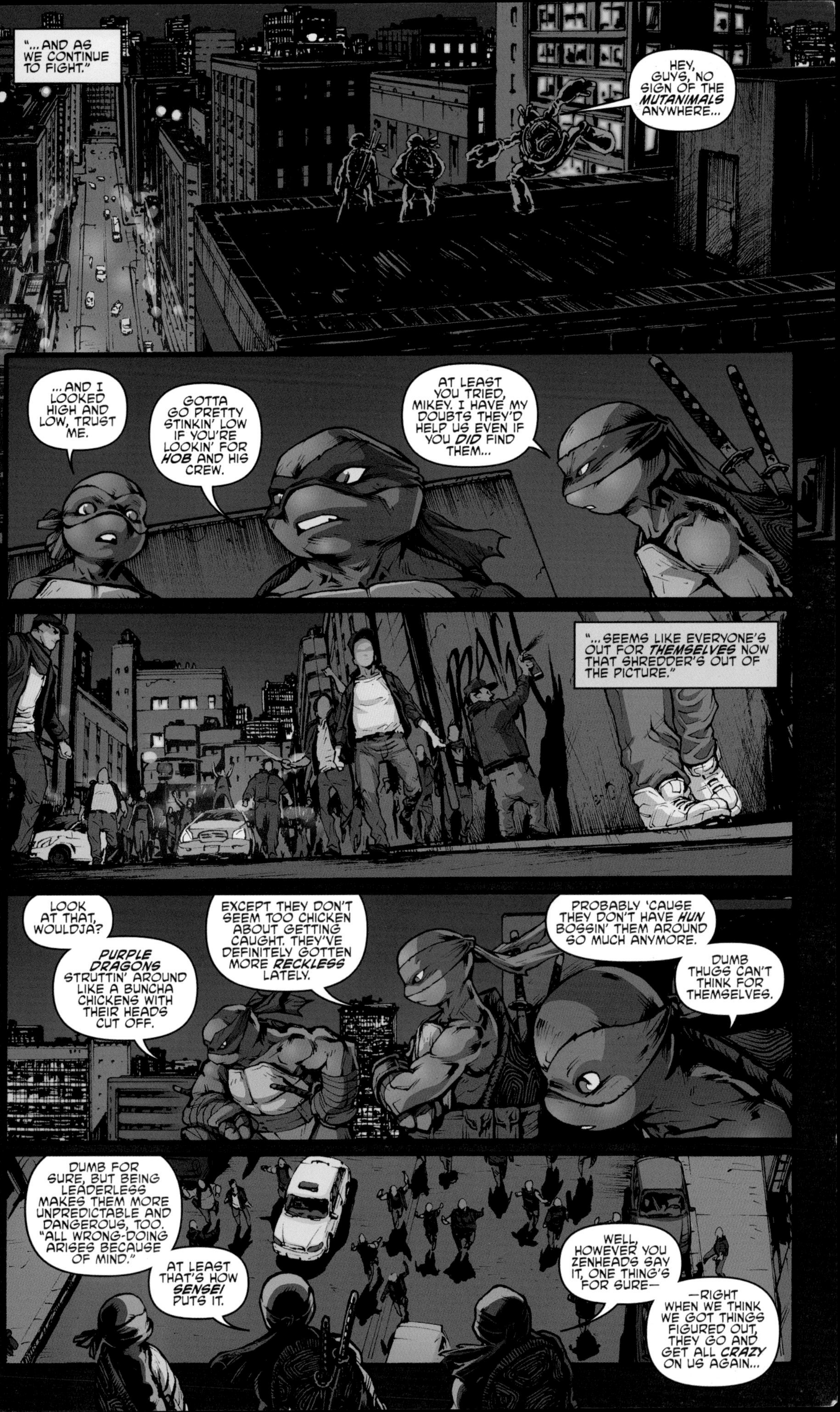
"...AND AS WE CONTINUE TO FIGHT."
HEY, GUYS, NO SIGN OF THE MUTANIMALS ANYWHERE...
...AND I LOOKED HIGH AND LOW, TRUST ME.
GOTTA GO PRETTY STINKIN' LOW IF YOU'RE LOOKIN' FOR HOB AND HIS CREW.
AT LEAST YOU TRIED, MIKEY. I HAVE MY DOUBTS THEY'D HELP US EVEN IF YOU DID FIND THEM...
"...SEEMS LIKE EVERYONE'S OUT FOR THEMSELVES NOW THAT SHREDDER'S OUT OF THE PICTURE."
LOOK AT THAT, WOULDJA?
PURPLE DRAGONS STRUTTIN' AROUND LIKE A BUNCHA CHICKENS WITH THEIR HEADS CUT OFF.
EXCEPT THEY DON'T SEEM TOO CHICKEN ABOUT GETTING CAUGHT. THEY'VE DEFINITELY GOTTEN MORE RECKLESS LATELY.
PROBABLY 'CAUSE THEY DON'T HAVE HUN BOSSIN' THEM AROUND SO MUCH ANYMORE.
DUMB THUGS CAN'T THINK FOR THEMSELVES.
DUMB FOR SURE, BUT BEING LEADERLESS MAKES THEM MORE UNPREDICTABLE AND DANGEROUS, TOO. "ALL WRONG-DOING ARISES BECAUSE OF MIND."
AT LEAST THAT'S HOW SENSEI PUTS IT.
WELL, HOWEVER YOU ZENHEADS SAY IT, ONE THING'S FOR SURE—
—RIGHT WHEN WE THINK WE GOT THINGS FIGURED OUT, THEY GO AND GET ALL CRAZY ON US AGAIN...

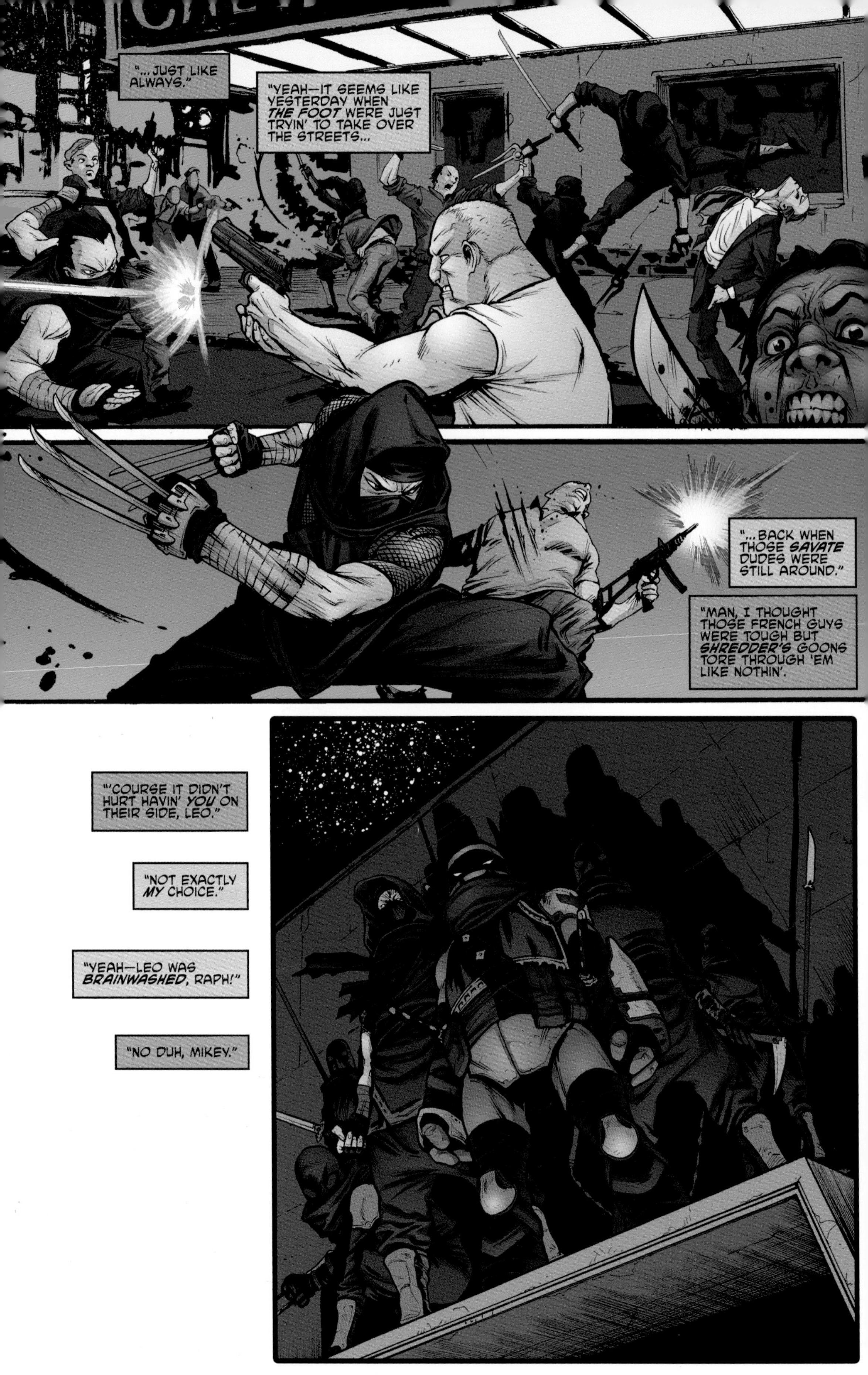
"...JUST LIKE ALWAYS."
"YEAH—IT SEEMS LIKE YESTERDAY WHEN *THE FOOT* WERE JUST TRYIN' TO TAKE OVER THE STREETS...
"...BACK WHEN THOSE *SAVATE* DUDES WERE STILL AROUND."
"MAN, I THOUGHT THOSE FRENCH GUYS WERE TOUGH BUT *SHREDDER'S* GOONS TORE THROUGH 'EM LIKE NOTHIN'.
"'COURSE IT DIDN'T HURT HAVIN' *YOU* ON THEIR SIDE, LEO."
"NOT EXACTLY *MY* CHOICE."
"YEAH—LEO WAS *BRAINWASHED*, RAPH!"
"NO DUH, MIKEY."

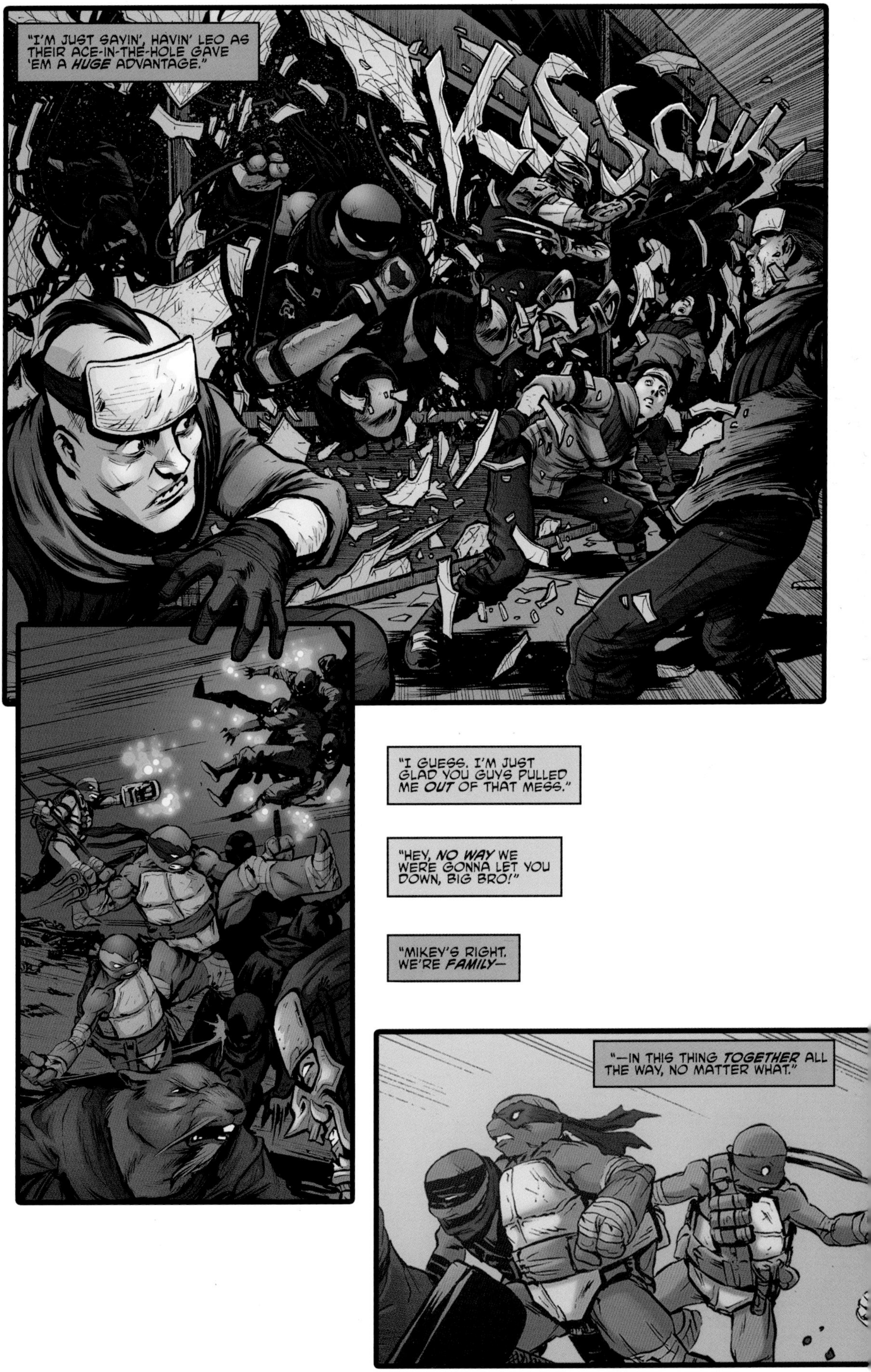
"I'M JUST SAYIN', HAVIN' LEO AS THEIR ACE-IN-THE-HOLE GAVE 'EM A *HUGE* ADVANTAGE."
"I GUESS. I'M JUST GLAD YOU GUYS PULLED ME *OUT* OF THAT MESS."
"HEY, *NO WAY* WE WERE GONNA LET YOU DOWN, BIG BRO!"
"MIKEY'S RIGHT. WE'RE *FAMILY*—
"—IN THIS THING *TOGETHER* ALL THE WAY, NO MATTER WHAT."

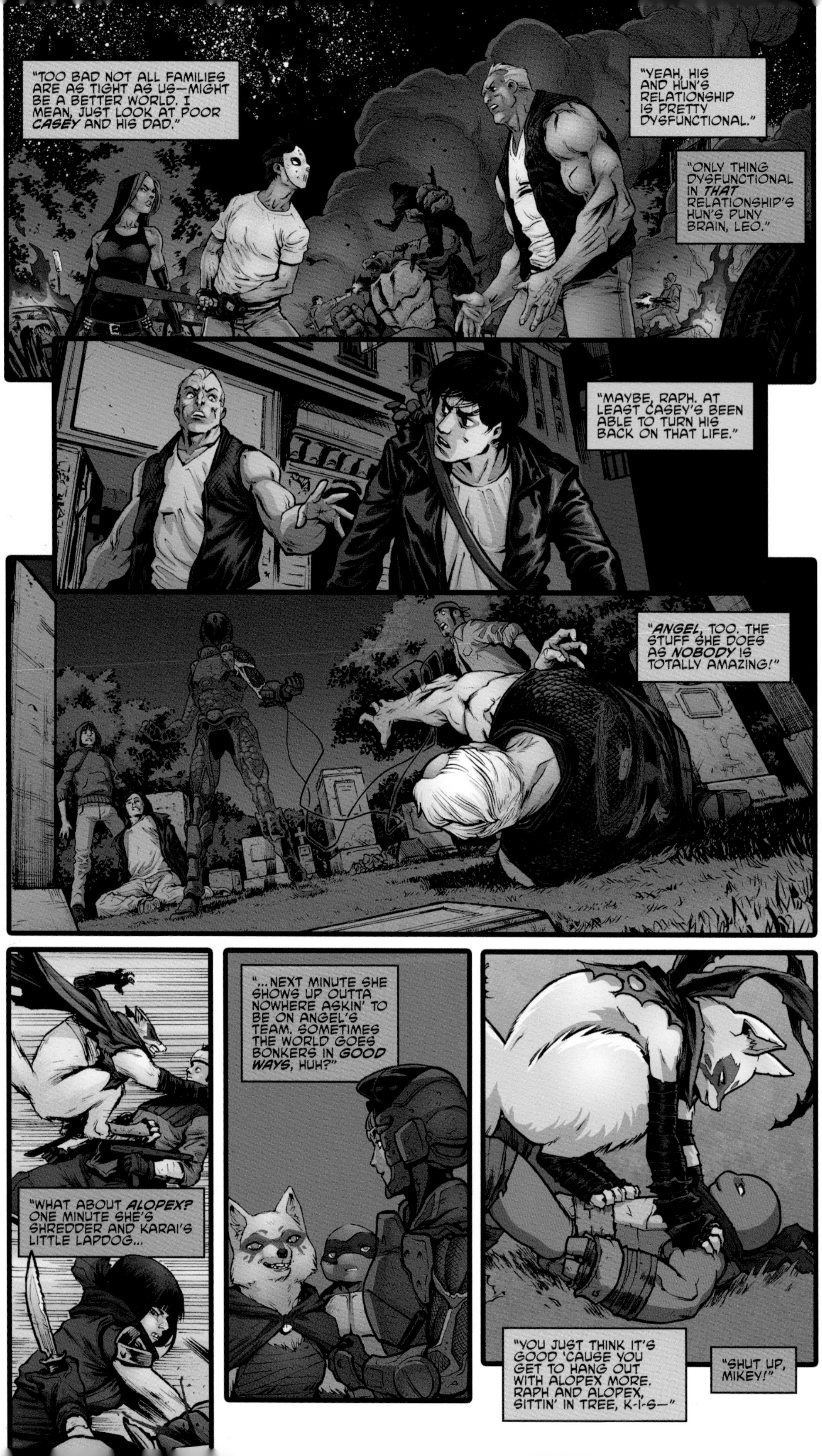
"TOO BAD NOT ALL FAMILIES ARE AS TIGHT AS US—MIGHT BE A BETTER WORLD. I MEAN, JUST LOOK AT POOR CASEY AND HIS DAD."
"YEAH, HIS AND HUN'S RELATIONSHIP IS PRETTY DYSFUNCTIONAL."
"ONLY THING DYSFUNCTIONAL IN THAT RELATIONSHIP'S HUN'S PUNY BRAIN, LEO."
"MAYBE, RAPH. AT LEAST CASEY'S BEEN ABLE TO TURN HIS BACK ON THAT LIFE."
"ANGEL, TOO. THE STUFF SHE DOES AS NOBODY IS TOTALLY AMAZING!"
"WHAT ABOUT ALOPEX? ONE MINUTE SHE'S SHREDDER AND KARAI'S LITTLE LAPDOG...
"...NEXT MINUTE SHE SHOWS UP OUTTA NOWHERE ASKIN' TO BE ON ANGEL'S TEAM. SOMETIMES THE WORLD GOES BONKERS IN GOOD WAYS, HUH?"
"YOU JUST THINK IT'S GOOD 'CAUSE YOU GET TO HANG OUT WITH ALOPEX MORE. RAPH AND ALOPEX, SITTIN' IN TREE, K-I-S—"
"SHUT UP, MIKEY!"

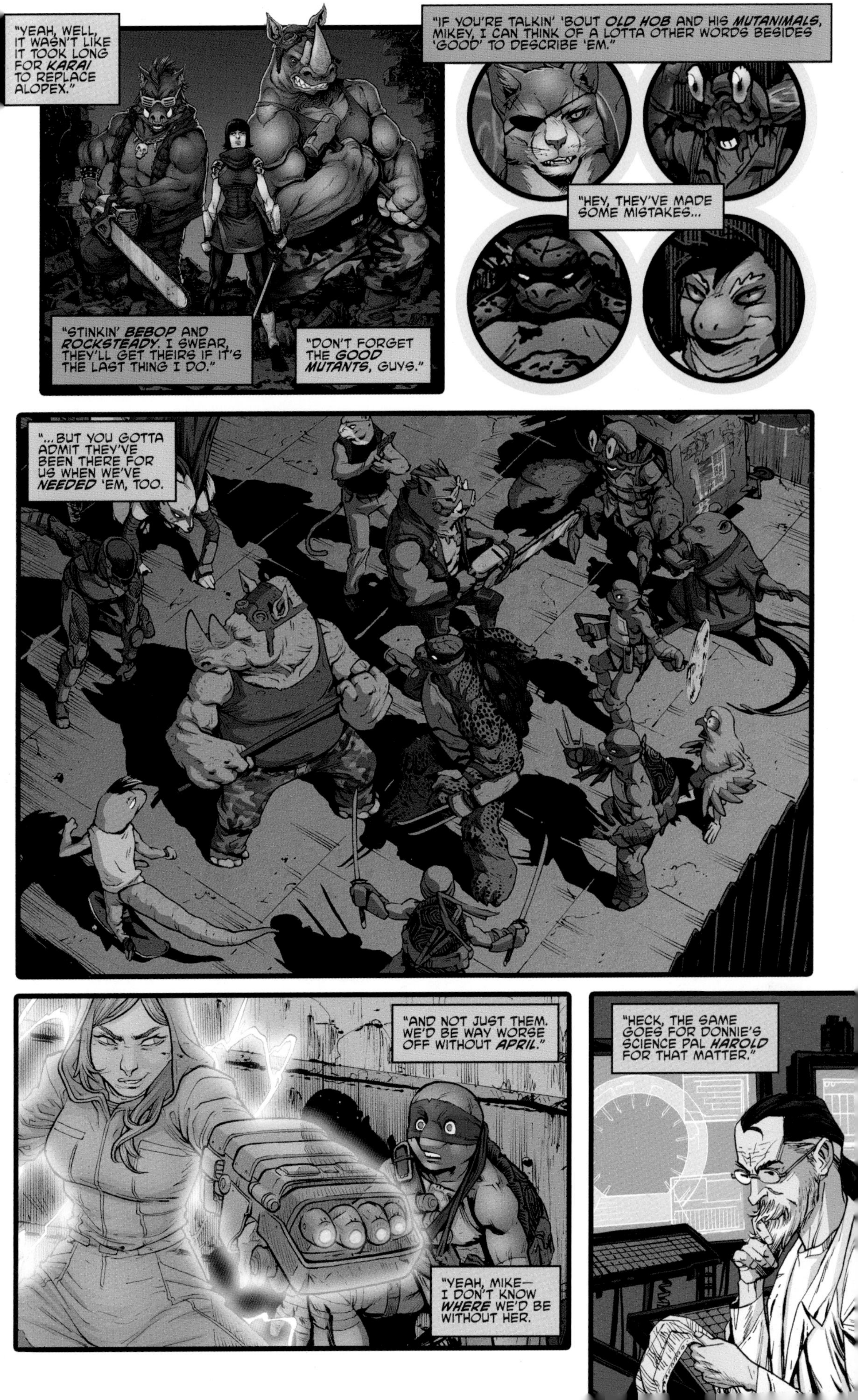

"YEAH, WELL, IT WASN'T LIKE IT TOOK LONG FOR KARAI TO REPLACE ALOPEX."
"STINKIN' BEBOP AND ROCKSTEADY. I SWEAR, THEY'LL GET THEIRS IF IT'S THE LAST THING I DO."
"DON'T FORGET THE GOOD MUTANTS, GUYS."
"IF YOU'RE TALKIN' 'BOUT OLD HOB AND HIS MUTANIMALS, MIKEY, I CAN THINK OF A LOTTA OTHER WORDS BESIDES 'GOOD' TO DESCRIBE 'EM."
"HEY, THEY'VE MADE SOME MISTAKES...
"...BUT YOU GOTTA ADMIT THEY'VE BEEN THERE FOR US WHEN WE'VE NEEDED 'EM, TOO.
"AND NOT JUST THEM. WE'D BE WAY WORSE OFF WITHOUT APRIL."
"YEAH, MIKE— I DON'T KNOW WHERE WE'D BE WITHOUT HER.
"HECK, THE SAME GOES FOR DONNIE'S SCIENCE PAL HAROLD FOR THAT MATTER."

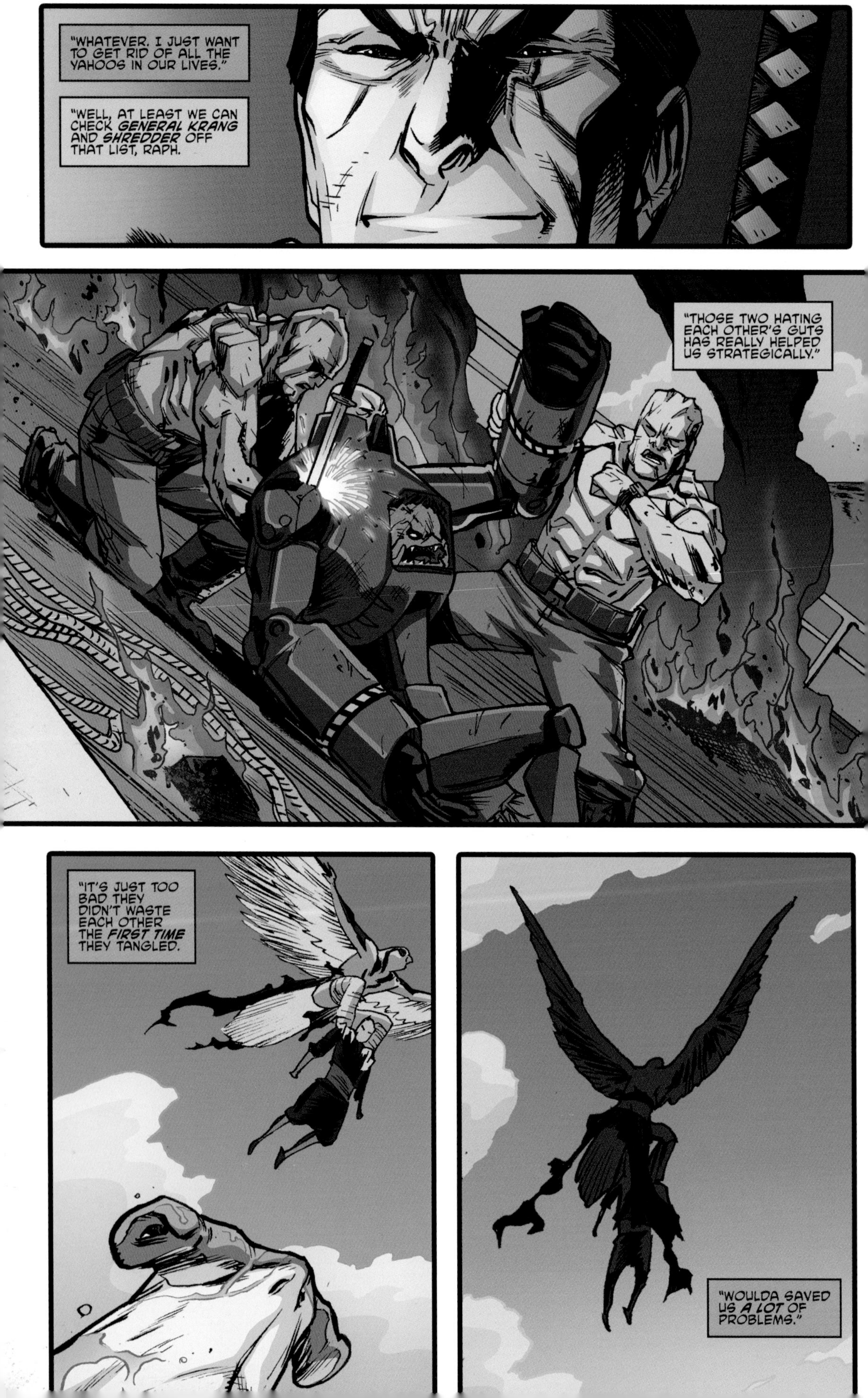
"WHATEVER. I JUST WANT TO GET RID OF ALL THE YAHOOS IN OUR LIVES."
"WELL, AT LEAST WE CAN CHECK *GENERAL KRANG* AND *SHREDDER* OFF THAT LIST, RAPH.
"THOSE TWO HATING EACH OTHER'S GUTS HAS REALLY HELPED US STRATEGICALLY."
"IT'S JUST TOO BAD THEY DIDN'T WASTE EACH OTHER THE *FIRST TIME* THEY TANGLED.
"WOULDA SAVED US *A LOT* OF PROBLEMS."

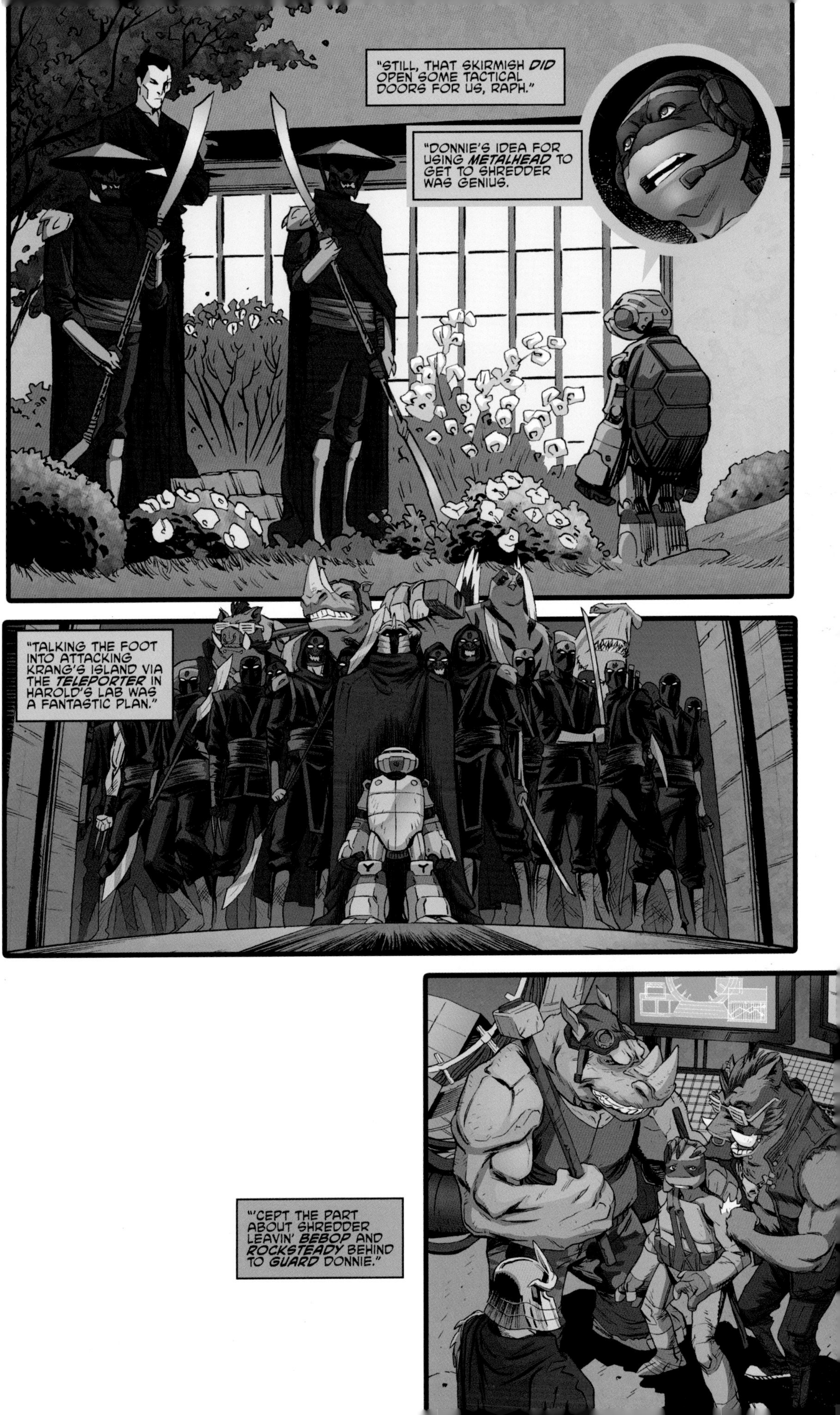
"STILL, THAT SKIRMISH *DID* OPEN SOME TACTICAL DOORS FOR US, RAPH."
"DONNIE'S IDEA FOR USING *METALHEAD* TO GET TO SHREDDER WAS GENIUS.
"TALKING THE FOOT INTO ATTACKING KRANG'S ISLAND VIA THE *TELEPORTER* IN HAROLD'S LAB WAS A FANTASTIC PLAN."
"'CEPT THE PART ABOUT SHREDDER LEAVIN' *BEBOP* AND *ROCKSTEADY* BEHIND TO *GUARD* DONNIE."

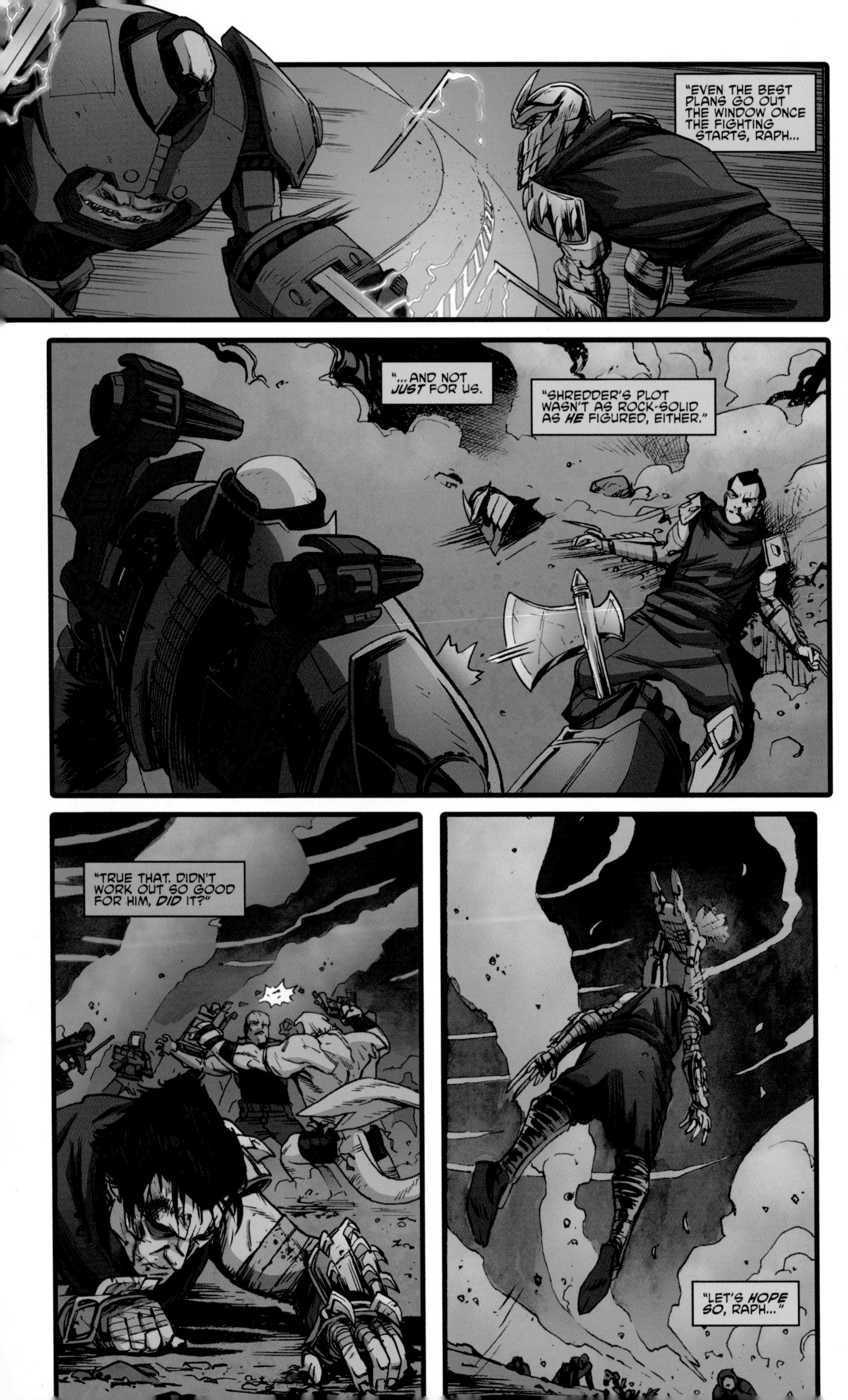
"EVEN THE BEST PLANS GO OUT THE WINDOW ONCE THE FIGHTING STARTS, RAPH...
"...AND NOT *JUST* FOR US.
"SHREDDER'S PLOT WASN'T AS ROCK-SOLID AS *HE* FIGURED, EITHER."
"TRUE THAT. DIDN'T WORK OUT SO GOOD FOR HIM, *DID* IT?"
"LET'S *HOPE* SO, RAPH..."

"...BECAUSE AFTER WHAT THOSE *PSYCHOS* DID TO DONNIE..."

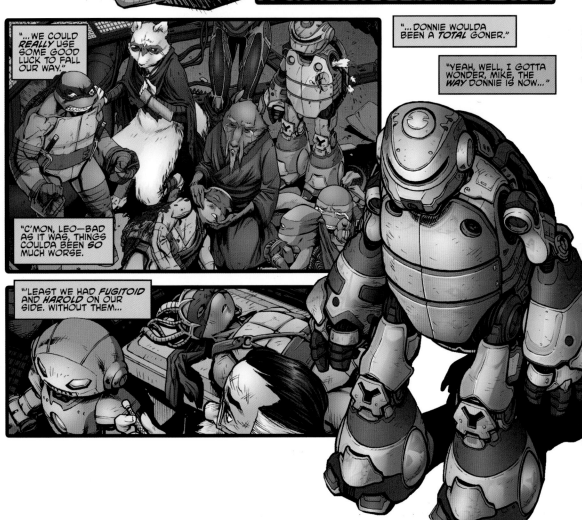

"...WE COULD *REALLY* USE SOME GOOD LUCK TO FALL OUR WAY."

"C'MON, LEO—BAD AS IT WAS, THINGS COULDA BEEN *SO* MUCH WORSE."

"LEAST WE HAD *FUGITOID* AND *HAROLD* ON OUR SIDE. WITHOUT THEM..."

"...DONNIE WOULDA BEEN A *TOTAL* GONER."

"YEAH, WELL, I GOTTA WONDER, MIKE, THE *WAY* DONNIE IS NOW..."

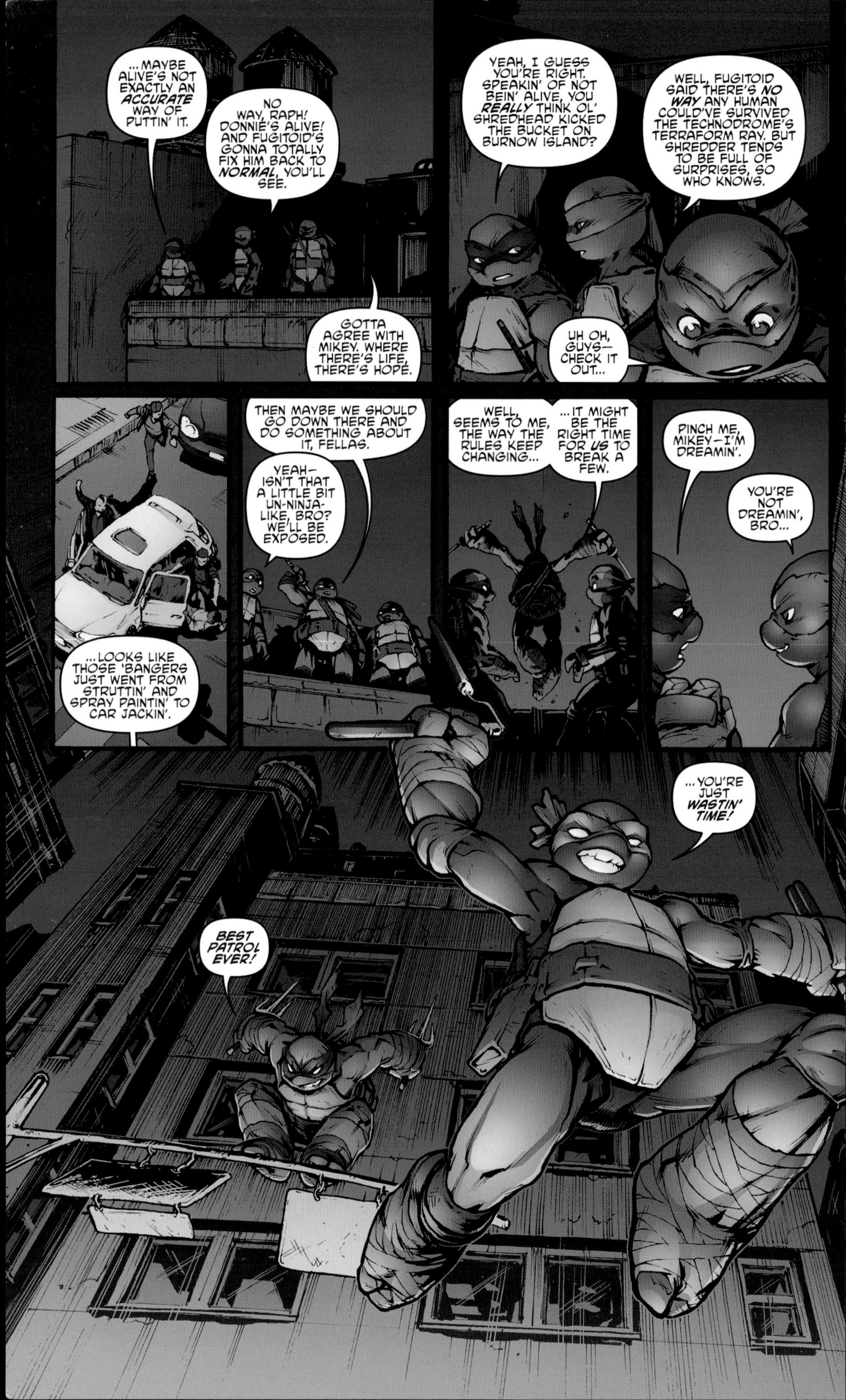
...MAYBE ALIVE'S NOT EXACTLY AN ACCURATE WAY OF PUTTIN' IT.
NO WAY, RAPH! DONNIE'S ALIVE! AND FUGITOID'S GONNA TOTALLY FIX HIM BACK TO NORMAL, YOU'LL SEE.
GOTTA AGREE WITH MIKEY. WHERE THERE'S LIFE, THERE'S HOPE.
YEAH, I GUESS YOU'RE RIGHT. SPEAKIN' OF NOT BEIN' ALIVE, YOU REALLY THINK OL' SHREDHEAD KICKED THE BUCKET ON BURNOW ISLAND?
WELL, FUGITOID SAID THERE'S NO WAY ANY HUMAN COULD'VE SURVIVED THE TECHNODROME'S TERRAFORM RAY. BUT SHREDDER TENDS TO BE FULL OF SURPRISES, SO WHO KNOWS.
UH OH, GUYS— CHECK IT OUT...
...LOOKS LIKE THOSE 'BANGERS JUST WENT FROM STRUTTIN' AND SPRAY PAINTIN' TO CAR JACKIN'.
THEN MAYBE WE SHOULD GO DOWN THERE AND DO SOMETHING ABOUT IT, FELLAS.
YEAH— ISN'T THAT A LITTLE BIT UN-NINJA-LIKE, BRO? WE'LL BE EXPOSED.
WELL, SEEMS TO ME, THE WAY THE RULES KEEP CHANGING...
...IT MIGHT BE THE RIGHT TIME FOR US TO BREAK A FEW.
PINCH ME, MIKEY—I'M DREAMIN'.
YOU'RE NOT DREAMIN', BRO...
...YOU'RE JUST WASTIN' TIME!
BEST PATROL EVER!

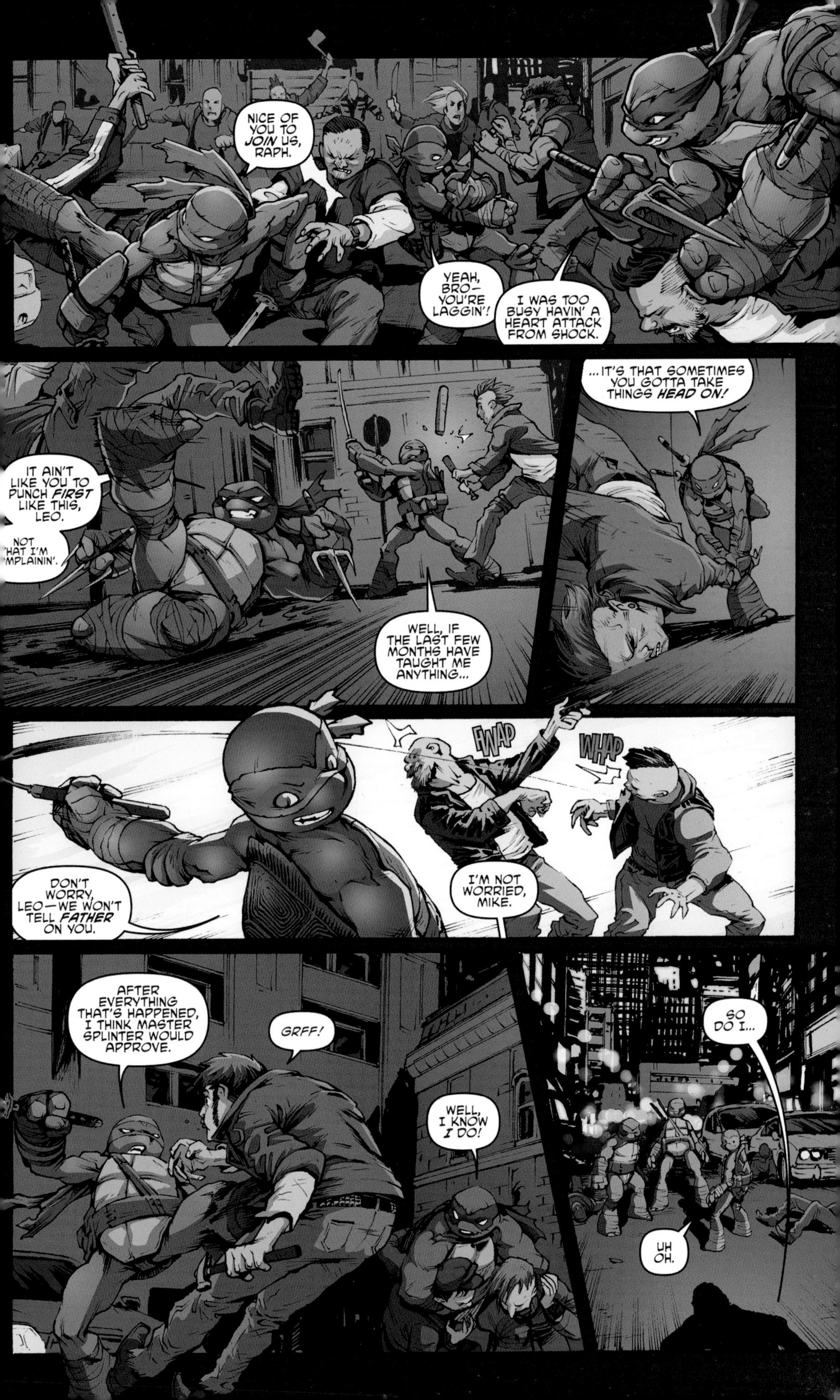
NICE OF YOU TO *JOIN* US, RAPH.
YEAH, BRO— YOU'RE LAGGIN'!
I WAS TOO BUSY HAVIN' A HEART ATTACK FROM SHOCK.
IT AIN'T LIKE YOU TO PUNCH *FIRST* LIKE THIS, LEO.
NOT THAT I'M COMPLAININ'.
WELL, IF THE LAST FEW MONTHS HAVE TAUGHT ME ANYTHING...
...IT'S THAT SOMETIMES YOU GOTTA TAKE THINGS *HEAD ON!*
FWAP
WHAP
DON'T WORRY, LEO—WE WON'T TELL *FATHER* ON YOU.
I'M NOT WORRIED, MIKE.
AFTER EVERYTHING THAT'S HAPPENED, I THINK MASTER SPLINTER WOULD APPROVE.
GRFF!
WELL, I KNOW *I* DO!
SO DO I...
UH OH.

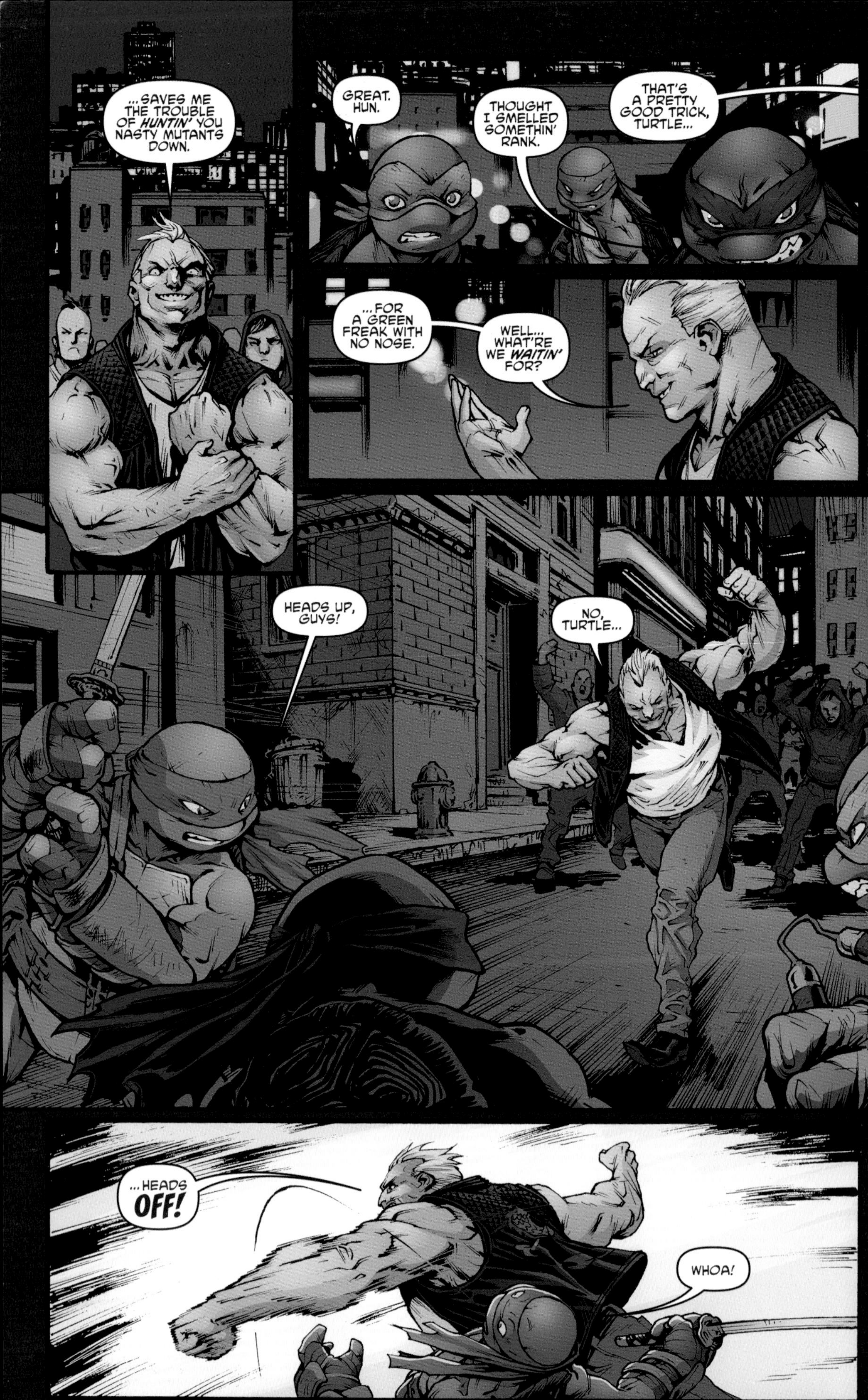
...SAVES ME THE TROUBLE OF HUNTIN' YOU NASTY MUTANTS DOWN.
GREAT. HUN.
THOUGHT I SMELLED SOMETHIN' RANK.
THAT'S A PRETTY GOOD TRICK, TURTLE...
...FOR A GREEN FREAK WITH NO NOSE.
WELL... WHAT'RE WE WAITIN' FOR?
HEADS UP, GUYS!
NO, TURTLE...
...HEADS OFF!
WHOA!

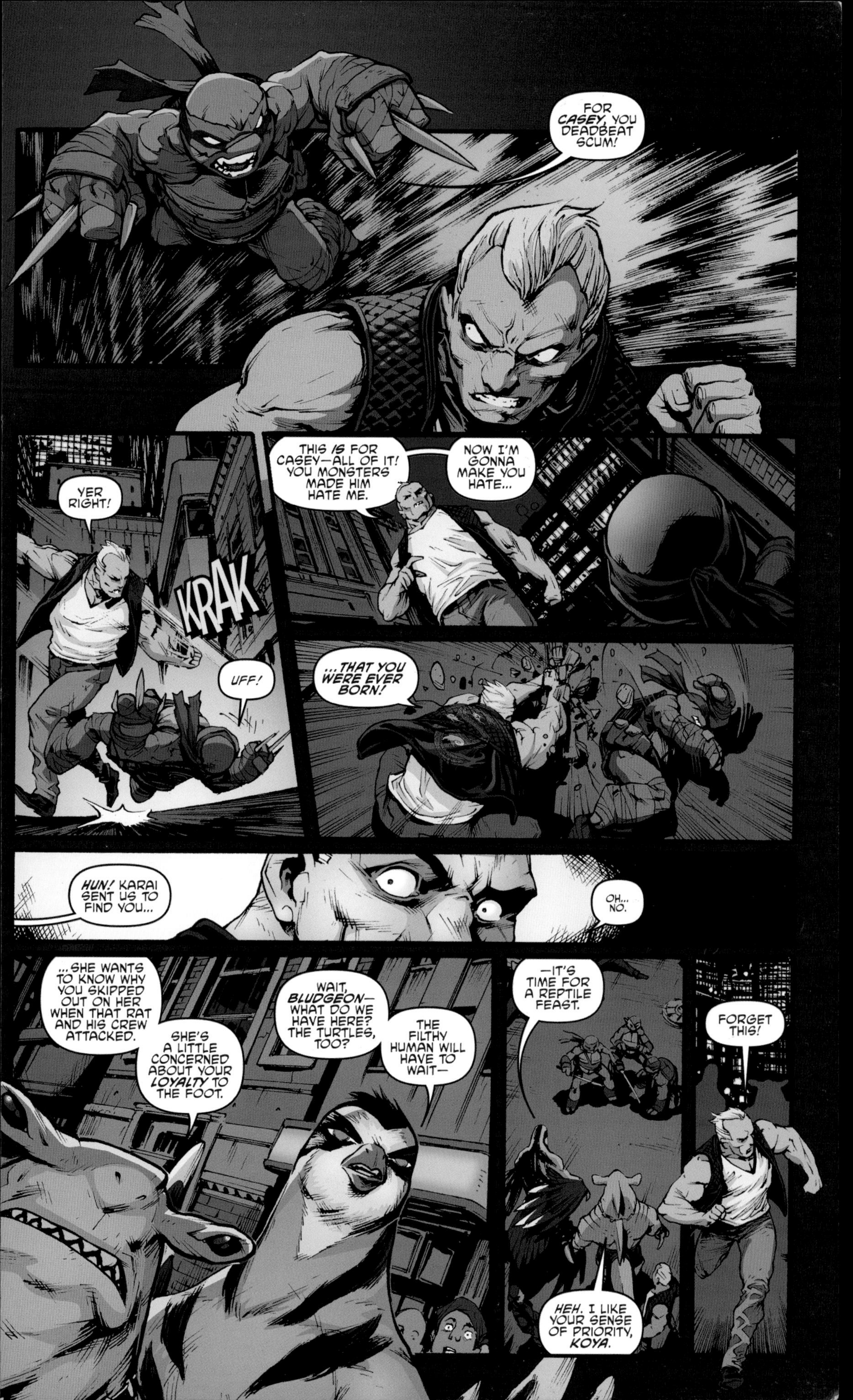

FOR *CASEY*, YOU DEADBEAT SCUM!
YER RIGHT!
KRAK
UFF!
THIS *IS* FOR CASEY—ALL OF IT! YOU MONSTERS MADE HIM HATE ME.
NOW I'M GONNA MAKE YOU HATE...
...THAT YOU WERE EVER BORN!
HUN! KARAI SENT US TO FIND YOU...
OH... NO.
...SHE WANTS TO KNOW WHY YOU SKIPPED OUT ON HER WHEN THAT RAT AND HIS CREW ATTACKED.
SHE'S A LITTLE CONCERNED ABOUT YOUR *LOYALTY* TO THE FOOT.
WAIT, *BLUDGEON*—WHAT DO WE HAVE HERE? THE TURTLES, TOO?
THE FILTHY HUMAN WILL HAVE TO WAIT—
—IT'S TIME FOR A REPTILE FEAST.
HEH. I LIKE YOUR SENSE OF PRIORITY, *KOYA*.
FORGET THIS!

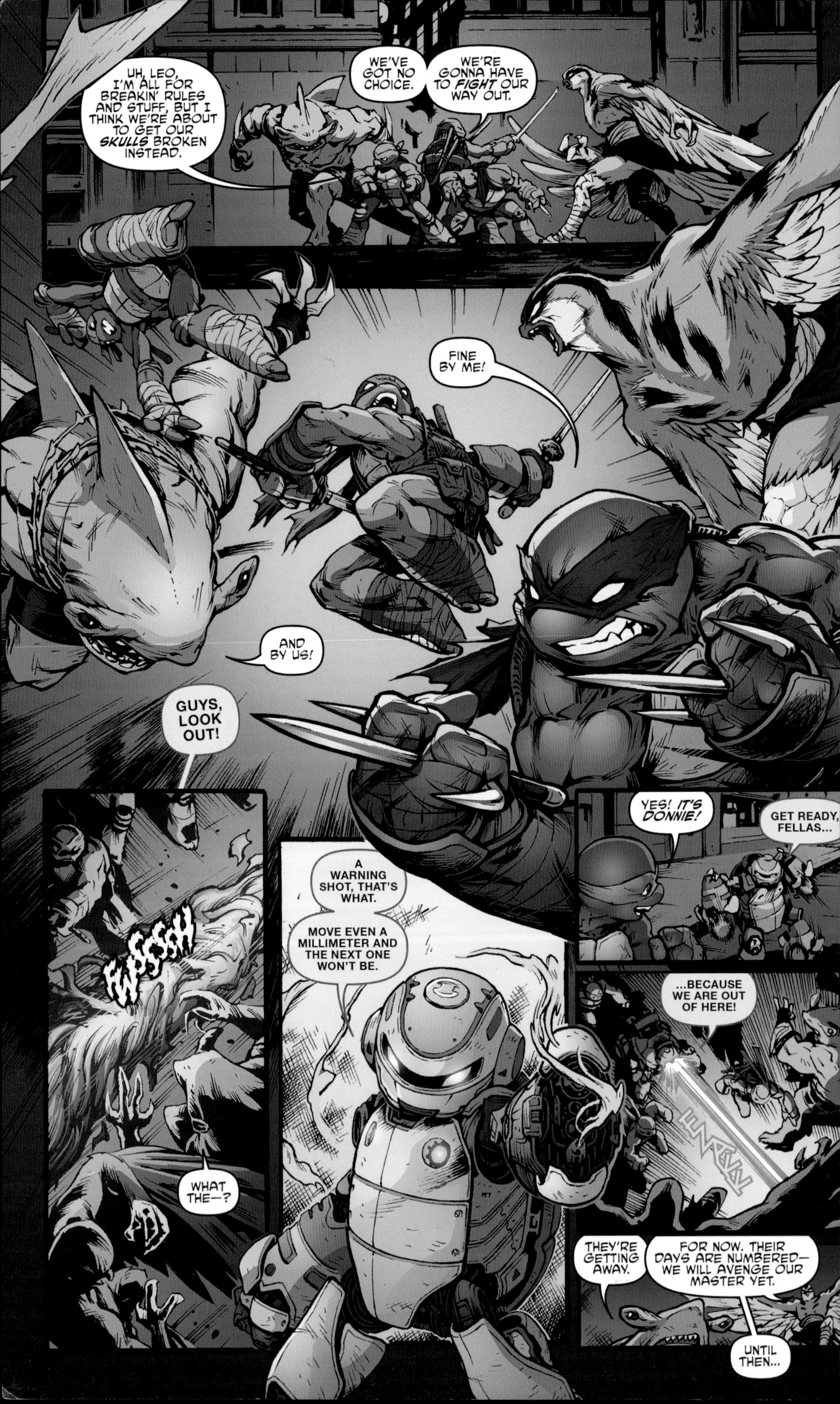
UH, LEO, I'M ALL FOR BREAKIN' RULES AND STUFF, BUT I THINK WE'RE ABOUT TO GET OUR SKULLS BROKEN INSTEAD.
WE'VE GOT NO CHOICE.
WE'RE GONNA HAVE TO FIGHT OUR WAY OUT.
FINE BY ME!
AND BY US!
GUYS, LOOK OUT!
FWSSSH
WHAT THE—?
A WARNING SHOT, THAT'S WHAT.
MOVE EVEN A MILLIMETER AND THE NEXT ONE WON'T BE.
YES! IT'S DONNIE!
GET READY, FELLAS...
...BECAUSE WE ARE OUT OF HERE!
THEY'RE GETTING AWAY.
FOR NOW. THEIR DAYS ARE NUMBERED— WE WILL AVENGE OUR MASTER YET.
UNTIL THEN...

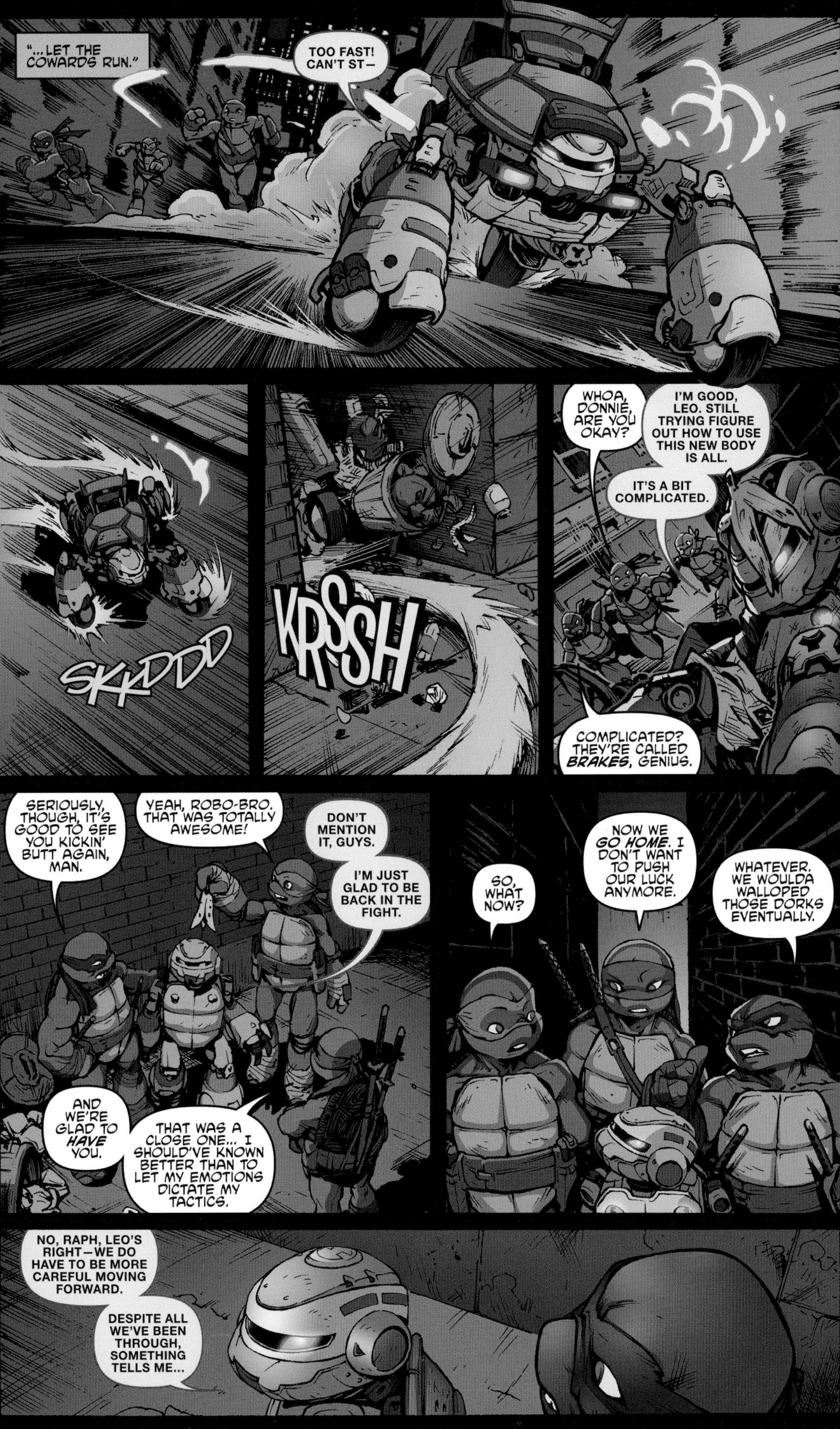
"...LET THE COWARDS RUN."
TOO FAST! CAN'T ST—
SKKDDD
KRSSH
WHOA, DONNIE, ARE YOU OKAY?
I'M GOOD, LEO. STILL TRYING FIGURE OUT HOW TO USE THIS NEW BODY IS ALL.
IT'S A BIT COMPLICATED.
COMPLICATED? THEY'RE CALLED ***BRAKES***, GENIUS.
SERIOUSLY, THOUGH, IT'S GOOD TO SEE YOU KICKIN' BUTT AGAIN, MAN.
YEAH, ROBO-BRO. THAT WAS TOTALLY AWESOME!
DON'T MENTION IT, GUYS.
I'M JUST GLAD TO BE BACK IN THE FIGHT.
AND WE'RE GLAD TO ***HAVE*** YOU.
THAT WAS A CLOSE ONE... I SHOULD'VE KNOWN BETTER THAN TO LET MY EMOTIONS DICTATE MY TACTICS.
SO, WHAT NOW?
NOW WE ***GO HOME***. I DON'T WANT TO PUSH OUR LUCK ANYMORE.
WHATEVER. WE WOULDA WALLOPED THOSE DORKS EVENTUALLY.
NO, RAPH, LEO'S RIGHT—WE DO HAVE TO BE MORE CAREFUL MOVING FORWARD.
DESPITE ALL WE'VE BEEN THROUGH, SOMETHING TELLS ME...

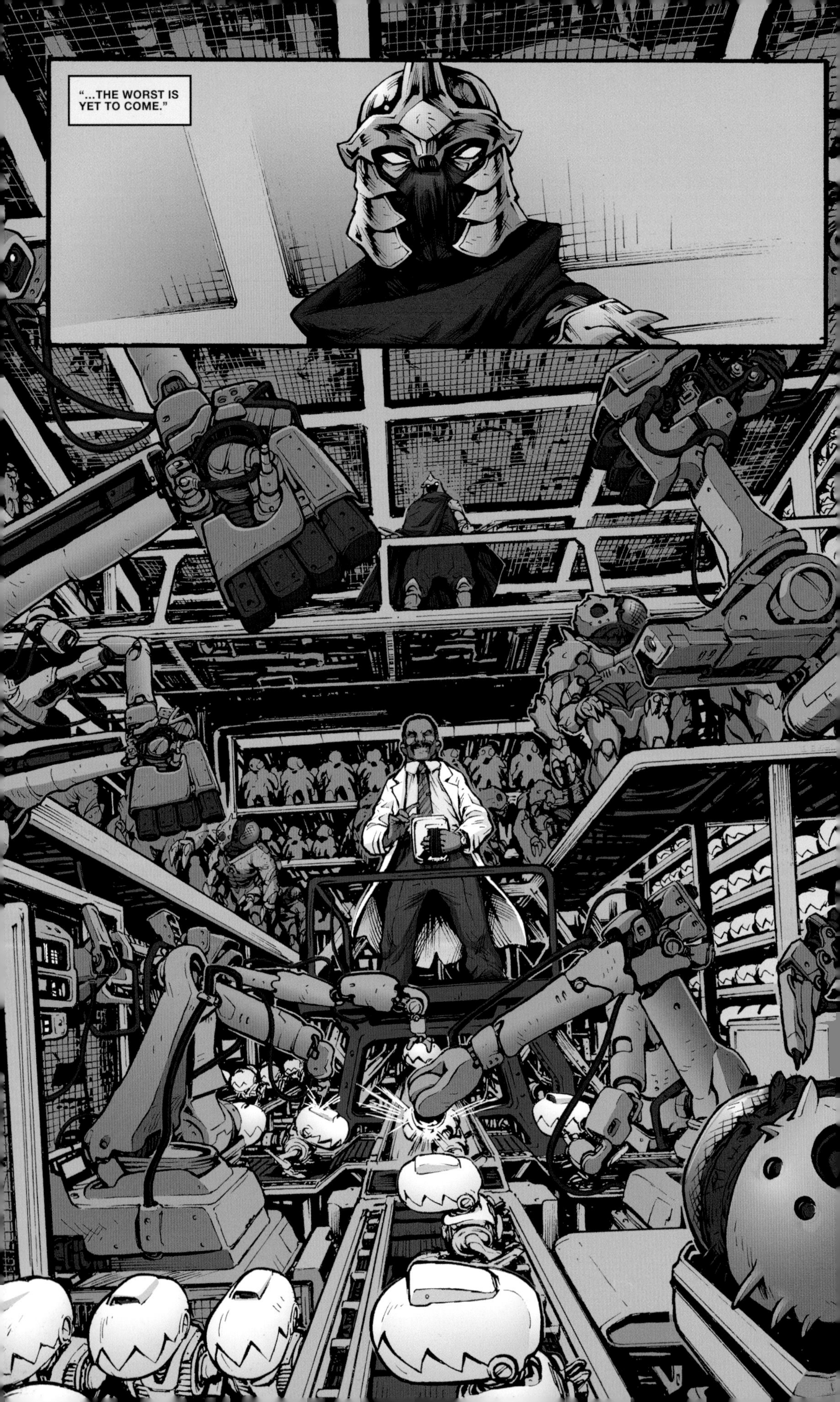
"...THE WORST IS YET TO COME."

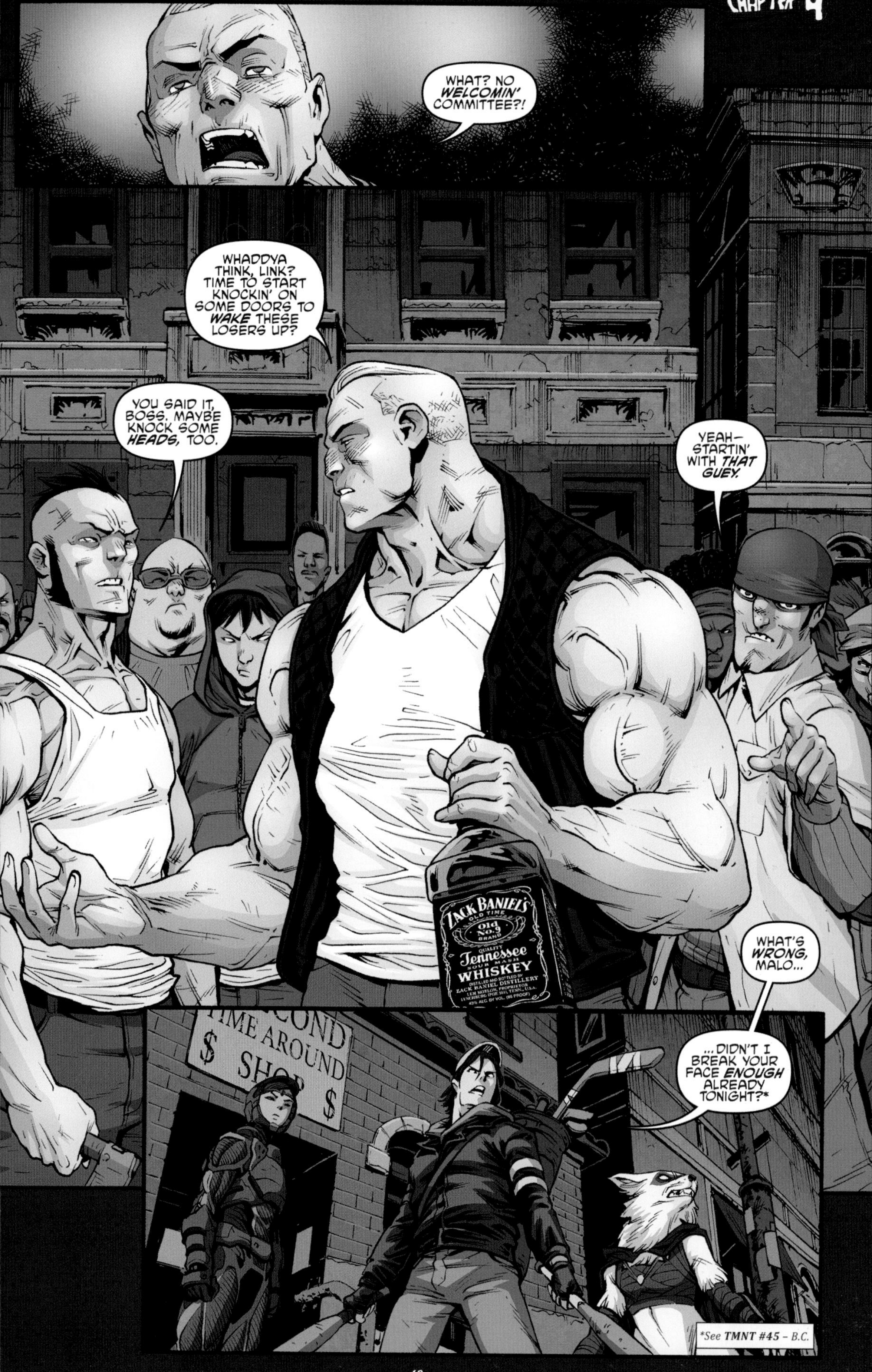
CHAPTER 4
WHAT? NO WELCOMIN' COMMITTEE?!
WHADDYA THINK, LINK? TIME TO START KNOCKIN' ON SOME DOORS TO WAKE THESE LOSERS UP?
YOU SAID IT, BOSS. MAYBE KNOCK SOME HEADS, TOO.
YEAH—STARTIN' WITH THAT GUEY.
ZACK BANIEL'S
OLD TIME
Old No.9 BRAND
QUALITY
Tennessee
SOUR MASH
WHISKEY
WHAT'S WRONG, MALO...
SECOND TIME AROUND $ SHOP $
...DIDN'T I BREAK YOUR FACE ENOUGH ALREADY TONIGHT?*
*See TMNT #45 – B.C.

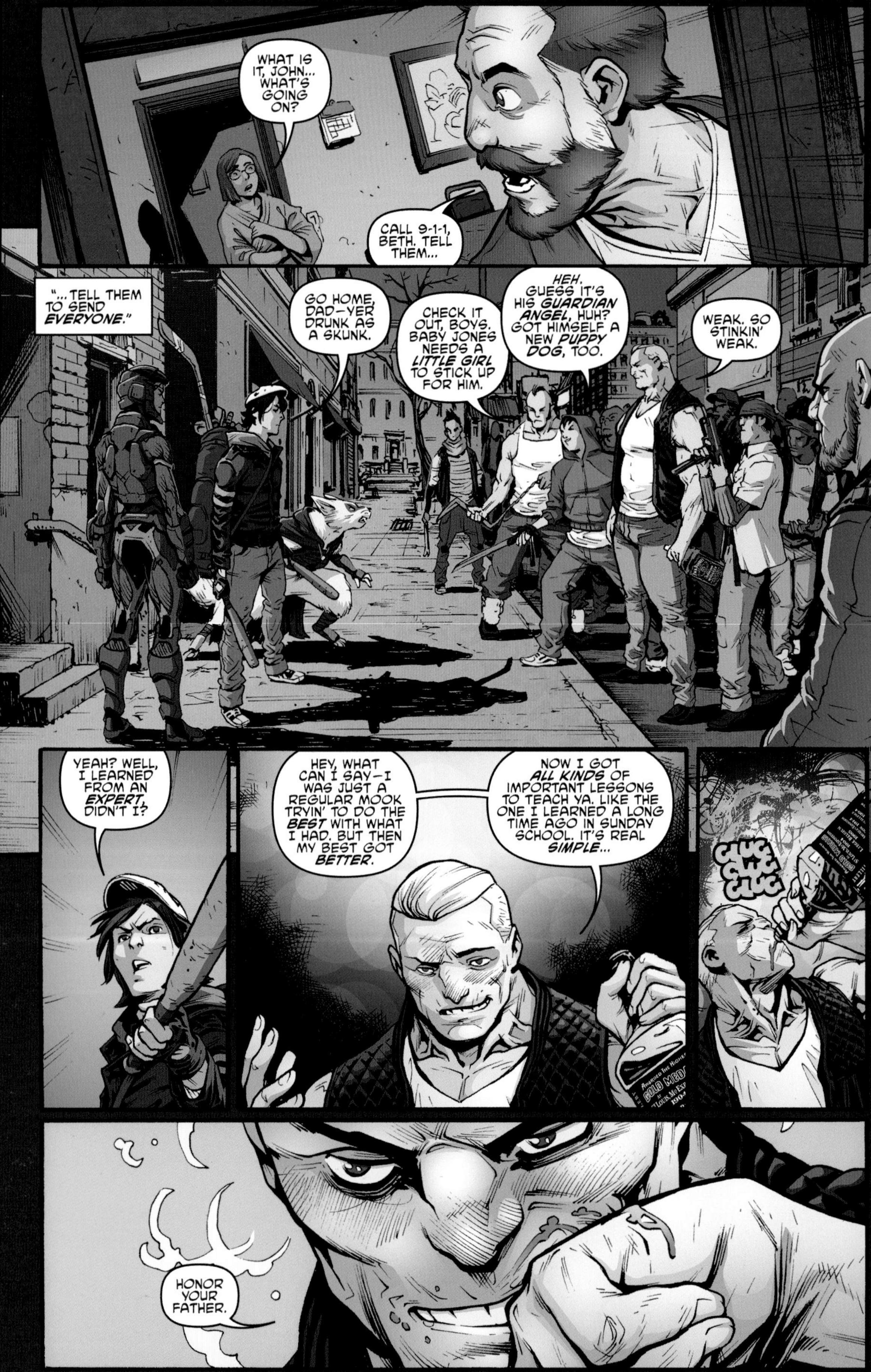

WHAT IS IT, JOHN... WHAT'S GOING ON?
CALL 9-1-1, BETH. TELL THEM...
"...TELL THEM TO SEND EVERYONE."
GO HOME, DAD—YER DRUNK AS A SKUNK.
CHECK IT OUT, BOYS. BABY JONES NEEDS A LITTLE GIRL TO STICK UP FOR HIM.
HEH. GUESS IT'S HIS GUARDIAN ANGEL, HUH? GOT HIMSELF A NEW PUPPY DOG, TOO.
WEAK. SO STINKIN' WEAK.
YEAH? WELL, I LEARNED FROM AN EXPERT, DIDN'T I?
HEY, WHAT CAN I SAY—I WAS JUST A REGULAR MOOK TRYIN' TO DO THE BEST WITH WHAT I HAD. BUT THEN MY BEST GOT BETTER.
NOW I GOT ALL KINDS OF IMPORTANT LESSONS TO TEACH YA. LIKE THE ONE I LEARNED A LONG TIME AGO IN SUNDAY SCHOOL. IT'S REAL SIMPLE...
GLUG GLUG GLUG
HONOR YOUR FATHER.

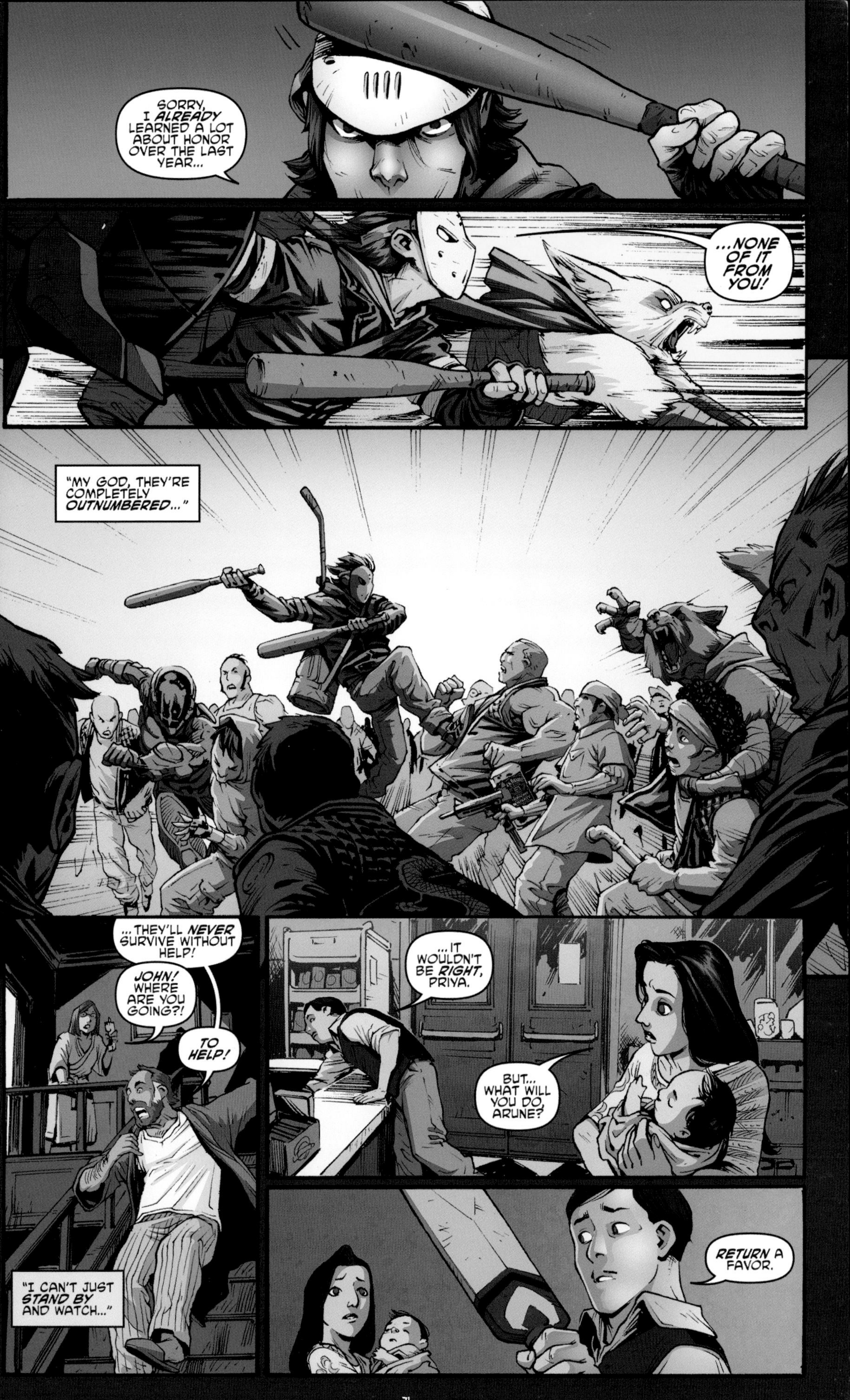
SORRY, I *ALREADY* LEARNED A LOT ABOUT HONOR OVER THE LAST YEAR...
...*NONE OF IT FROM YOU!*
"MY GOD, THEY'RE COMPLETELY *OUTNUMBERED*..."
...THEY'LL *NEVER* SURVIVE WITHOUT HELP!
JOHN! WHERE ARE YOU GOING?!
TO HELP!
"I CAN'T JUST *STAND BY* AND WATCH..."
...IT WOULDN'T BE *RIGHT*, PRIYA.
BUT... WHAT WILL YOU DO, ARUNE?
RETURN A FAVOR.

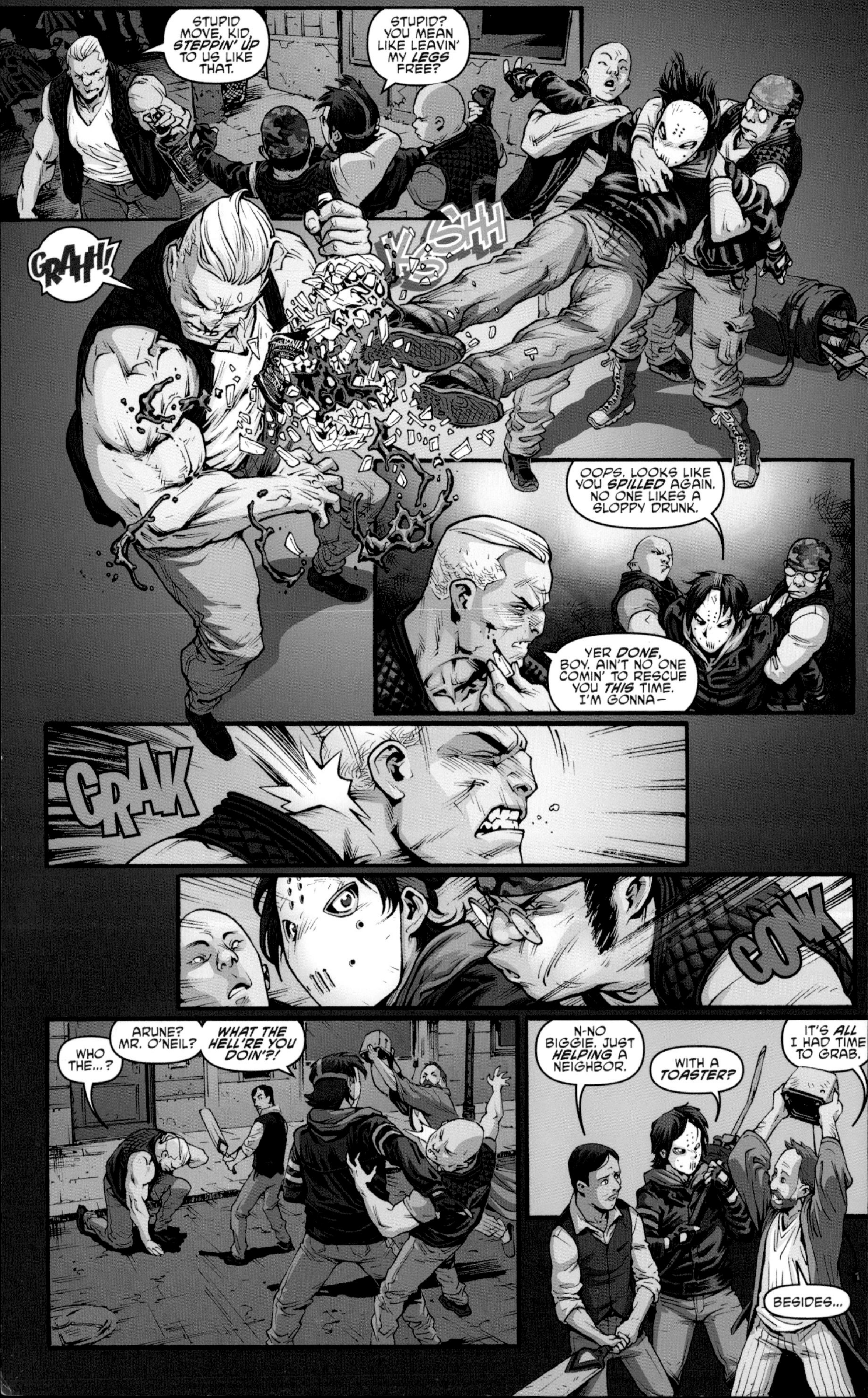

STUPID MOVE, KID, STEPPIN' UP TO US LIKE THAT.
STUPID? YOU MEAN LIKE LEAVIN' MY LEGS FREE?
GRAHH!
KSHH
OOPS. LOOKS LIKE YOU SPILLED AGAIN. NO ONE LIKES A SLOPPY DRUNK.
YER DONE, BOY. AIN'T NO ONE COMIN' TO RESCUE YOU THIS TIME. I'M GONNA—
CRAK
GONK
WHO THE...?
ARUNE? MR. O'NEIL?
WHAT THE HELL'RE YOU DOIN'?!
N-NO BIGGIE. JUST HELPING A NEIGHBOR.
WITH A TOASTER?
IT'S ALL I HAD TIME TO GRAB.
BESIDES...

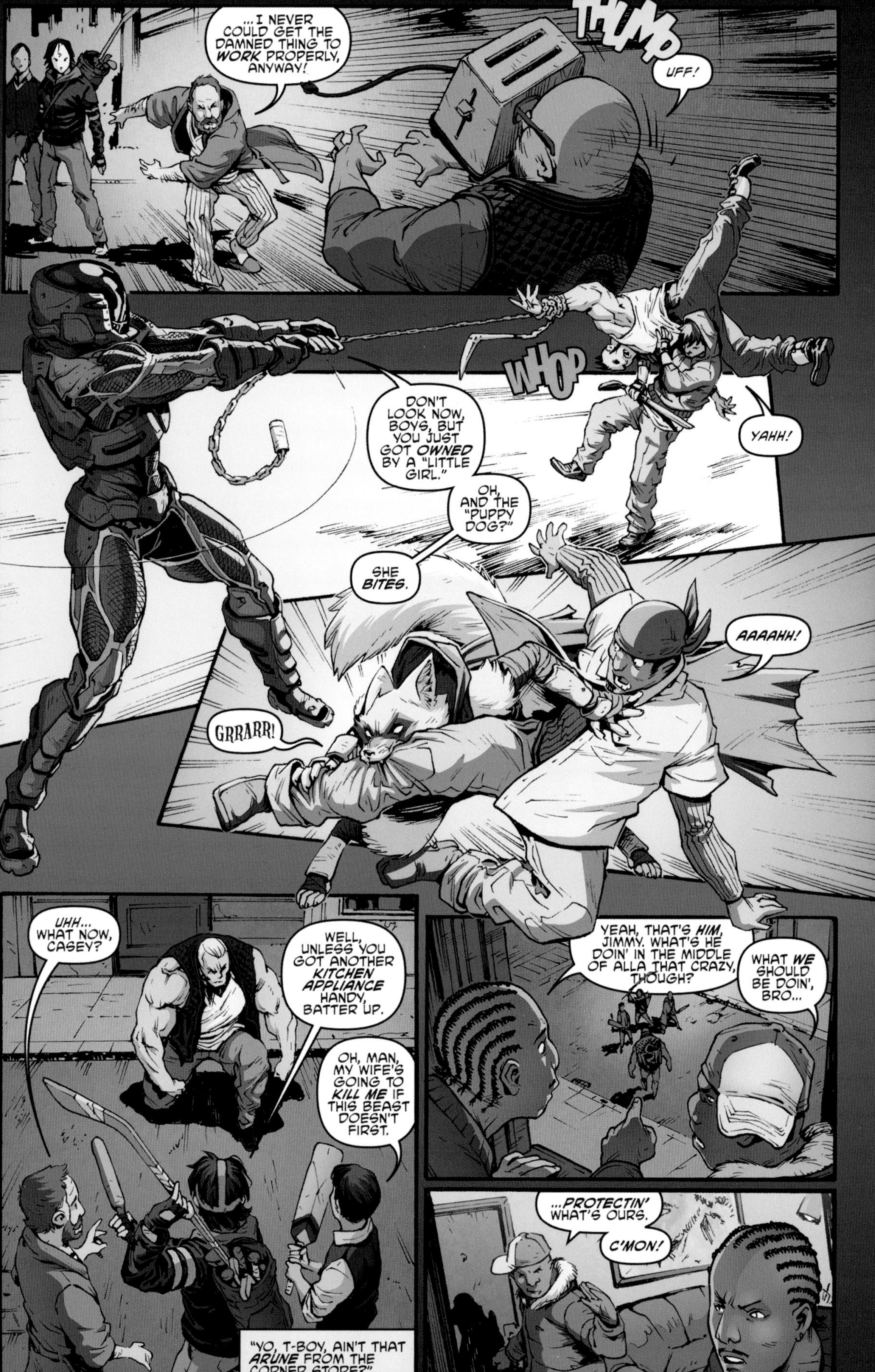
...I NEVER COULD GET THE DAMNED THING TO WORK PROPERLY, ANYWAY!
THUMP
UFF!
WHOP
DON'T LOOK NOW, BOYS, BUT YOU JUST GOT OWNED BY A "LITTLE GIRL."
OH, AND THE "PUPPY DOG?"
SHE BITES.
YAHH!
AAAAHH!
GRRARR!
UHH... WHAT NOW, CASEY?
WELL, UNLESS YOU GOT ANOTHER KITCHEN APPLIANCE HANDY, BATTER UP.
OH, MAN, MY WIFE'S GOING TO KILL ME IF THIS BEAST DOESN'T FIRST.
"YO, T-BOY, AIN'T THAT ARUNE FROM THE CORNER STORE?"
YEAH, THAT'S HIM, JIMMY. WHAT'S HE DOIN' IN THE MIDDLE OF ALLA THAT CRAZY, THOUGH?
WHAT WE SHOULD BE DOIN', BRO...
...PROTECTIN' WHAT'S OURS.
C'MON!

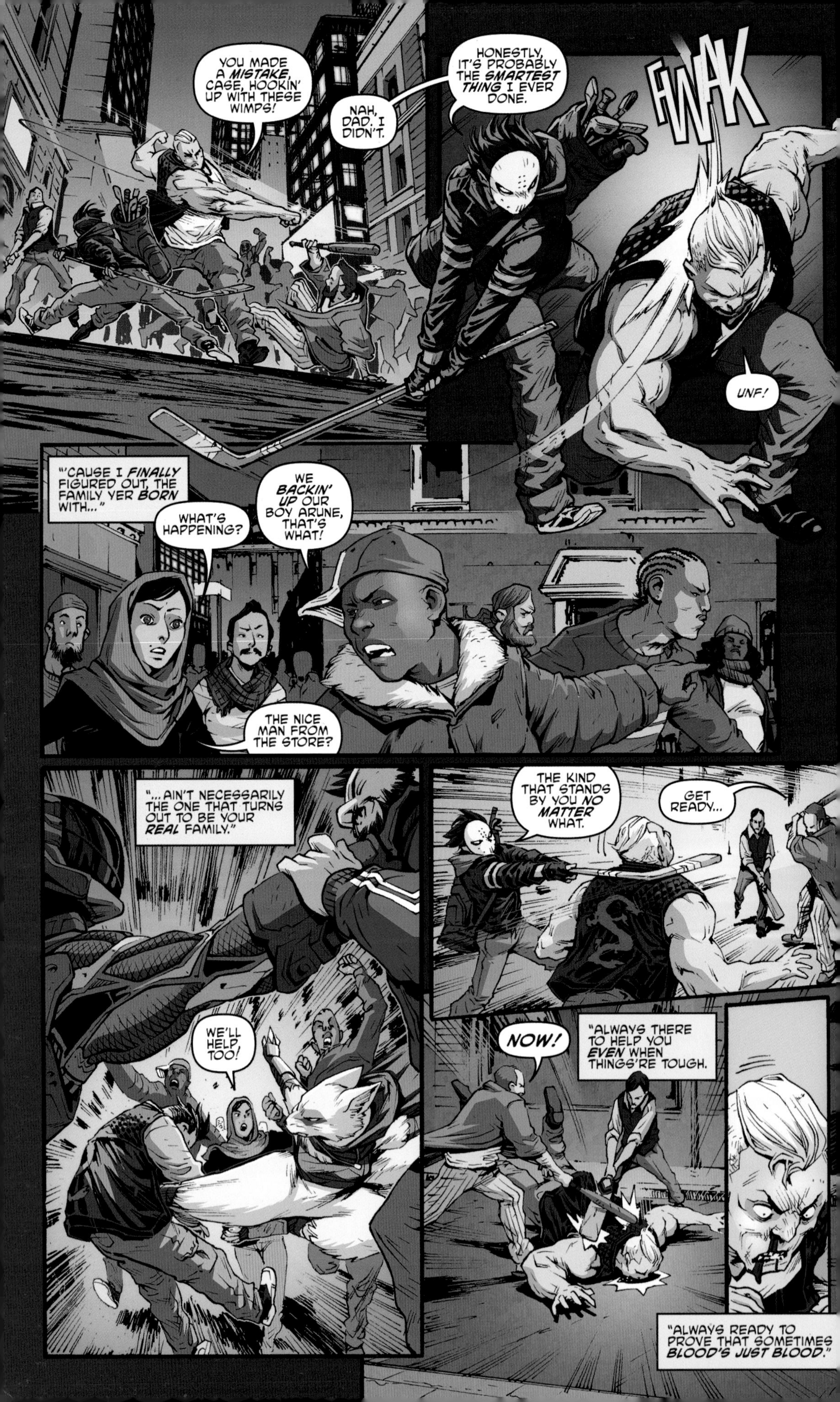

YOU MADE A *MISTAKE*, CASE, HOOKIN' UP WITH THESE WIMPS!
NAH, DAD. I DIDN'T.
HONESTLY, IT'S PROBABLY THE *SMARTEST THING* I EVER DONE.
FWAK
UNF!
"'CAUSE I *FINALLY* FIGURED OUT, THE FAMILY YER *BORN* WITH..."
WHAT'S HAPPENING?
WE *BACKIN' UP* OUR BOY ARUNE, THAT'S WHAT!
THE NICE MAN FROM THE STORE?
"...AIN'T NECESSARILY THE ONE THAT TURNS OUT TO BE YOUR *REAL* FAMILY."
WE'LL HELP, TOO!
THE KIND THAT STANDS BY YOU *NO MATTER* WHAT.
GET READY...
NOW!
"ALWAYS THERE TO HELP YOU *EVEN* WHEN THINGS'RE TOUGH.
"ALWAYS READY TO PROVE THAT SOMETIMES *BLOOD'S JUST BLOOD*."

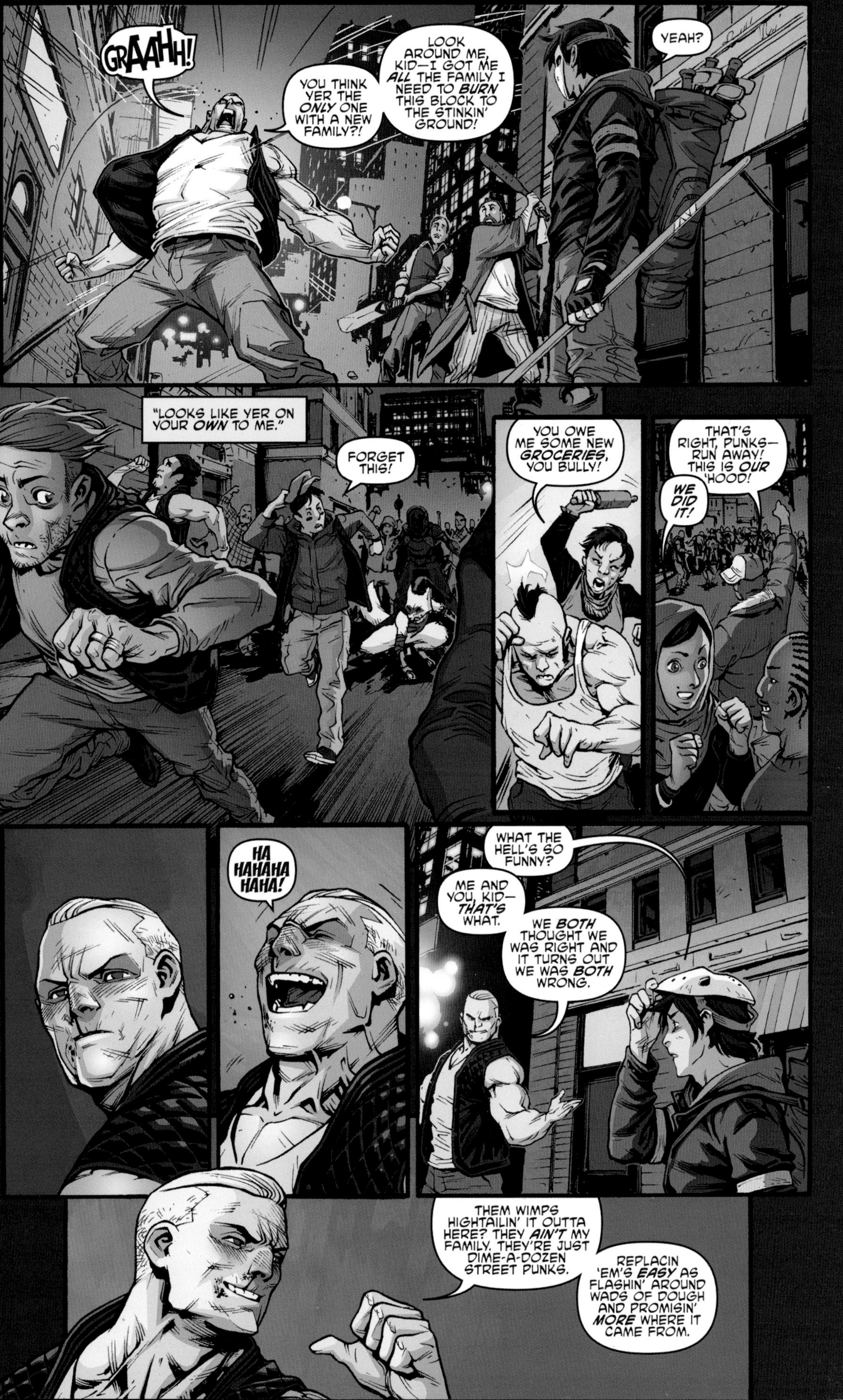
GRAAHH!
YOU THINK YER THE ONLY ONE WITH A NEW FAMILY?!
LOOK AROUND ME, KID—I GOT ME ALL THE FAMILY I NEED TO BURN THIS BLOCK TO THE STINKIN' GROUND!
YEAH?
"LOOKS LIKE YER ON YOUR OWN TO ME."
FORGET THIS!
YOU OWE ME SOME NEW GROCERIES, YOU BULLY!
THAT'S RIGHT, PUNKS—RUN AWAY! THIS IS OUR 'HOOD!
WE DID IT!
HA HAHAHA HAHA!
WHAT THE HELL'S SO FUNNY?
ME AND YOU, KID—THAT'S WHAT.
WE BOTH THOUGHT WE WAS RIGHT AND IT TURNS OUT WE WAS BOTH WRONG.
THEM WIMPS HIGHTAILIN' IT OUTTA HERE? THEY AIN'T MY FAMILY. THEY'RE JUST DIME-A-DOZEN STREET PUNKS.
REPLACIN 'EM'S EASY AS FLASHIN' AROUND WADS OF DOUGH AND PROMISIN' MORE WHERE IT CAME FROM.

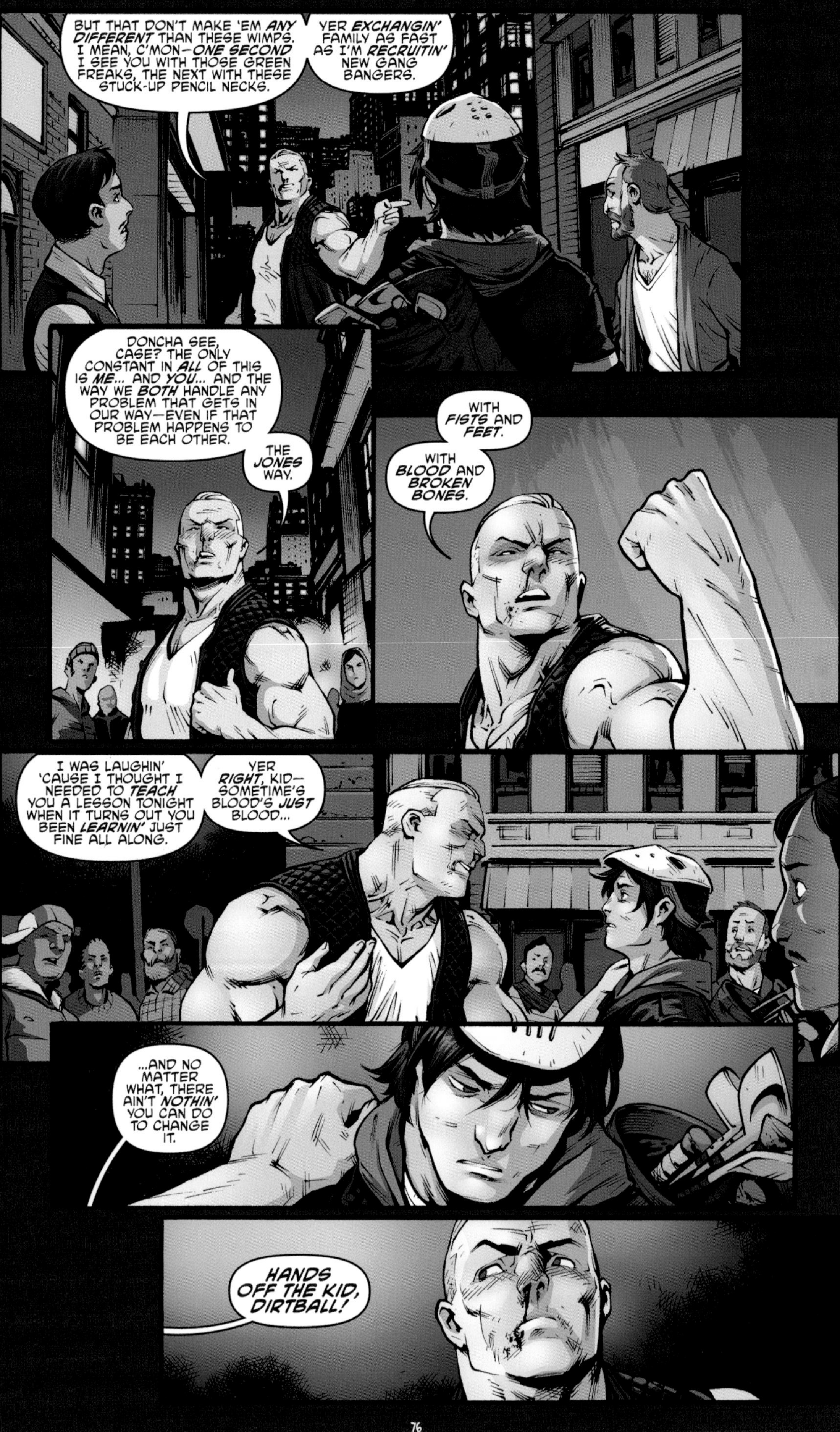
BUT THAT DON'T MAKE 'EM ANY DIFFERENT THAN THESE WIMPS. I MEAN, C'MON—ONE SECOND I SEE YOU WITH THOSE GREEN FREAKS, THE NEXT WITH THESE STUCK-UP PENCIL NECKS.
YER EXCHANGIN' FAMILY AS FAST AS I'M RECRUITIN' NEW GANG BANGERS.
DONCHA SEE, CASE? THE ONLY CONSTANT IN ALL OF THIS IS ME... AND YOU... AND THE WAY WE BOTH HANDLE ANY PROBLEM THAT GETS IN OUR WAY—EVEN IF THAT PROBLEM HAPPENS TO BE EACH OTHER.
THE JONES WAY.
WITH FISTS AND FEET.
WITH BLOOD AND BROKEN BONES.
I WAS LAUGHIN' 'CAUSE I THOUGHT I NEEDED TO TEACH YOU A LESSON TONIGHT WHEN IT TURNS OUT YOU BEEN LEARNIN' JUST FINE ALL ALONG.
YER RIGHT, KID—SOMETIME'S BLOOD'S JUST BLOOD...
...AND NO MATTER WHAT, THERE AIN'T NOTHIN' YOU CAN DO TO CHANGE IT.
HANDS OFF THE KID, DIRTBALL!

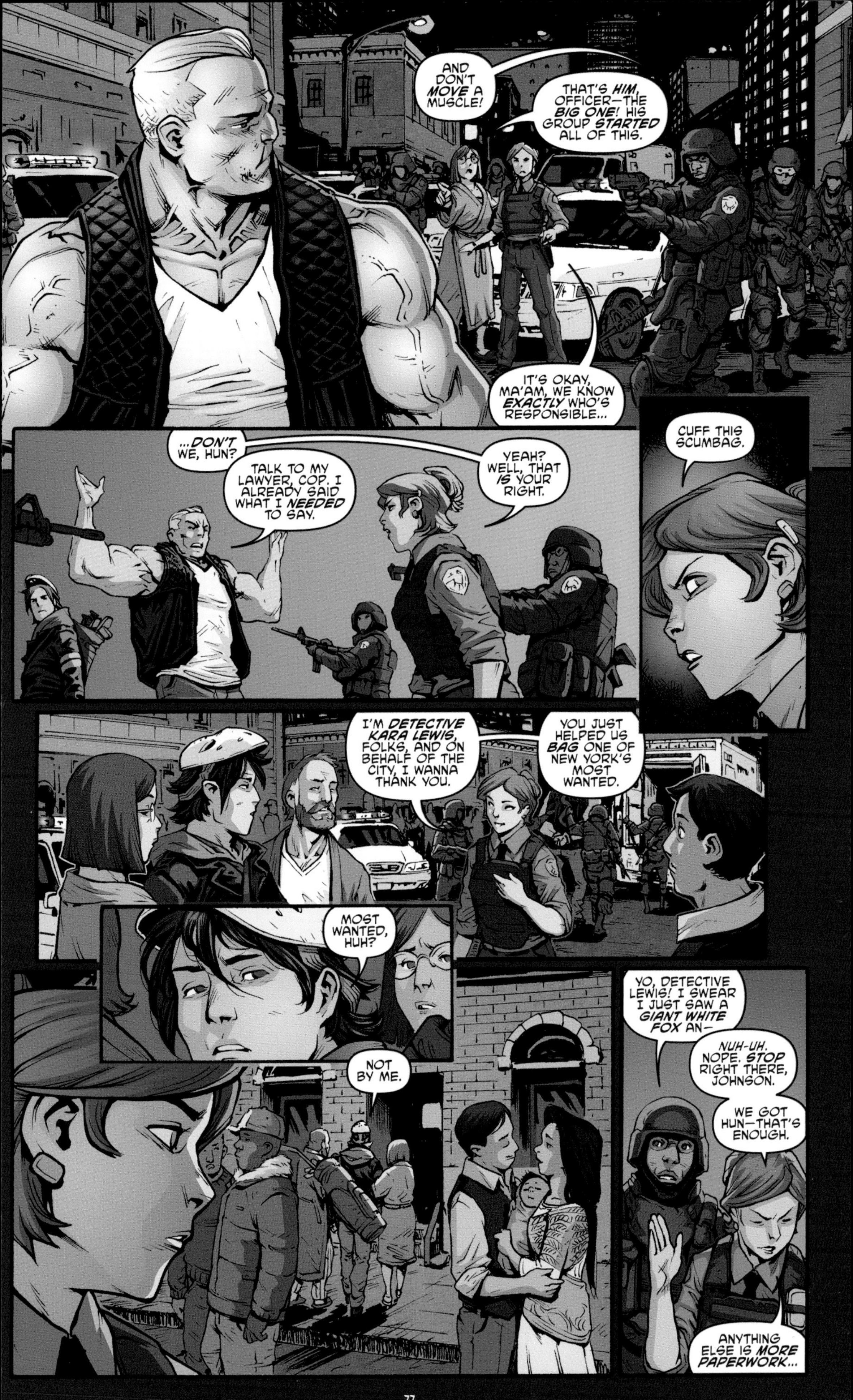
AND DON'T MOVE A MUSCLE!
THAT'S HIM, OFFICER—THE BIG ONE! HIS GROUP STARTED ALL OF THIS.
IT'S OKAY, MA'AM, WE KNOW EXACTLY WHO'S RESPONSIBLE...
...DON'T WE, HUN?
TALK TO MY LAWYER, COP. I ALREADY SAID WHAT I NEEDED TO SAY.
YEAH? WELL, THAT IS YOUR RIGHT.
CUFF THIS SCUMBAG.
I'M DETECTIVE KARA LEWIS, FOLKS, AND ON BEHALF OF THE CITY, I WANNA THANK YOU.
YOU JUST HELPED US BAG ONE OF NEW YORK'S MOST WANTED.
MOST WANTED, HUH?
NOT BY ME.
YO, DETECTIVE LEWIS! I SWEAR I JUST SAW A GIANT WHITE FOX AN—
NUH-UH. NOPE. STOP RIGHT THERE, JOHNSON.
WE GOT HUN—THAT'S ENOUGH.
ANYTHING ELSE IS MORE PAPERWORK...

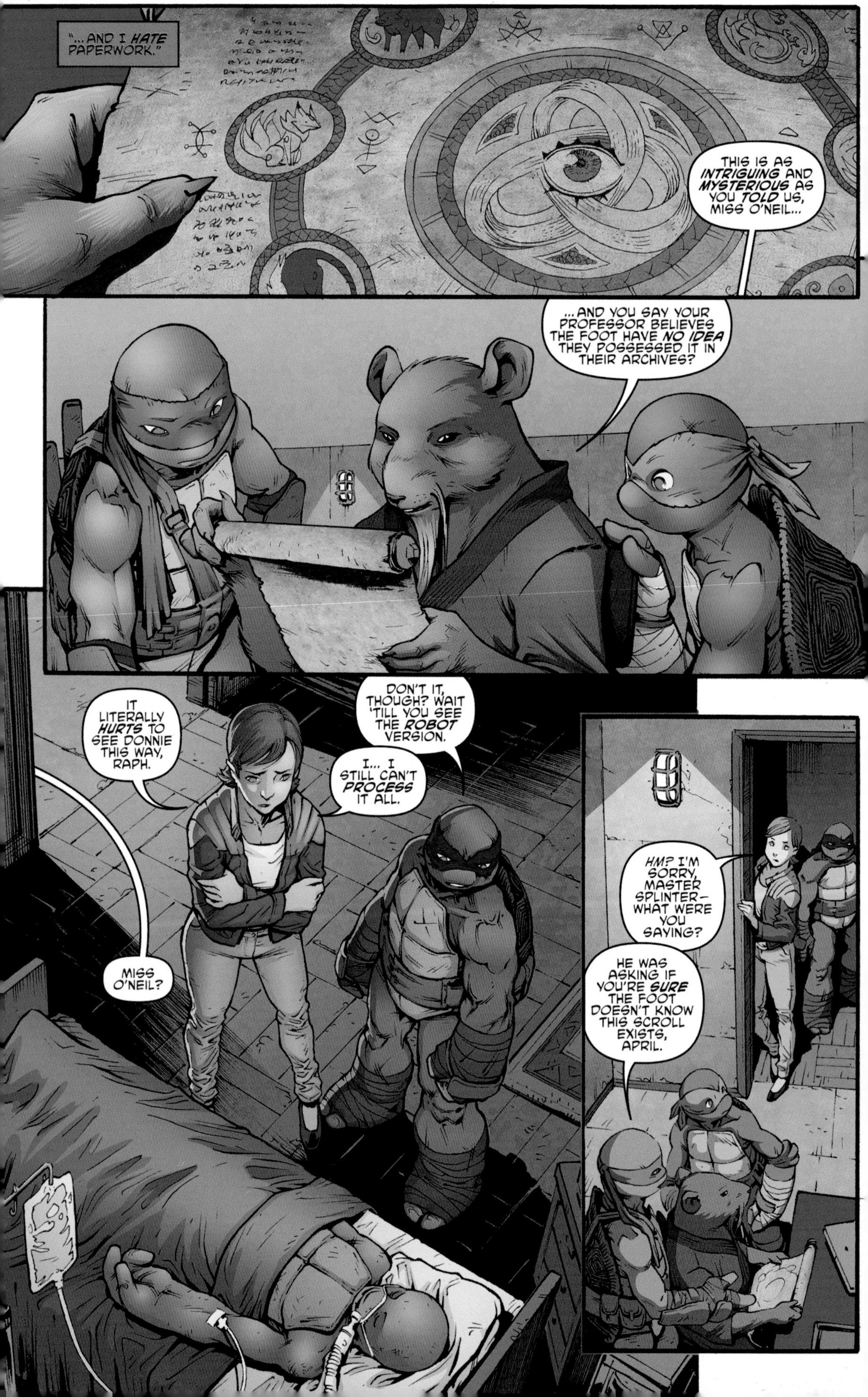
"...AND I *HATE* PAPERWORK."
THIS IS AS *INTRIGUING* AND *MYSTERIOUS* AS YOU *TOLD* US, MISS O'NEIL...
...AND YOU SAY YOUR PROFESSOR BELIEVES THE FOOT HAVE *NO IDEA* THEY POSSESSED IT IN THEIR ARCHIVES?
IT LITERALLY *HURTS* TO SEE DONNIE THIS WAY, RAPH.
I... I STILL CAN'T *PROCESS* IT ALL.
DON'T IT, THOUGH? WAIT 'TILL YOU SEE THE *ROBOT* VERSION.
MISS O'NEIL?
HM? I'M SORRY, MASTER SPLINTER— WHAT WERE YOU SAYING?
HE WAS ASKING IF YOU'RE *SURE* THE FOOT DOESN'T KNOW THIS SCROLL EXISTS, APRIL.

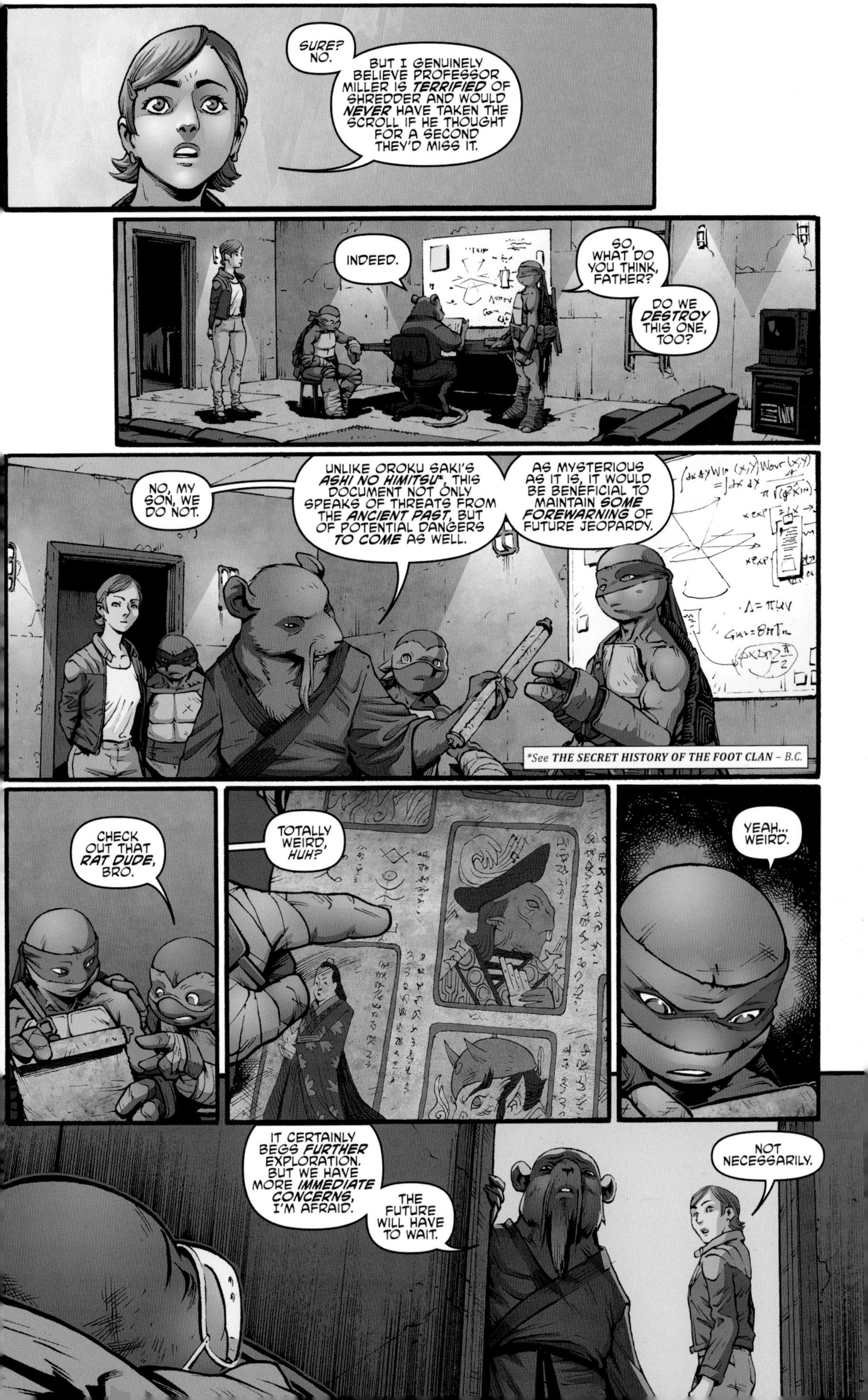
SURE? NO.
BUT I GENUINELY BELIEVE PROFESSOR MILLER IS TERRIFIED OF SHREDDER AND WOULD NEVER HAVE TAKEN THE SCROLL IF HE THOUGHT FOR A SECOND THEY'D MISS IT.
INDEED.
SO, WHAT DO YOU THINK, FATHER?
DO WE DESTROY THIS ONE, TOO?
NO, MY SON, WE DO NOT.
UNLIKE OROKU SAKI'S ASHI NO HIMITSU*, THIS DOCUMENT NOT ONLY SPEAKS OF THREATS FROM THE ANCIENT PAST, BUT OF POTENTIAL DANGERS TO COME AS WELL.
AS MYSTERIOUS AS IT IS, IT WOULD BE BENEFICIAL TO MAINTAIN SOME FOREWARNING OF FUTURE JEOPARDY.
*See THE SECRET HISTORY OF THE FOOT CLAN – B.C.
CHECK OUT THAT RAT DUDE, BRO.
TOTALLY WEIRD, HUH?
YEAH... WEIRD.
IT CERTAINLY BEGS FURTHER EXPLORATION. BUT WE HAVE MORE IMMEDIATE CONCERNS, I'M AFRAID.
THE FUTURE WILL HAVE TO WAIT.
NOT NECESSARILY.

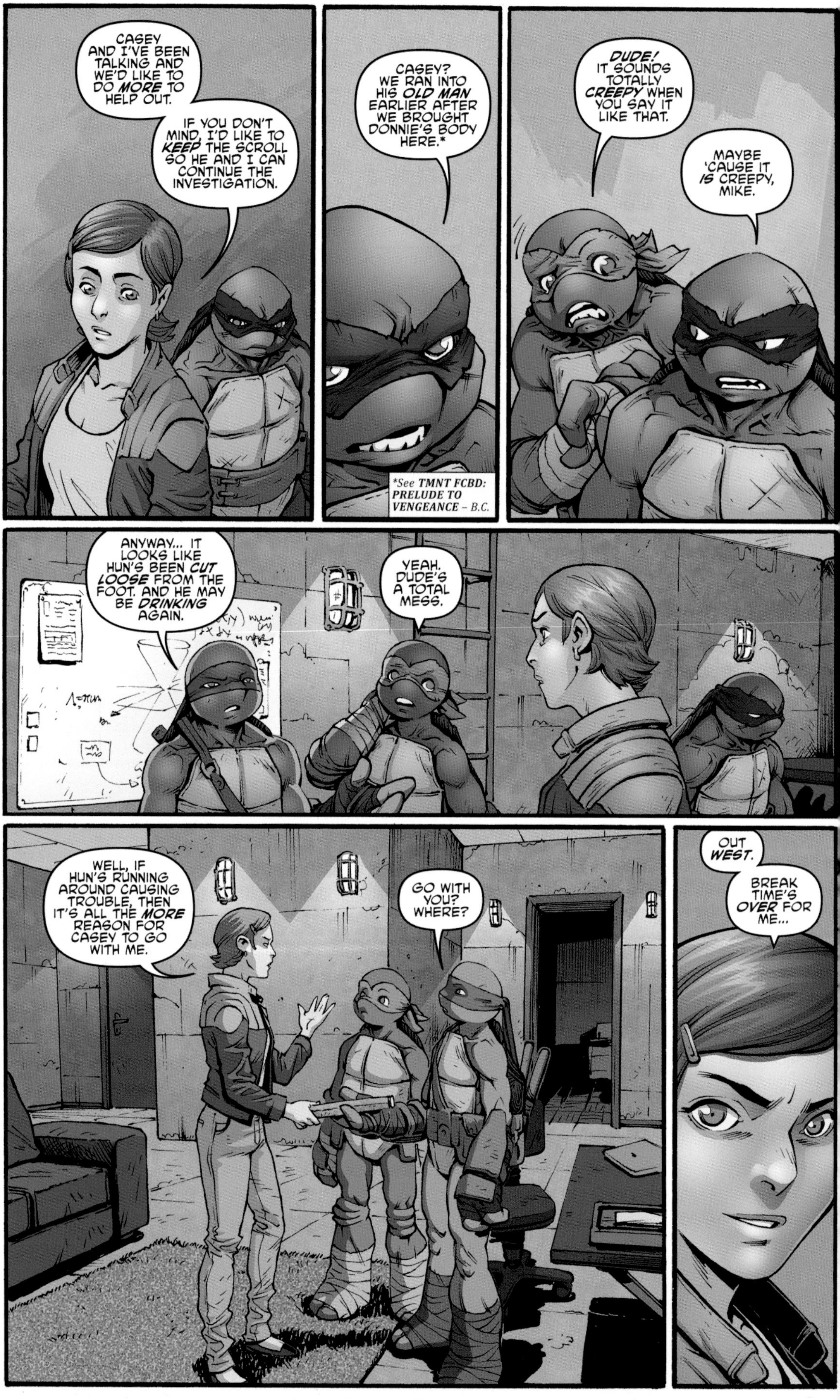

CASEY AND I'VE BEEN TALKING AND WE'D LIKE TO DO *MORE* TO HELP OUT.
IF YOU DON'T MIND, I'D LIKE TO *KEEP* THE SCROLL SO HE AND I CAN CONTINUE THE INVESTIGATION.
CASEY? WE RAN INTO HIS *OLD MAN* EARLIER AFTER WE BROUGHT DONNIE'S BODY HERE.*
*See TMNT FCBD: PRELUDE TO VENGEANCE – B.C.
DUDE! IT SOUNDS TOTALLY *CREEPY* WHEN YOU SAY IT LIKE THAT.
MAYBE 'CAUSE IT *IS* CREEPY, MIKE.
ANYWAY... IT LOOKS LIKE HUN'S BEEN *CUT LOOSE* FROM THE FOOT. AND HE MAY BE *DRINKING* AGAIN.
YEAH. DUDE'S A TOTAL MESS.
WELL, IF HUN'S RUNNING AROUND CAUSING TROUBLE, THEN IT'S ALL THE *MORE* REASON FOR CASEY TO GO WITH ME.
GO WITH YOU? WHERE?
OUT *WEST*.
BREAK TIME'S *OVER* FOR ME...

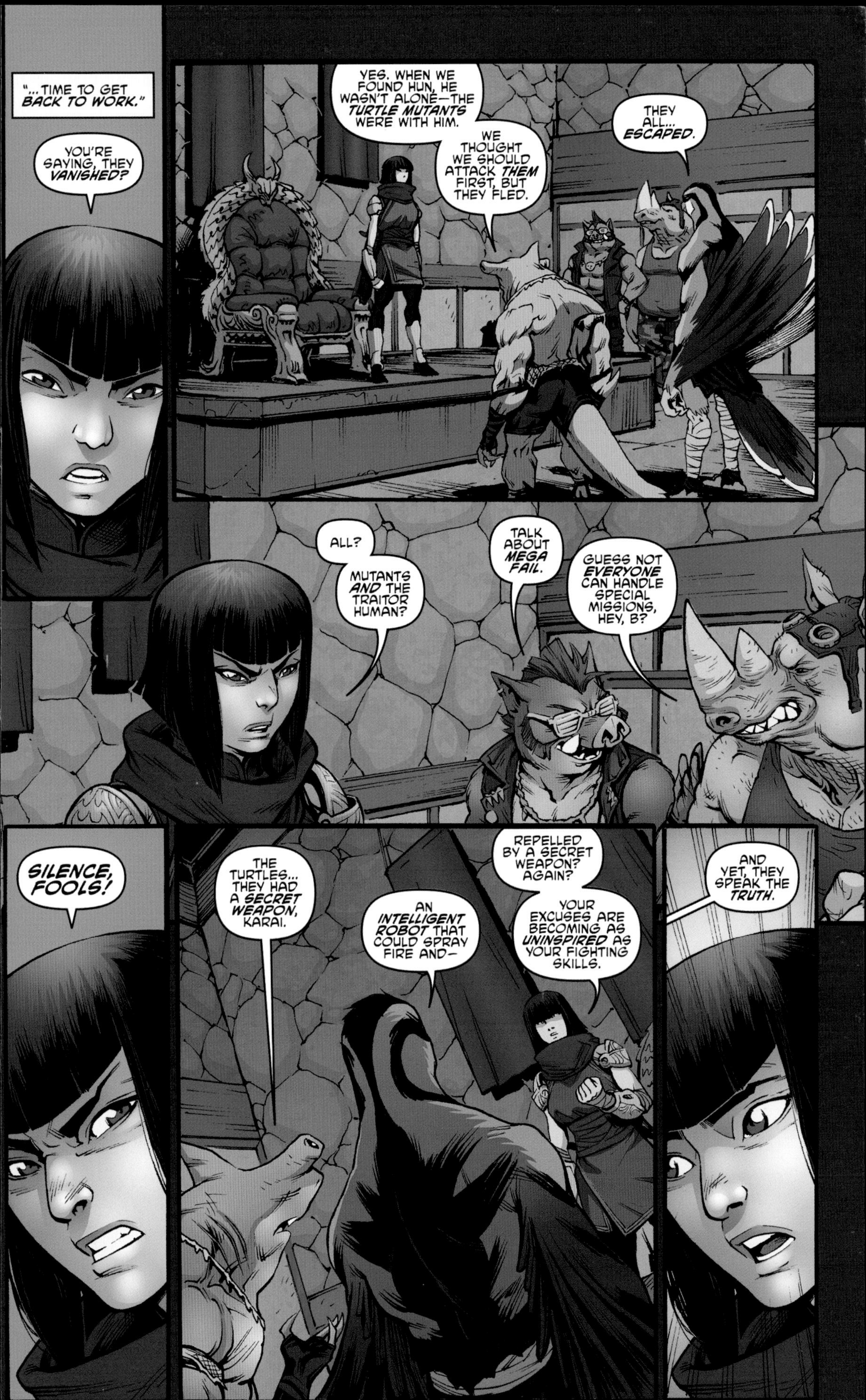

"...TIME TO GET BACK TO WORK."
YOU'RE SAYING, THEY VANISHED?
YES. WHEN WE FOUND HUN, HE WASN'T ALONE—THE TURTLE MUTANTS WERE WITH HIM.
WE THOUGHT WE SHOULD ATTACK THEM FIRST, BUT THEY FLED.
THEY ALL... ESCAPED.
ALL?
MUTANTS AND THE TRAITOR HUMAN?
TALK ABOUT MEGA FAIL.
GUESS NOT EVERYONE CAN HANDLE SPECIAL MISSIONS, HEY, B?
SILENCE, FOOLS!
THE TURTLES... THEY HAD A SECRET WEAPON, KARAI.
AN INTELLIGENT ROBOT THAT COULD SPRAY FIRE AND—
REPELLED BY A SECRET WEAPON? AGAIN?
YOUR EXCUSES ARE BECOMING AS UNINSPIRED AS YOUR FIGHTING SKILLS.
AND YET, THEY SPEAK THE TRUTH.

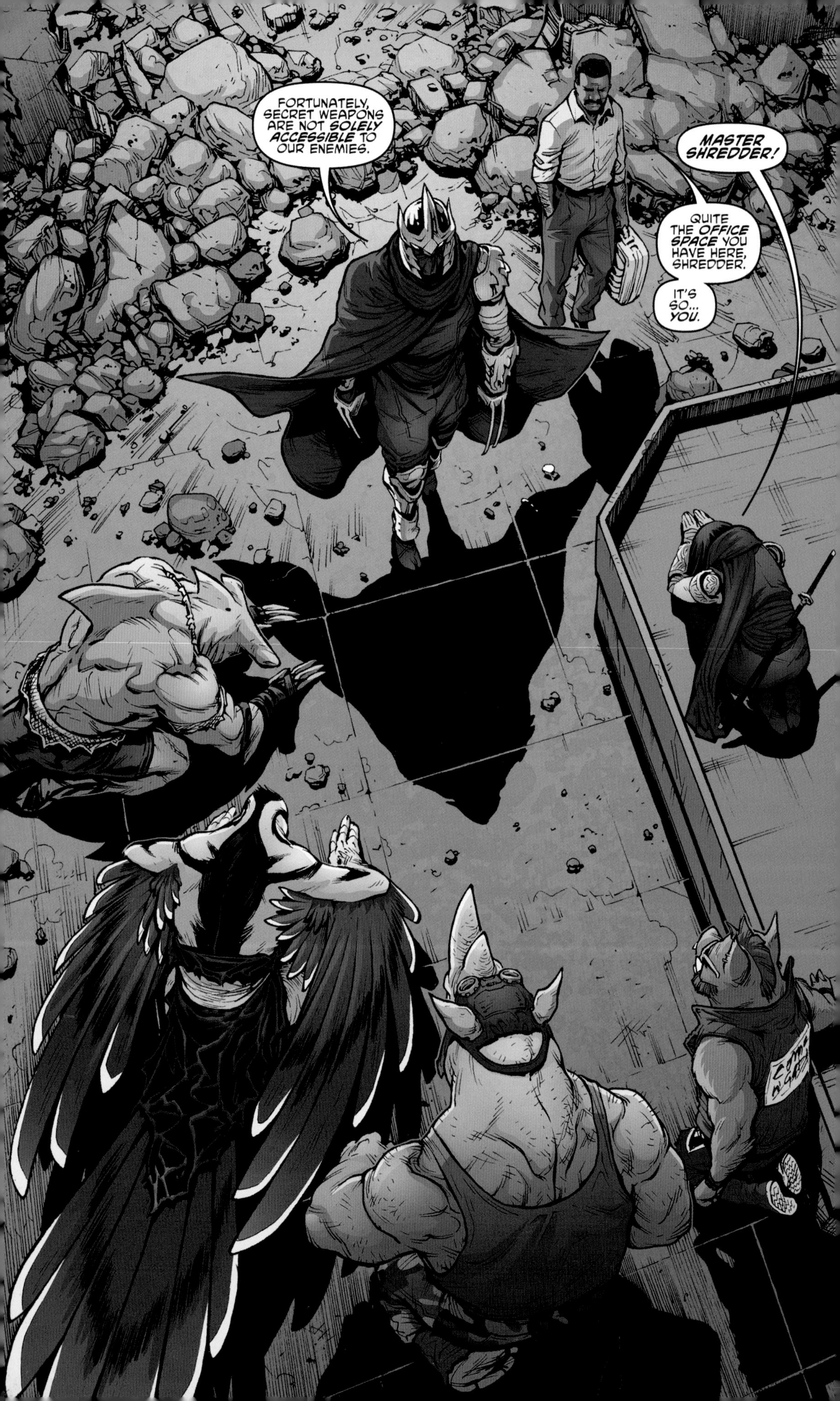
FORTUNATELY, SECRET WEAPONS ARE NOT SOLELY ACCESSIBLE TO OUR ENEMIES.
MASTER SHREDDER!
QUITE THE OFFICE SPACE YOU HAVE HERE, SHREDDER.
IT'S SO... YOU.

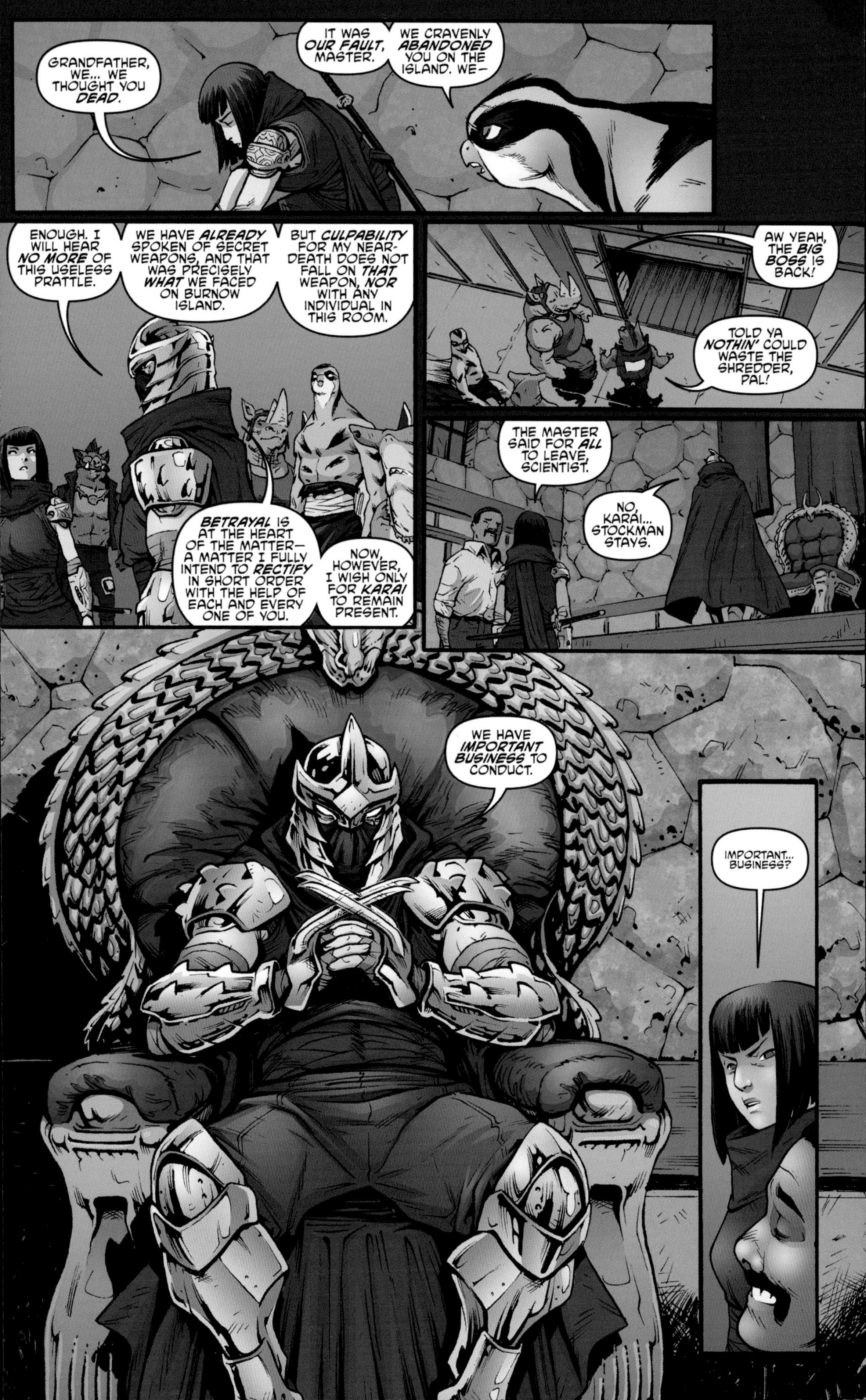

GRANDFATHER, WE... WE THOUGHT YOU DEAD.
IT WAS OUR FAULT, MASTER.
WE CRAVENLY ABANDONED YOU ON THE ISLAND. WE—
ENOUGH. I WILL HEAR NO MORE OF THIS USELESS PRATTLE.
WE HAVE ALREADY SPOKEN OF SECRET WEAPONS, AND THAT WAS PRECISELY WHAT WE FACED ON BURNOW ISLAND.
BUT CULPABILITY FOR MY NEAR-DEATH DOES NOT FALL ON THAT WEAPON, NOR WITH ANY INDIVIDUAL IN THIS ROOM.
BETRAYAL IS AT THE HEART OF THE MATTER— A MATTER I FULLY INTEND TO RECTIFY IN SHORT ORDER WITH THE HELP OF EACH AND EVERY ONE OF YOU.
NOW, HOWEVER, I WISH ONLY FOR KARAI TO REMAIN PRESENT.
AW YEAH, THE BIG BOSS IS BACK!
TOLD YA NOTHIN' COULD WASTE THE SHREDDER, PAL!
THE MASTER SAID FOR ALL TO LEAVE, SCIENTIST.
NO, KARAI... STOCKMAN STAYS.
WE HAVE IMPORTANT BUSINESS TO CONDUCT.
IMPORTANT... BUSINESS?

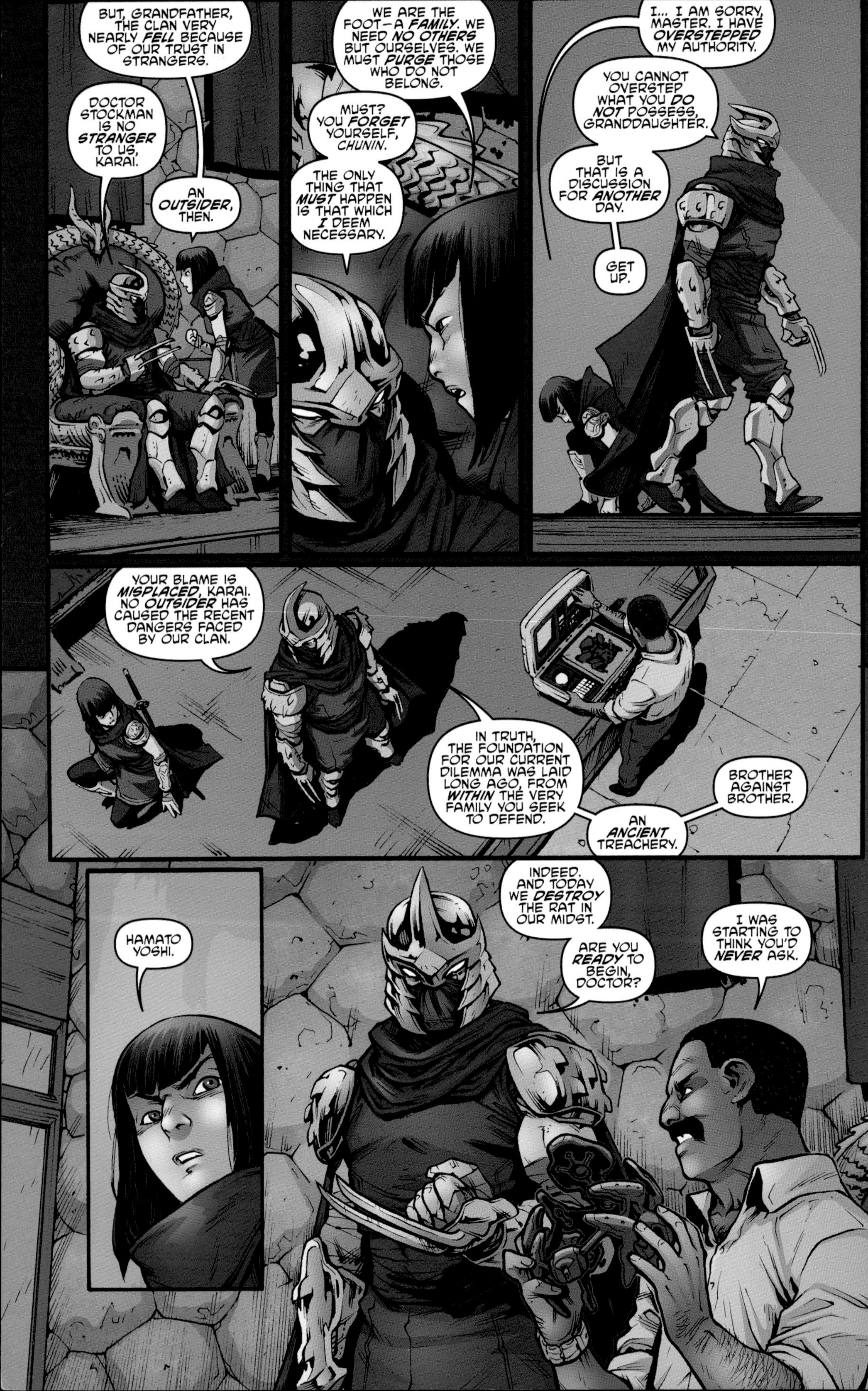

BUT, GRANDFATHER, THE CLAN VERY NEARLY FELL BECAUSE OF OUR TRUST IN STRANGERS.
DOCTOR STOCKMAN IS NO STRANGER TO US, KARAI.
AN OUTSIDER, THEN.
WE ARE THE FOOT—A FAMILY. WE NEED NO OTHERS BUT OURSELVES. WE MUST PURGE THOSE WHO DO NOT BELONG.
MUST? YOU FORGET YOURSELF, CHUNIN.
THE ONLY THING THAT MUST HAPPEN IS THAT WHICH I DEEM NECESSARY.
I... I AM SORRY, MASTER. I HAVE OVERSTEPPED MY AUTHORITY.
YOU CANNOT OVERSTEP WHAT YOU DO NOT POSSESS, GRANDDAUGHTER.
BUT THAT IS A DISCUSSION FOR ANOTHER DAY.
GET UP.
YOUR BLAME IS MISPLACED, KARAI. NO OUTSIDER HAS CAUSED THE RECENT DANGERS FACED BY OUR CLAN.
IN TRUTH, THE FOUNDATION FOR OUR CURRENT DILEMMA WAS LAID LONG AGO, FROM WITHIN THE VERY FAMILY YOU SEEK TO DEFEND.
AN ANCIENT TREACHERY.
BROTHER AGAINST BROTHER.
HAMATO YOSHI.
INDEED. AND TODAY WE DESTROY THE RAT IN OUR MIDST.
ARE YOU READY TO BEGIN, DOCTOR?
I WAS STARTING TO THINK YOU'D NEVER ASK.

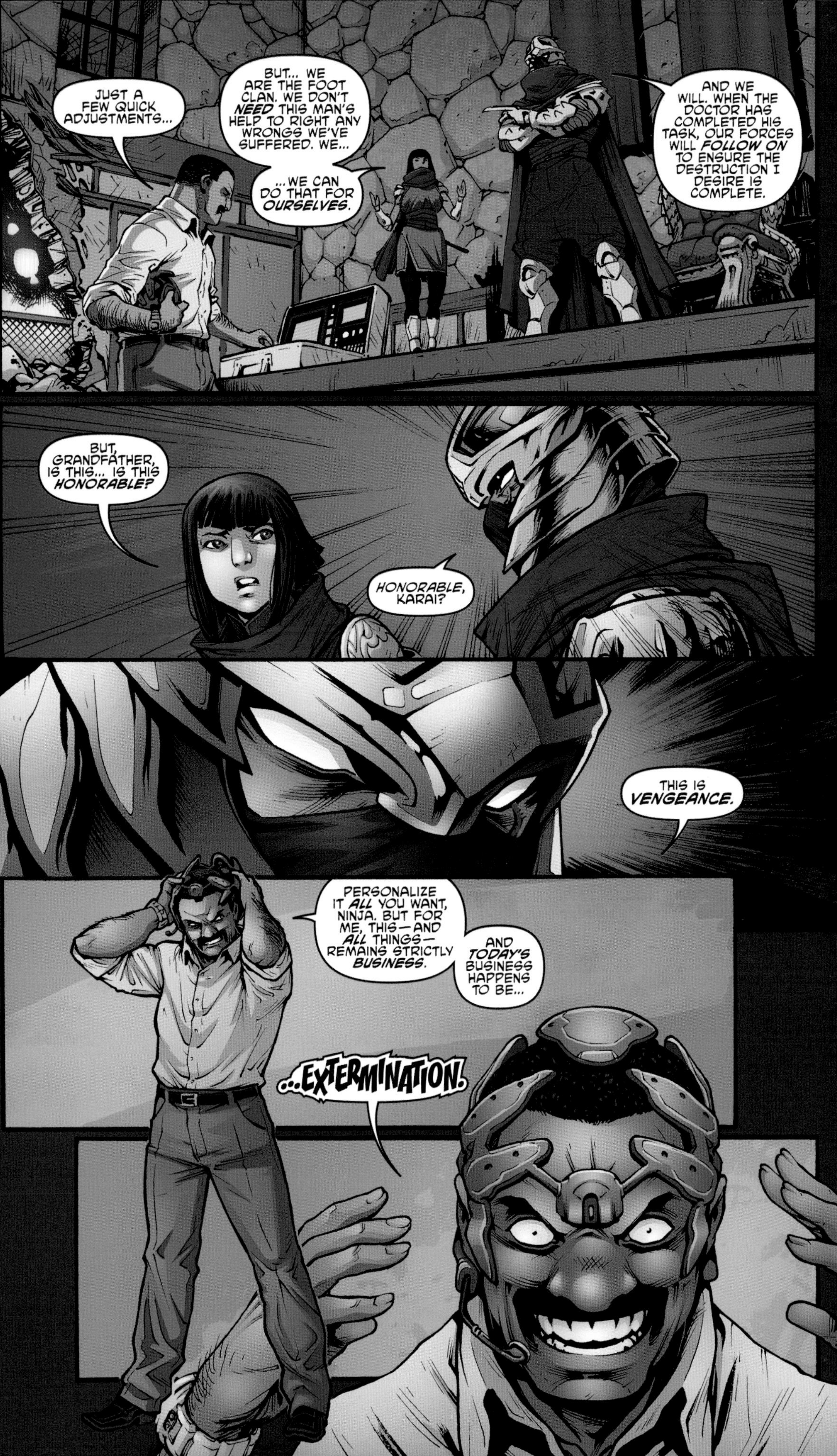
JUST A FEW QUICK ADJUSTMENTS...
BUT... WE ARE THE FOOT CLAN. WE DON'T NEED THIS MAN'S HELP TO RIGHT ANY WRONGS WE'VE SUFFERED. WE...
...WE CAN DO THAT FOR OURSELVES.
AND WE WILL. WHEN THE DOCTOR HAS COMPLETED HIS TASK, OUR FORCES WILL FOLLOW ON TO ENSURE THE DESTRUCTION I DESIRE IS COMPLETE.
BUT, GRANDFATHER, IS THIS... IS THIS HONORABLE?
HONORABLE, KARAI?
THIS IS VENGEANCE.
PERSONALIZE IT ALL YOU WANT, NINJA. BUT FOR ME, THIS—AND ALL THINGS—REMAINS STRICTLY BUSINESS.
AND TODAY'S BUSINESS HAPPENS TO BE...
...EXTERMINATION.

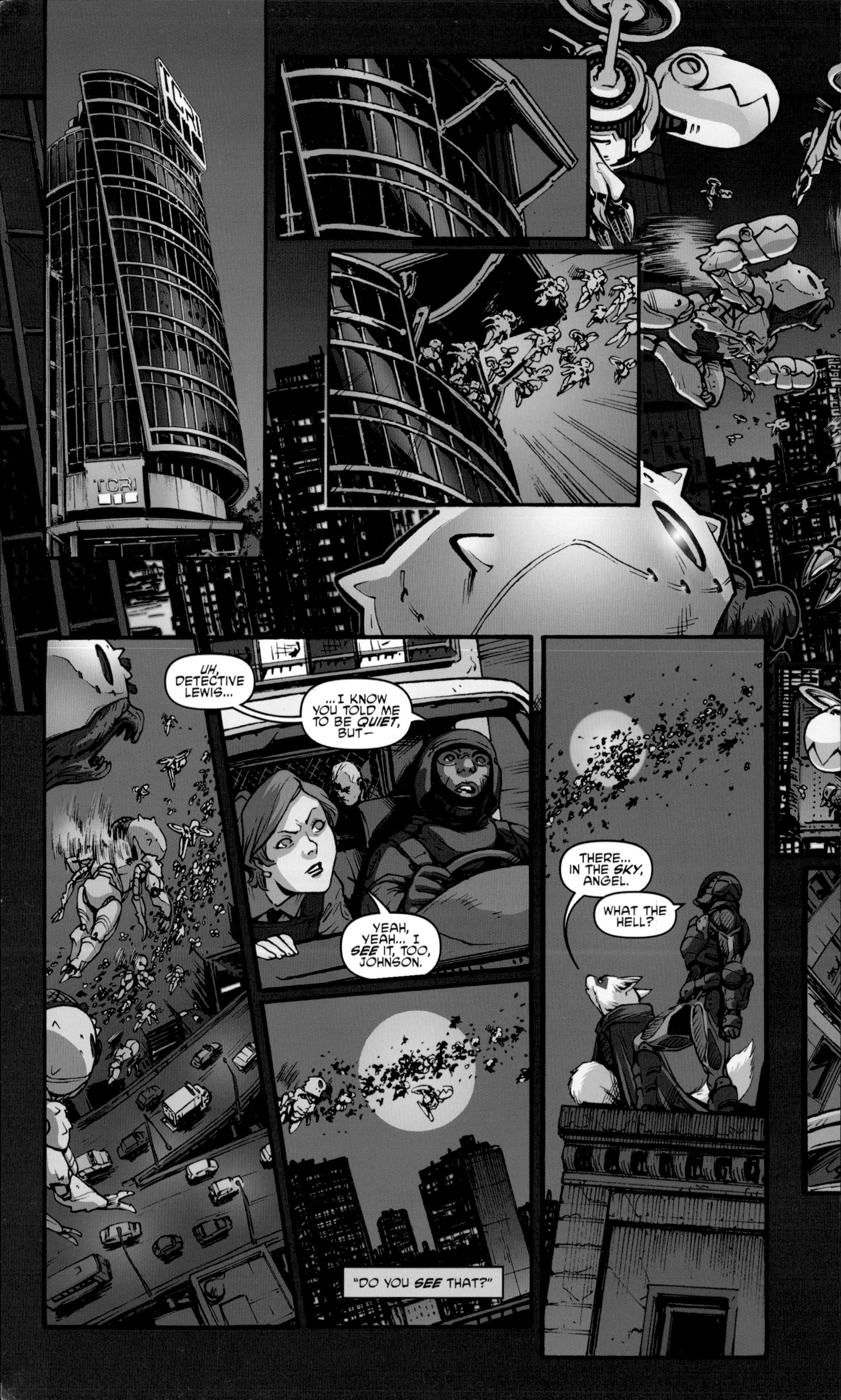
TCRI
UH, DETECTIVE LEWIS...
...I KNOW YOU TOLD ME TO BE QUIET, BUT—
YEAH, YEAH... I SEE IT, TOO, JOHNSON.
"DO YOU SEE THAT?"
THERE... IN THE SKY, ANGEL.
WHAT THE HELL?

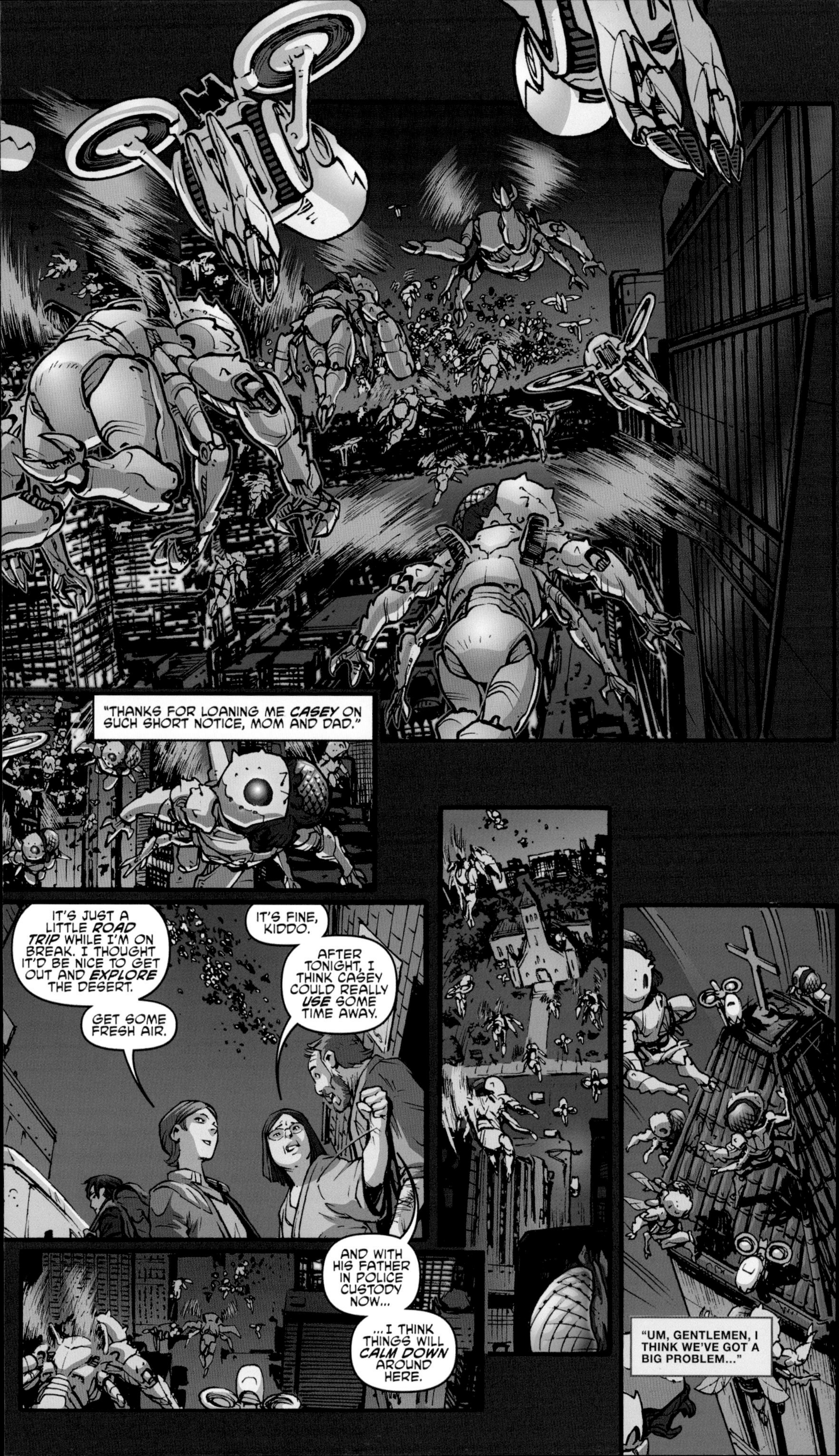
"THANKS FOR LOANING ME CASEY ON SUCH SHORT NOTICE, MOM AND DAD."
IT'S JUST A LITTLE ROAD TRIP WHILE I'M ON BREAK. I THOUGHT IT'D BE NICE TO GET OUT AND EXPLORE THE DESERT.
GET SOME FRESH AIR.
IT'S FINE, KIDDO.
AFTER TONIGHT, I THINK CASEY COULD REALLY USE SOME TIME AWAY.
AND WITH HIS FATHER IN POLICE CUSTODY NOW...
...I THINK THINGS WILL CALM DOWN AROUND HERE.
"UM, GENTLEMEN, I THINK WE'VE GOT A BIG PROBLEM..."

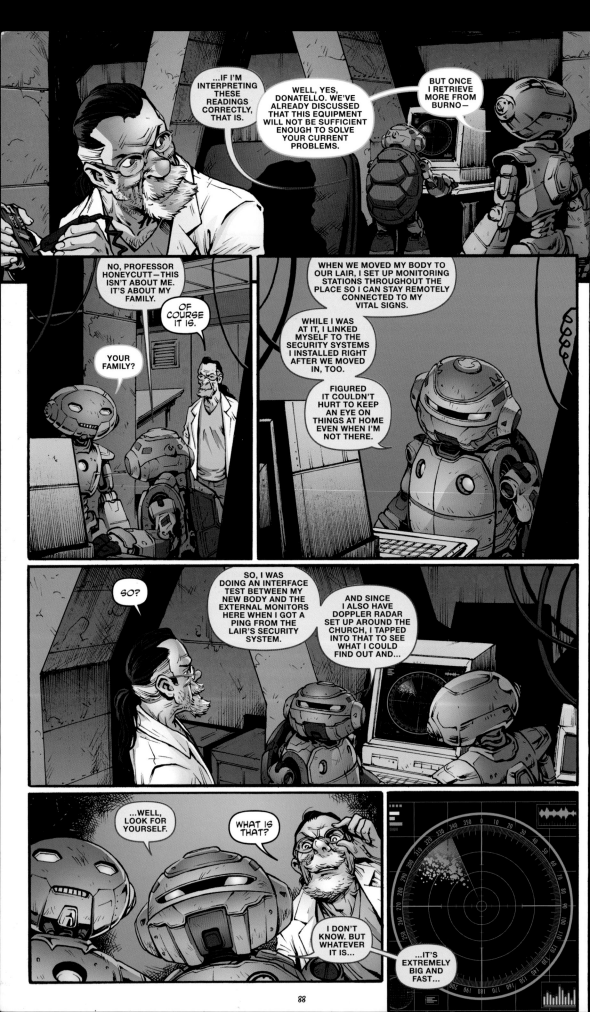

...IF I'M INTERPRETING THESE READINGS CORRECTLY, THAT IS.

WELL, YES, DONATELLO. WE'VE ALREADY DISCUSSED THAT THIS EQUIPMENT WILL NOT BE SUFFICIENT ENOUGH TO SOLVE YOUR CURRENT PROBLEMS.

BUT ONCE I RETRIEVE MORE FROM BURNO—

NO, PROFESSOR HONEYCUTT—THIS ISN'T ABOUT ME. IT'S ABOUT MY FAMILY.

OF COURSE IT IS.

YOUR FAMILY?

WHEN WE MOVED MY BODY TO OUR LAIR, I SET UP MONITORING STATIONS THROUGHOUT THE PLACE SO I CAN STAY REMOTELY CONNECTED TO MY VITAL SIGNS.

WHILE I WAS AT IT, I LINKED MYSELF TO THE SECURITY SYSTEMS I INSTALLED RIGHT AFTER WE MOVED IN, TOO.

FIGURED IT COULDN'T HURT TO KEEP AN EYE ON THINGS AT HOME EVEN WHEN I'M NOT THERE.

SO, I WAS DOING AN INTERFACE TEST BETWEEN MY NEW BODY AND THE EXTERNAL MONITORS HERE WHEN I GOT A PING FROM THE LAIR'S SECURITY SYSTEM.

SO?

AND SINCE I ALSO HAVE DOPPLER RADAR SET UP AROUND THE CHURCH, I TAPPED INTO THAT TO SEE WHAT I COULD FIND OUT AND...

...WELL, LOOK FOR YOURSELF.

WHAT IS THAT?

I DON'T KNOW. BUT WHATEVER IT IS...

...IT'S EXTREMELY BIG AND FAST...

88

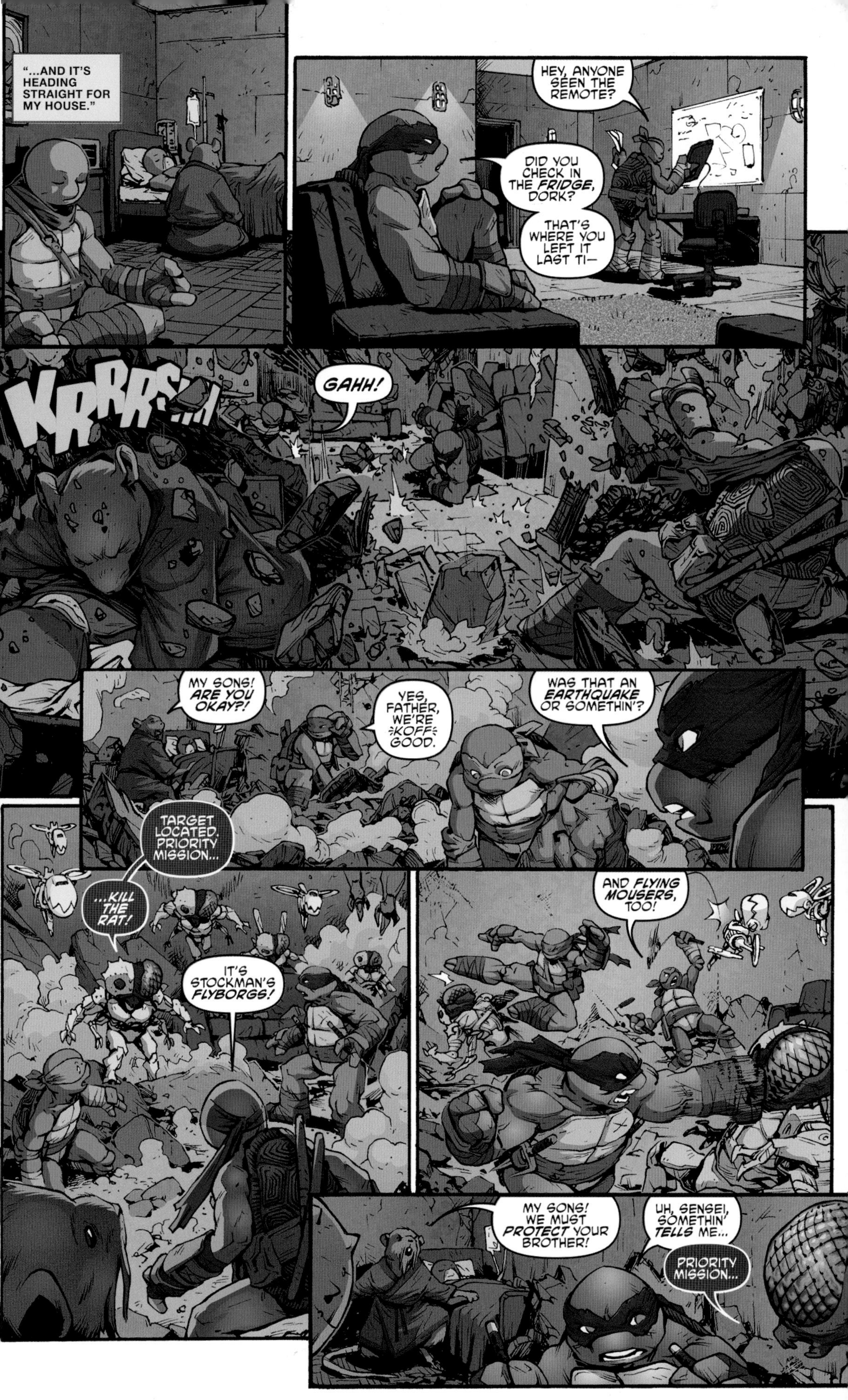
"...AND IT'S HEADING STRAIGHT FOR MY HOUSE."
HEY, ANYONE SEEN THE REMOTE?
DID YOU CHECK IN THE FRIDGE, DORK?
THAT'S WHERE YOU LEFT IT LAST TI—
KRRRSH!!
GAHH!
MY SONS! ARE YOU OKAY?!
YES, FATHER, WE'RE KOFF GOOD.
WAS THAT AN EARTHQUAKE OR SOMETHIN'?
TARGET LOCATED. PRIORITY MISSION...
...KILL THE RAT!
IT'S STOCKMAN'S FLYBORGS!
AND FLYING MOUSERS, TOO!
MY SONS! WE MUST PROTECT YOUR BROTHER!
UH, SENSEI, SOMETHIN' TELLS ME...
PRIORITY MISSION...

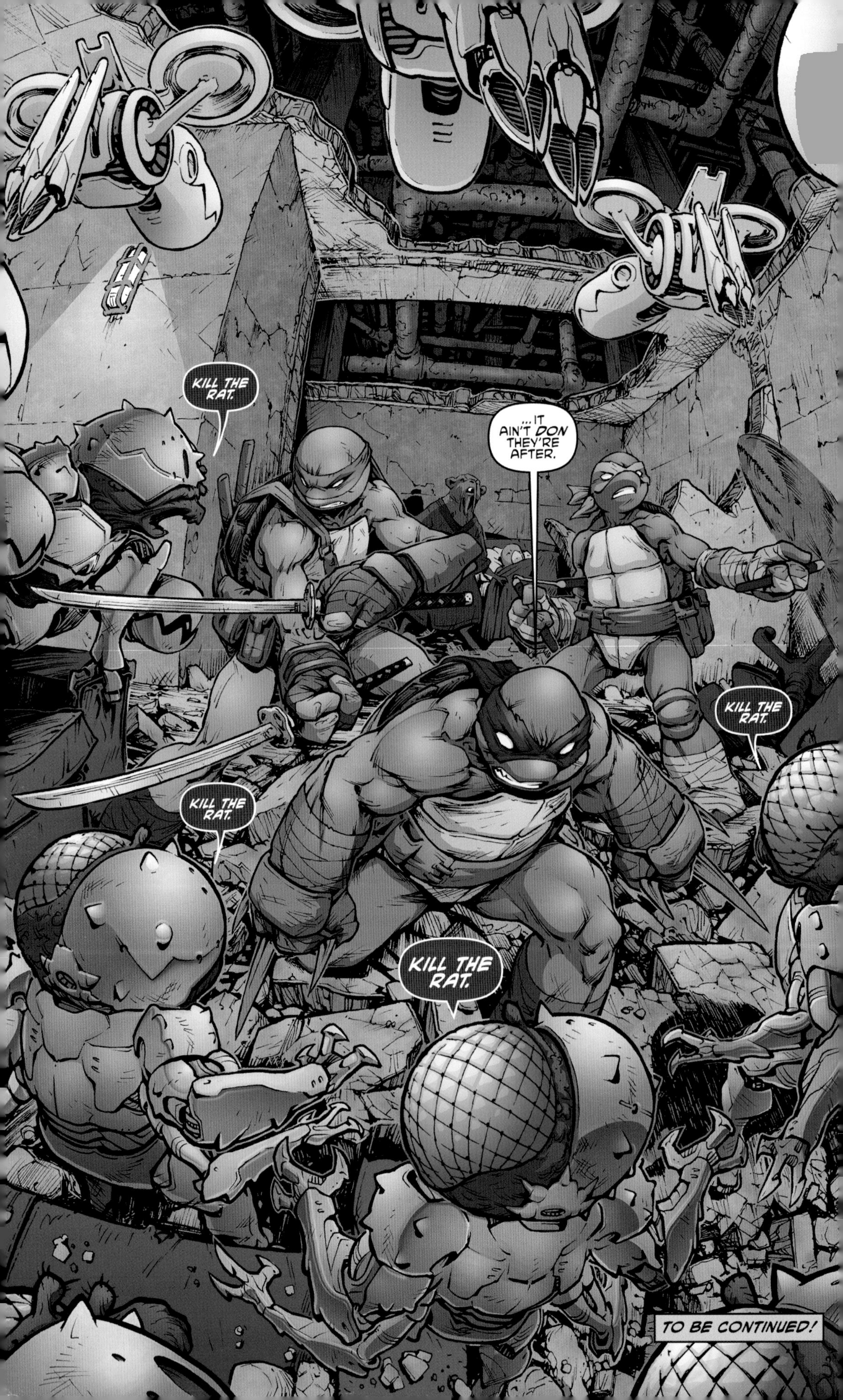

KILL THE RAT.
...IT AIN'T DON THEY'RE AFTER.
KILL THE RAT.
KILL THE RAT.
KILL THE RAT.
TO BE CONTINUED!

ART GALLERY

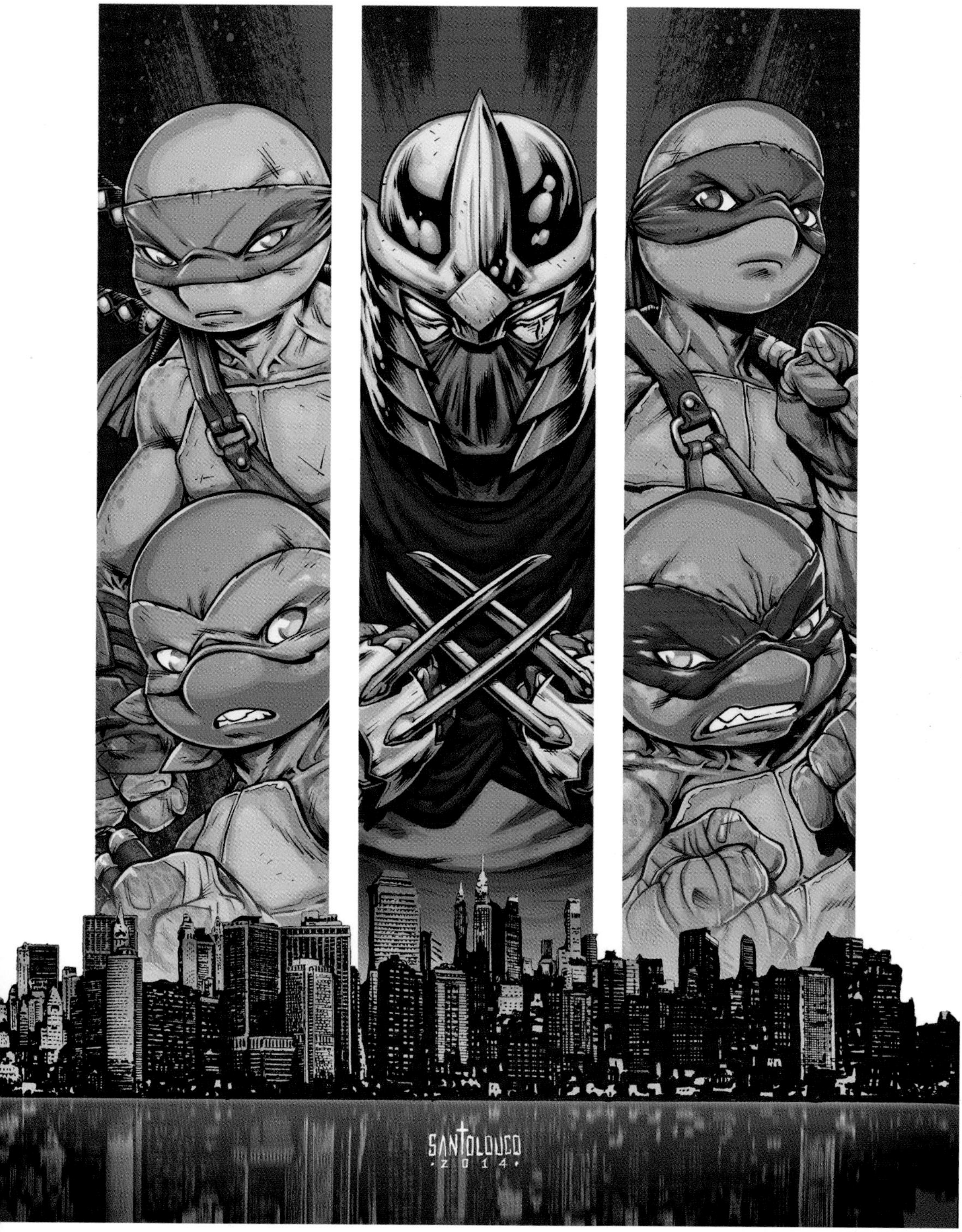
SANTOLOUCO
2014

ART BY MATEUS SANTOLOUCO

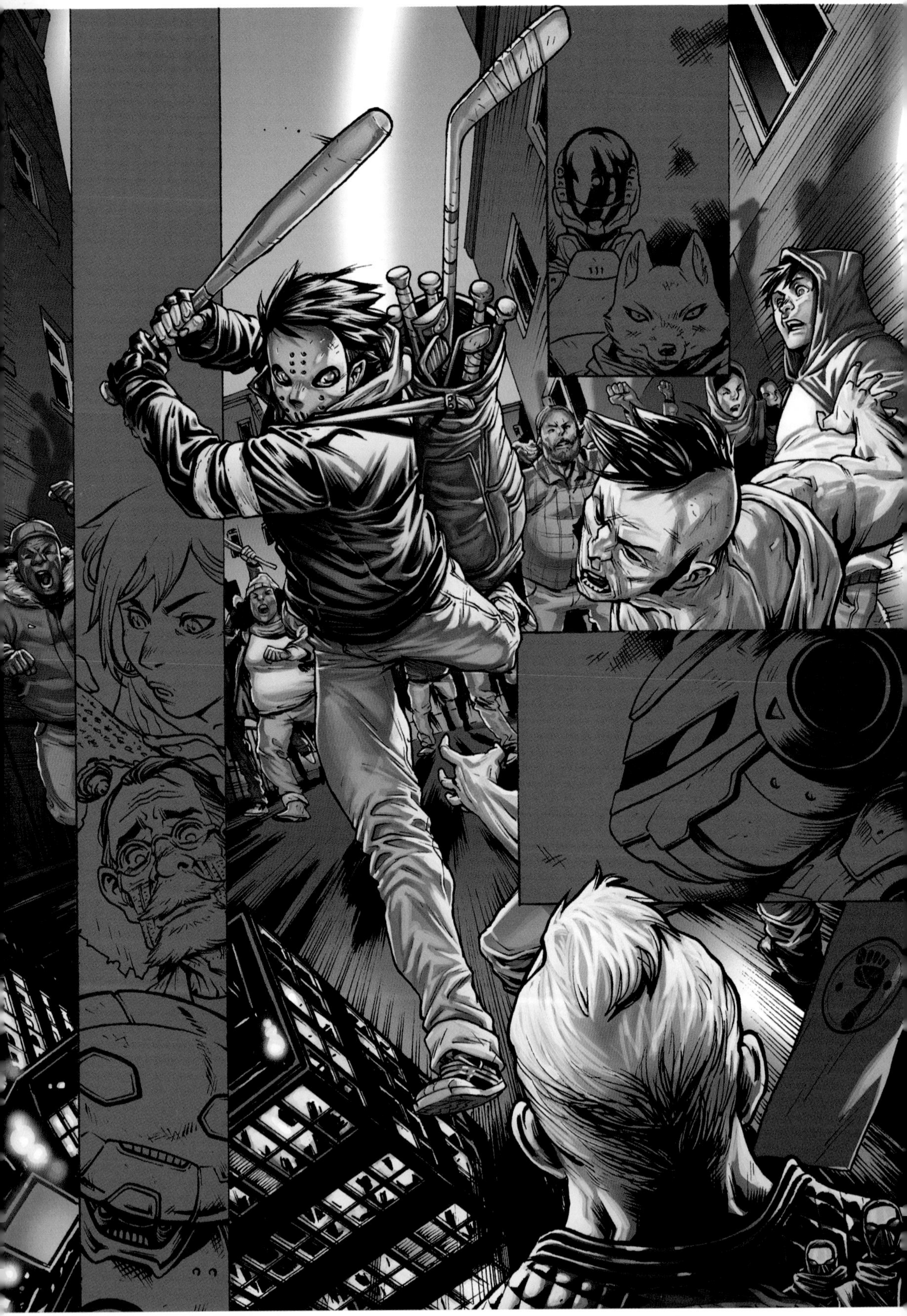

THIS PAGE AND OPPOSITE PAGE: ART BY **MATEUS SANTOLOUCO**

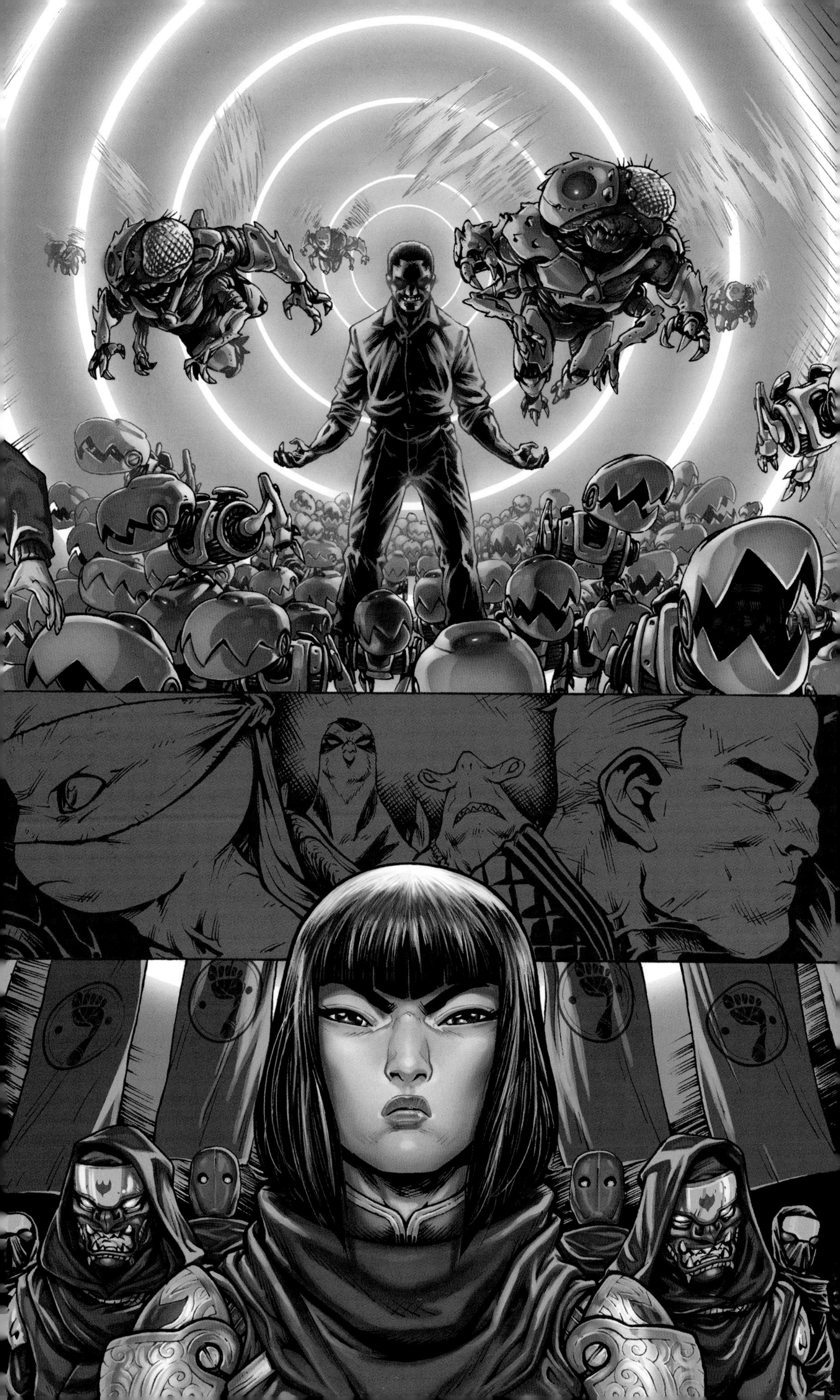

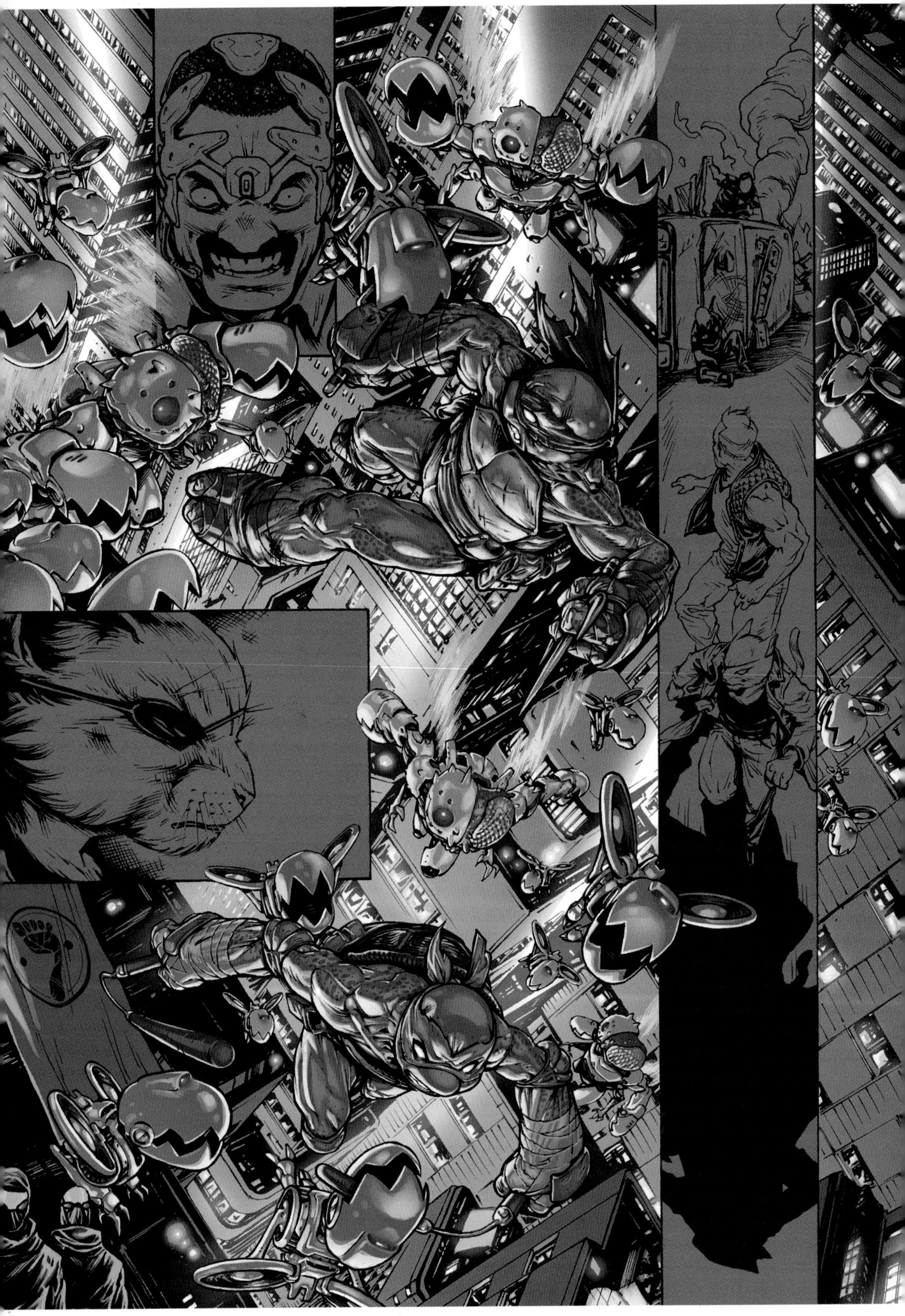

ART BY MATEUS SANTOLOUCO

OPPOSITE PAGE: ART BY KEVIN EASTMAN · COLORS BY RONDA PATTISON

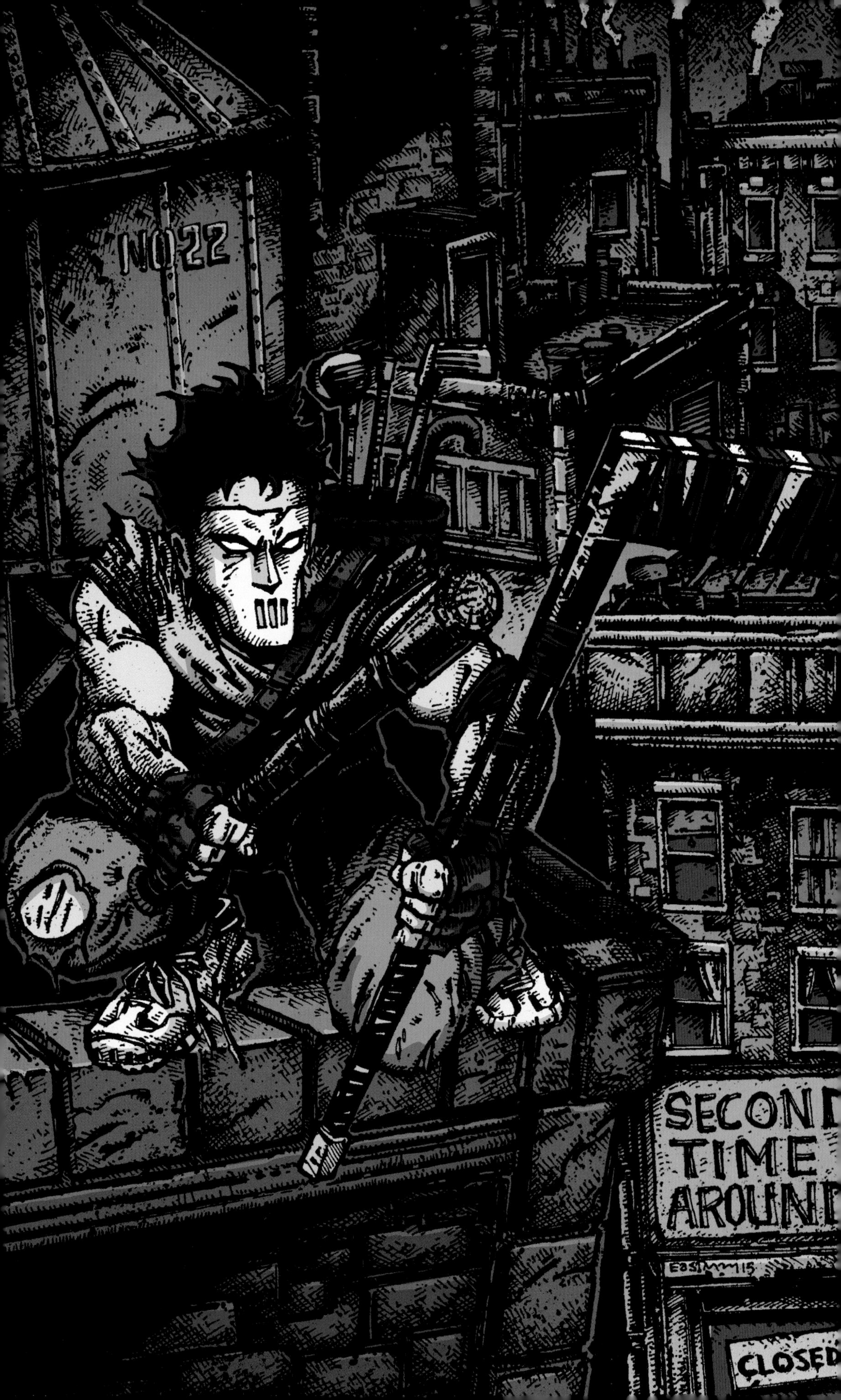

NO22
SECOND
TIME
AROUND
EASTMAN '15
CLOSED

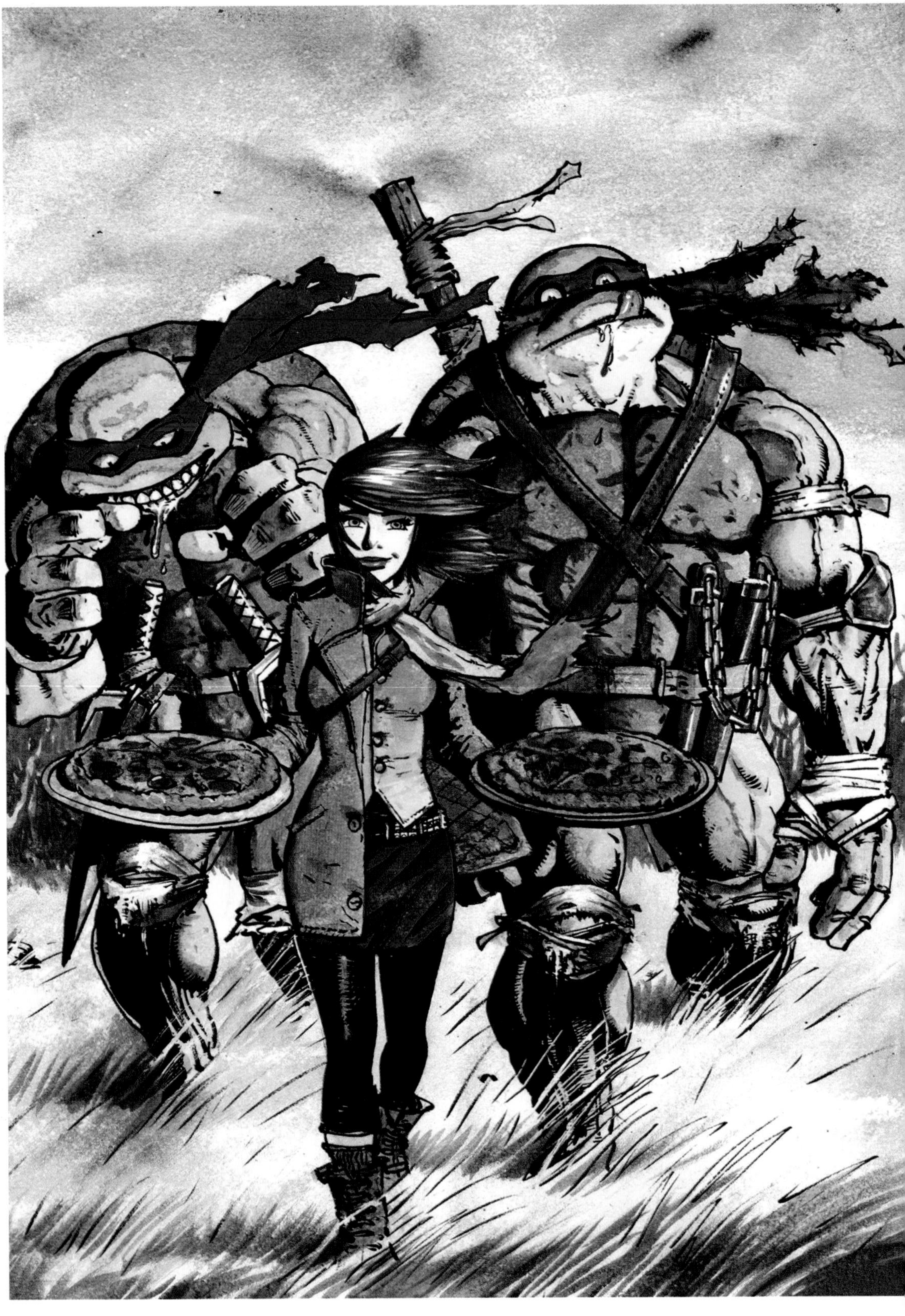

ART BY SIMON BISLEY

OPPOSITE PAGE: ART BY ADAM GORHAM · COLORS BY PARIS ALLEYNE

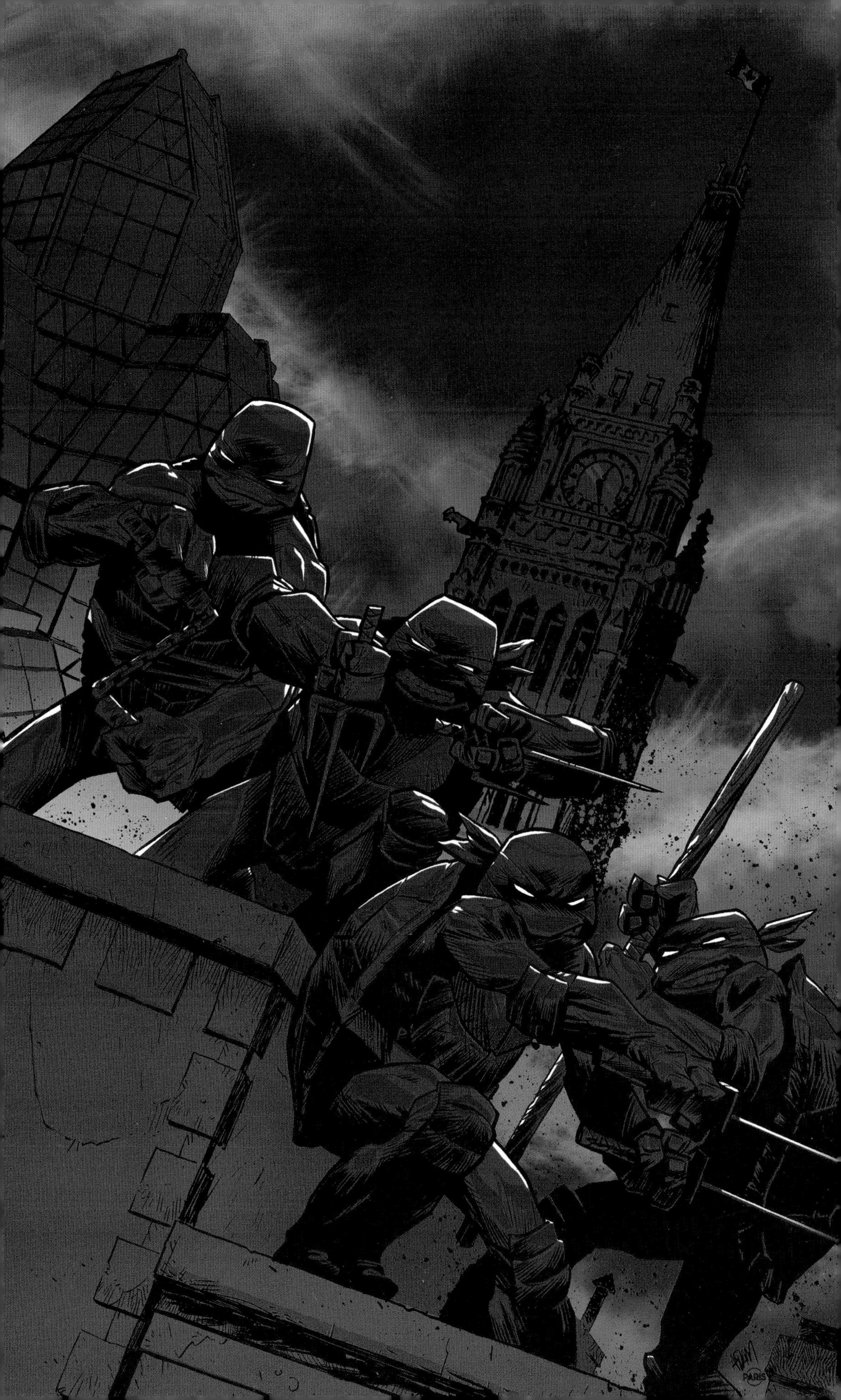
PARIS

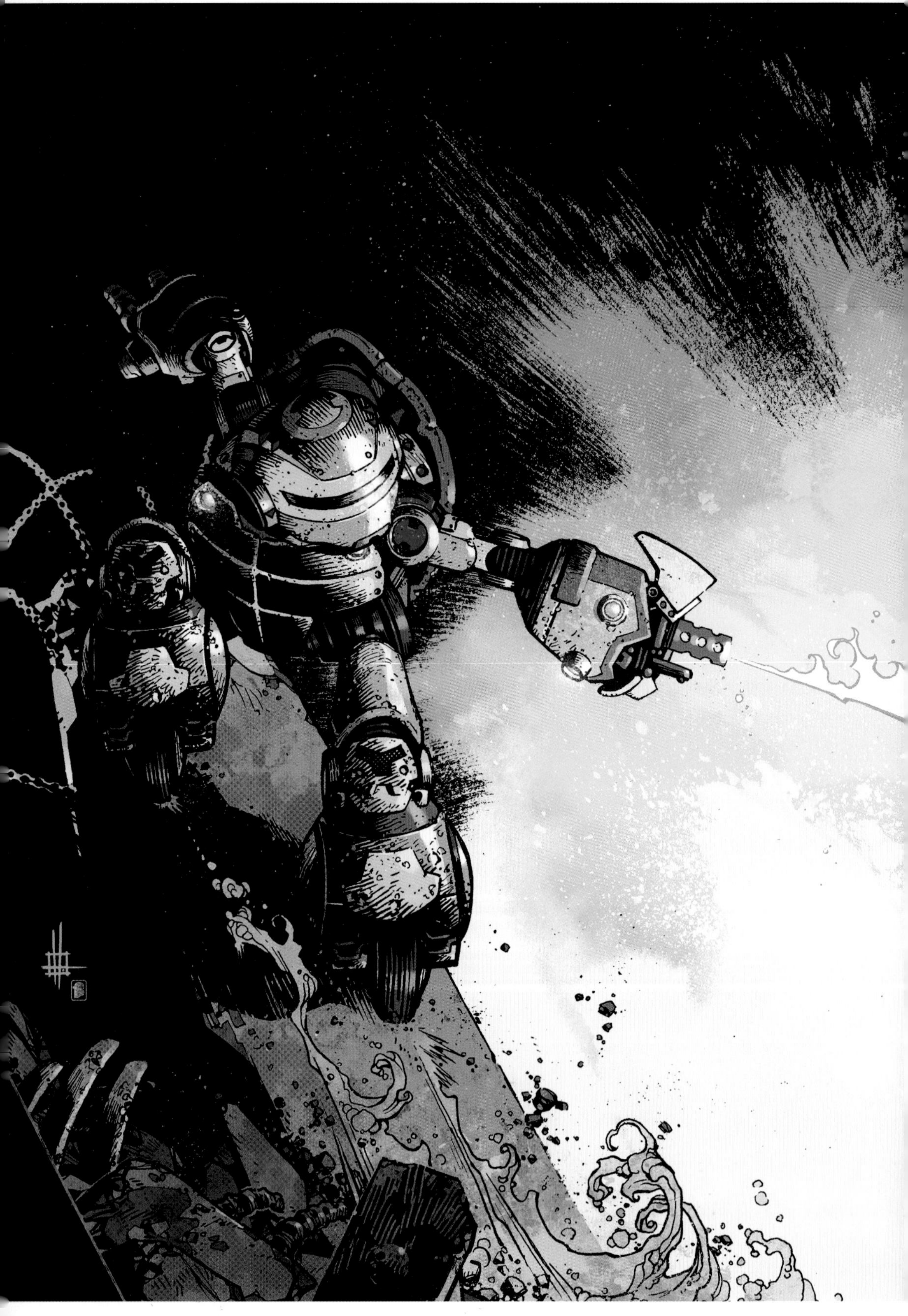

ART BY ZACH HOWARD

OPPOSITE PAGE: ART BY KEVIN EASTMAN · COLORS BY RONDA PATTISON

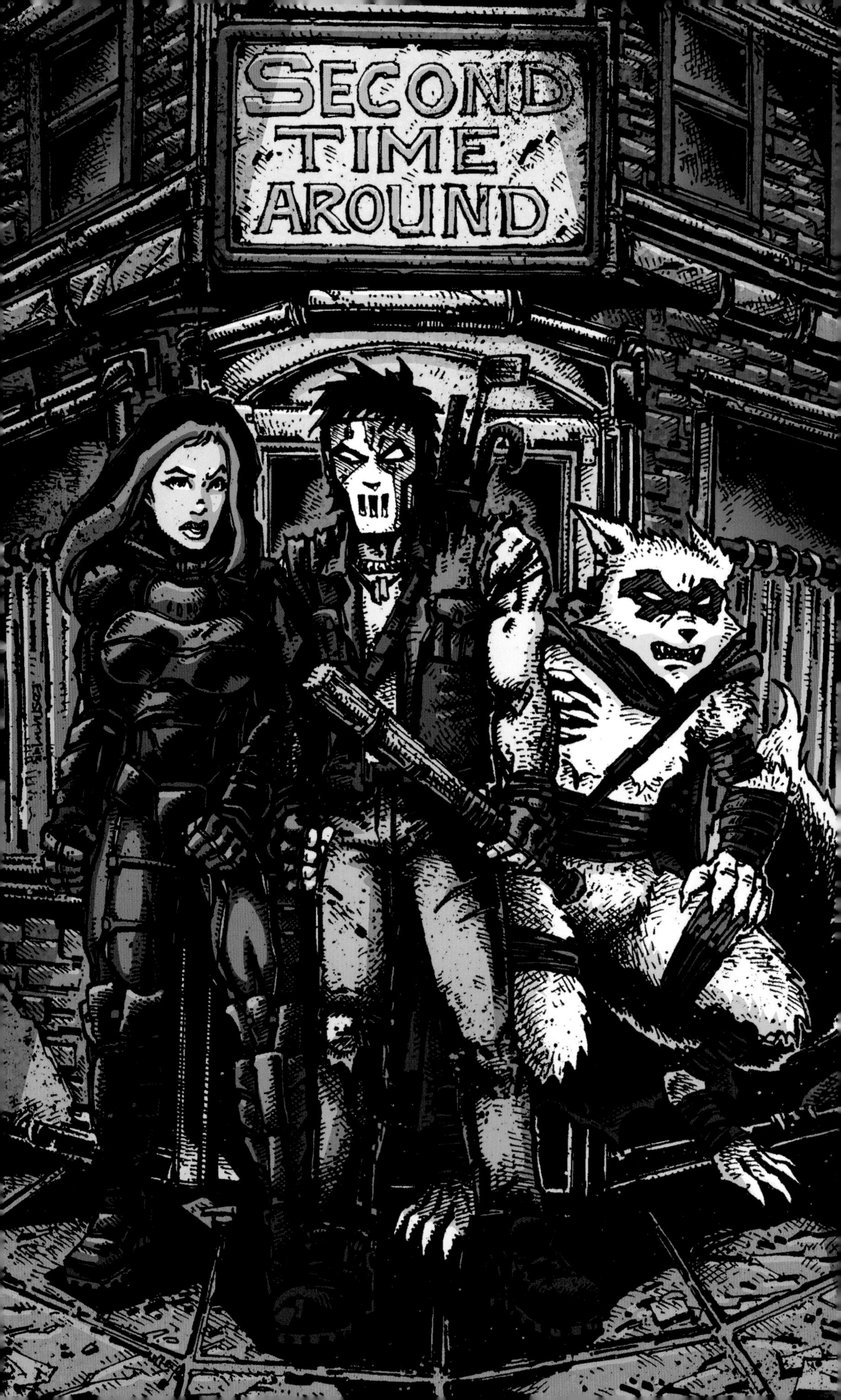
SECOND TIME AROUND

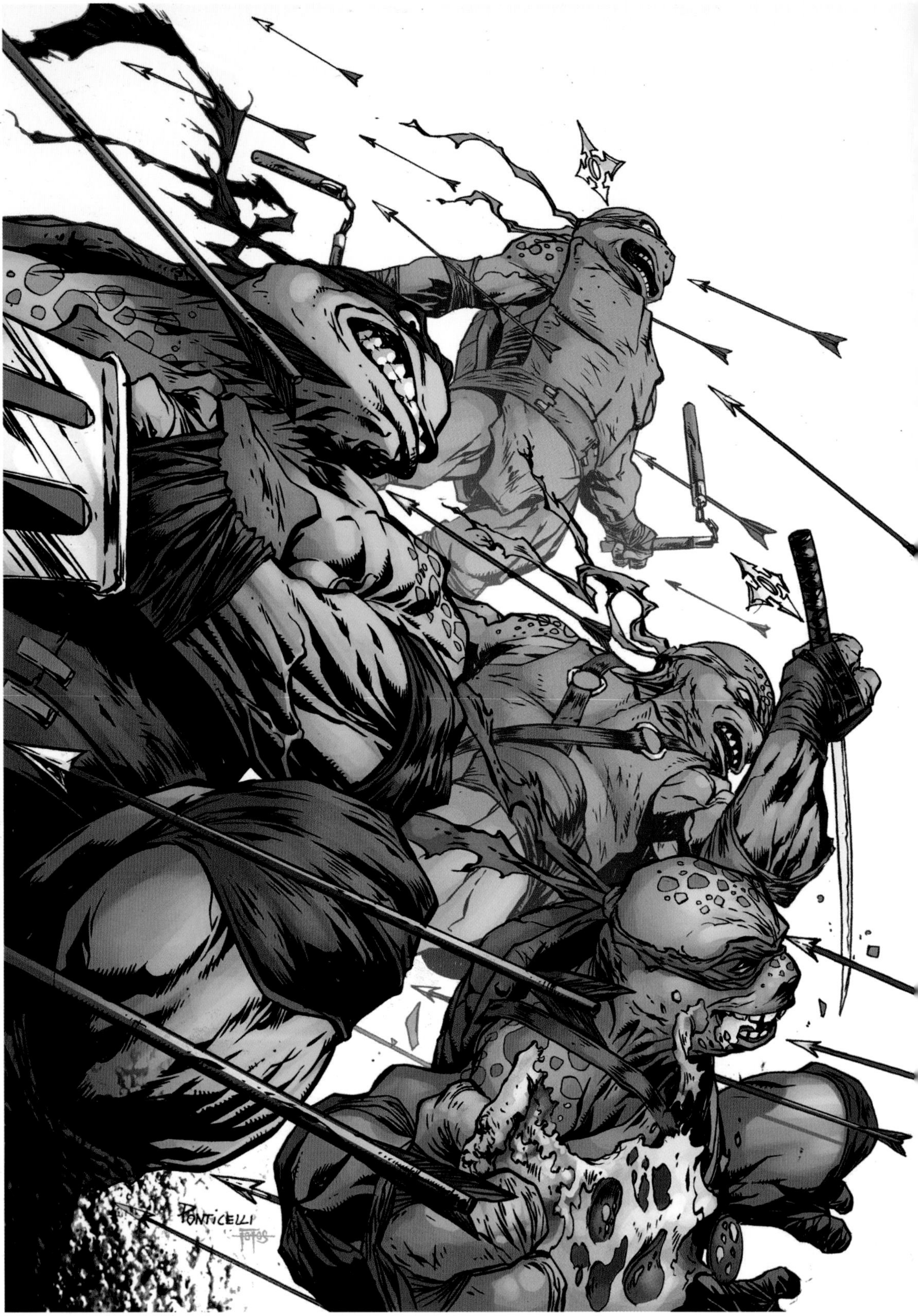
PONTICELLI

ART BY ALBERTO PONTICELLI · COLORS BY JAY FOTOS

OPPOSITE PAGE: ART BY KEVIN EASTMAN · COLORS BY RONDA PATTISON

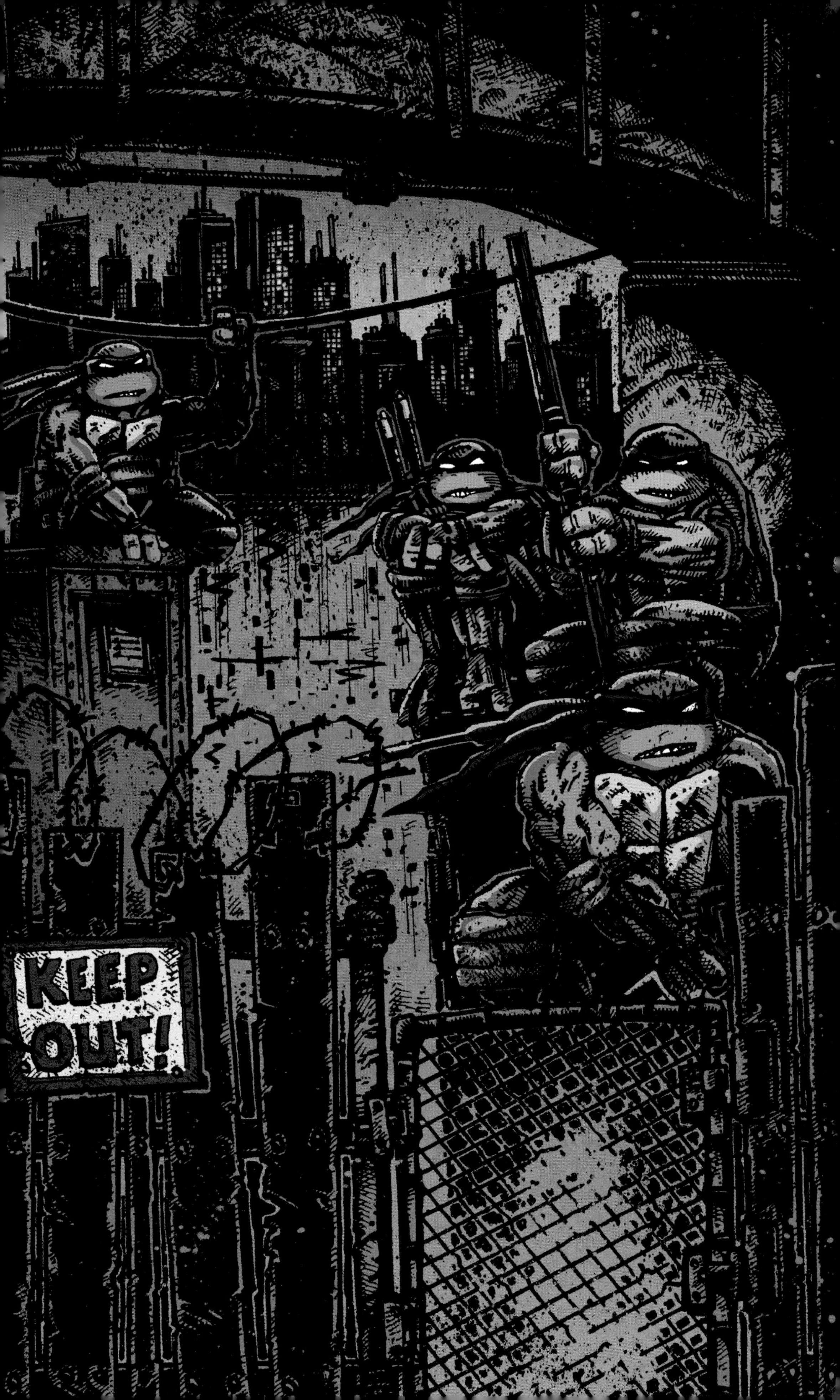
KEEP
OUT!

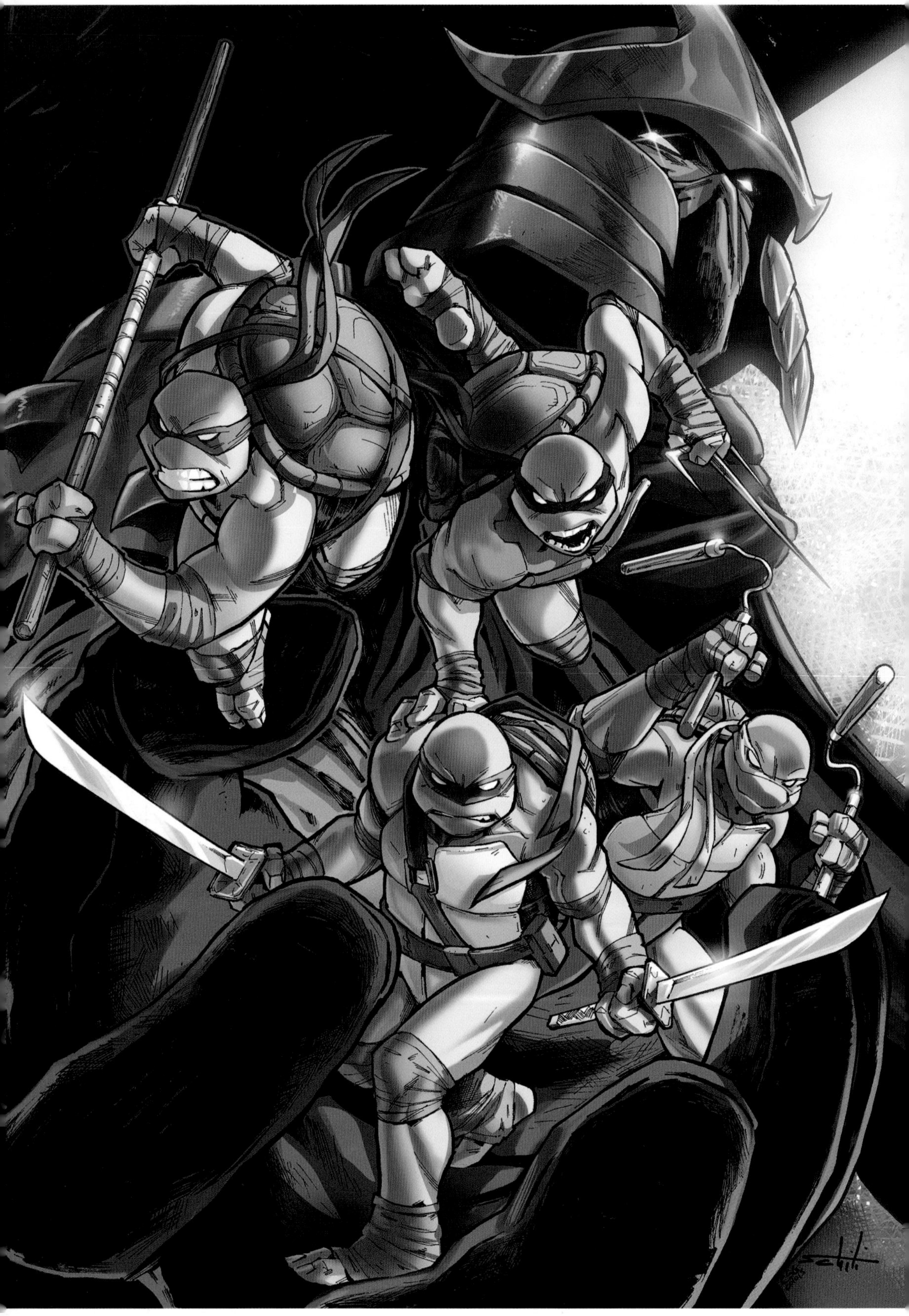

ART BY VALERIO SCHITI · COLORS BY CLAUDIA SG IANNICIELLO

OPPOSITE PAGE: ART BY MATEUS SANTOLOUCO

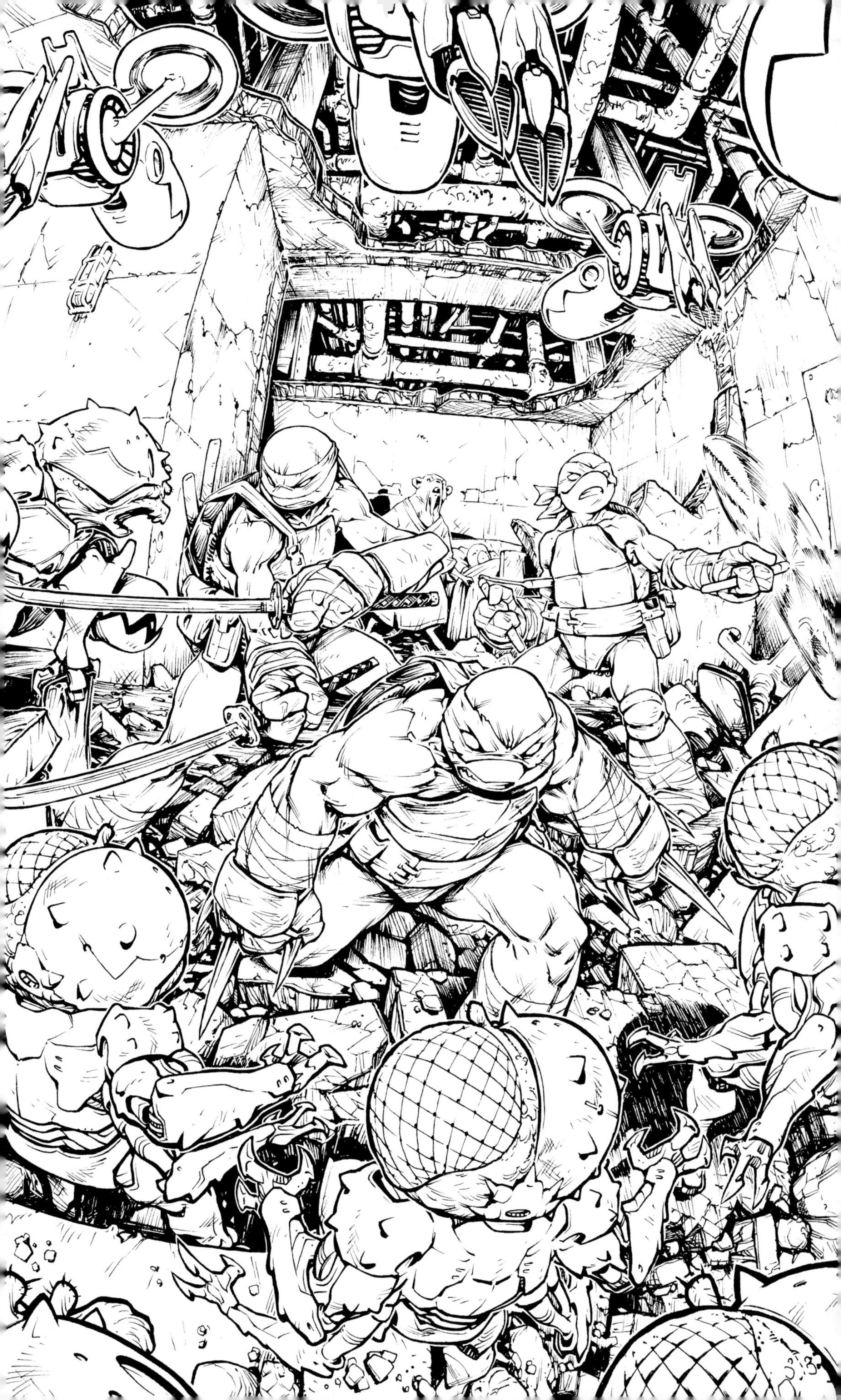

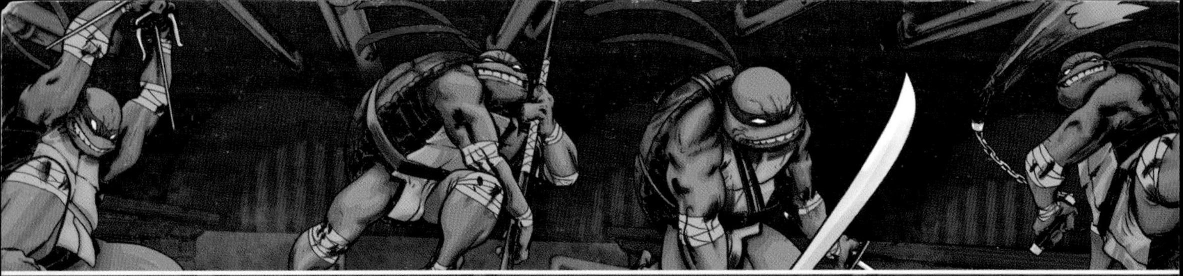

TEENAGE MUTANT NINJA TURTLES

MORE TURTLE ACTION!

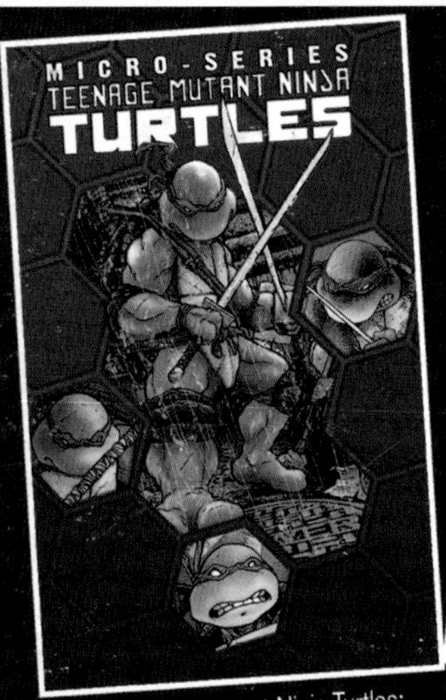
MICRO-SERIES
TEENAGE MUTANT NINJA
TURTLES

Teenage Mutant Ninja Turtles:
Micro-Series, Vol. 1
ISBN: 978-1-61377-232-4

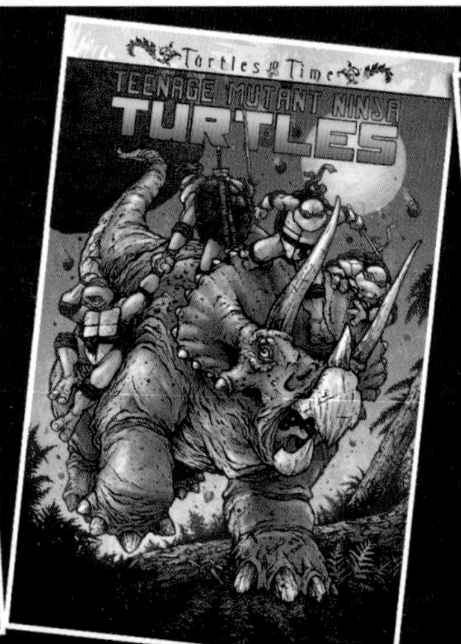
Turtles in Time
TEENAGE MUTANT NINJA
TURTLES

Teenage Mutant Ninja Turtles:
Turtles in Time
ISBN: 978-1-63140-181-7

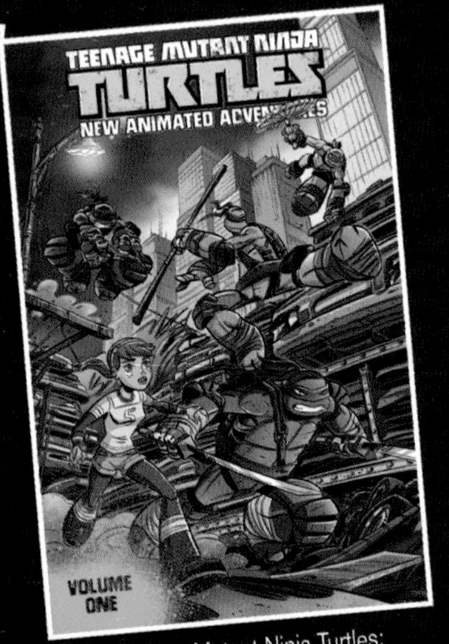
TEENAGE MUTANT NINJA
TURTLES
VOLUME ONE

Teenage Mutant Ninja Turtles:
New Animated Adventures, Vol. 1
ISBN: 978-1-61377-856-2

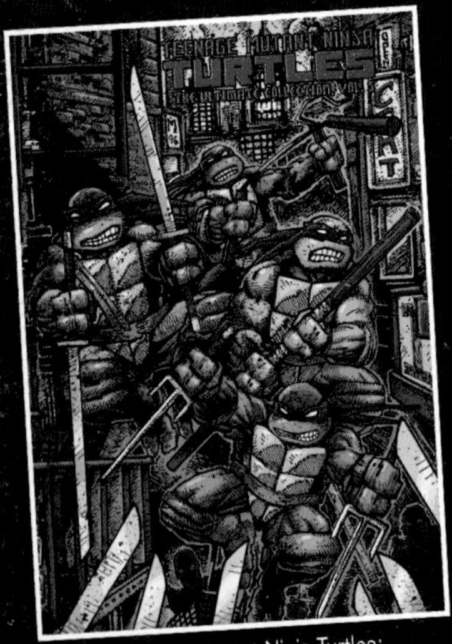
TEENAGE MUTANT NINJA
TURTLES

Teenage Mutant Ninja Turtles:
The Ultimate Collection, Vol. 5
ISBN: 978-1-61377-553-0

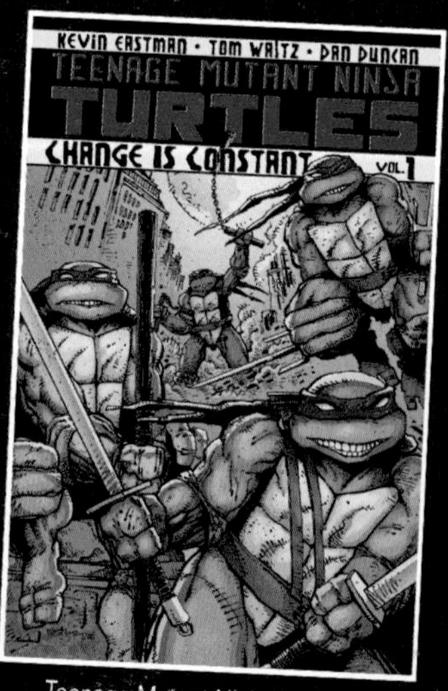
KEVIN EASTMAN • TOM WALTZ • DAN DUNCAN
TEENAGE MUTANT NINJA
TURTLES
CHANGE IS CONSTANT VOL. 1

Teenage Mutant Ninja Turtles:
Change Is Constant, Vol. 1
ISBN: 978-1-61377-139-6

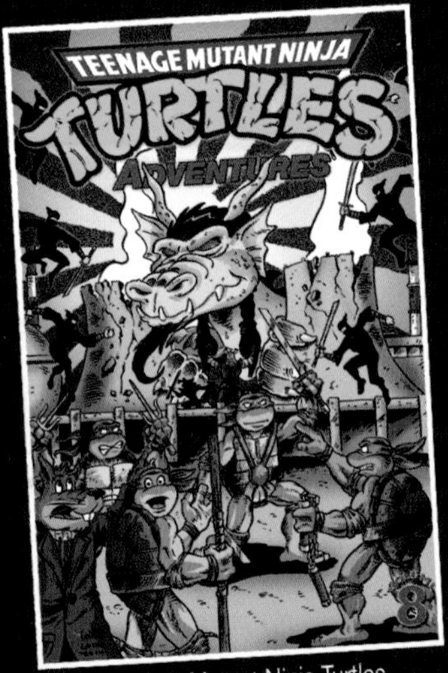
TEENAGE MUTANT NINJA
TURTLES
ADVENTURES
8

Teenage Mutant Ninja Turtles
Adventures, Vol. 8
ISBN: 978-1-63140-082-7

ON SALE NOW

www.idwpublishing.com

IDW

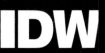